Passionate Longevity

The 10 secrets to growing younger

Elaine Dembe

Macmillan Canada

Canadian Cataloguing in Publication Data
Dembe, Elaine 1948–
    Passionate longevity : the 10 secrets to growing younger

Includes index.
ISBN 0-7715-7302-2

1. Longevity.   2. Health.   3. Nutrition.   4. Aging.
I. Title.

RA776.5.D45 1995   613   C94–932682–8

Macmillan Canada wishes to thank the Canada Council, the Ontario Arts Council and the Ontario Ministry of Culture and Communications for supporting its publishing program.

Cover design: Gillian Tsintziras

Macmillan Canada
A Division of Canada Publishing Corporation
Toronto, Canada

1 2 3 4 5   99 98 97 96 95

Printed in Canada

ACKNOWLEDGMENTS

This book was created with the wisdom and help of many people. I am deeply grateful to all of them. Many thanks to: David Talbot, my best friend, who provided the wind beneath my wings.

Major-General Richard Rohmer, my mentor, solicitor and friend, whose advice and guidance gave me the courage to charge on to the next windmill.

Bertha Madott, my guardian angel, sent to teach me about life, common sense and dangling participles.

Deanna Borda, for her tireless efforts above and beyond the call of duty, juggling the thousands of manuscript changes in between patient bookings.

Jennifer Glossop, whose careful editing and guidance helped me find my voice.

A special thank you to all the inspirational and extraordinary "life mentors" whose wisdom, values and experience represent the essence of *Passionate Longevity:* Dorothy Bates, Alex Beder, Anne Blair, Lil Brown, Ginger Eisen, Ida Farber, Natalie Fine, Max Goldhar, Bernie Herman, Joe Hillman, the late Ruth A. Hindmarsh, Catherine and Nicolson Holwell, Judith Kazdan, Gert Kushin, Allan Lamport, Grace Lawrence, Bill Lindo, Harry Malabar, the Hon. Pauline McGibbon, Bill McMullen, Eleanor Mills, Ed Mirvish, Sigga Moore, Fay and Harvey Morris, Elsie Palter, Donna Pasquale, Rabbi Gunther Plaut, George Richards, Major-General Richard Rohmer, Marjorie Rothstein, Max Sharp, the late Dr. George Sheehan, Frank Shuster, the late Sam Sigesman, Rose Wolfe, Joe Womersley, Helen and John Weinzweig, and Sol and Pearl Zucker.

And, for all those who shared their expertise with me including Erika Arndt, Burke Brown, Dr. Roberta Ferrence, Dr. Jack Goodman, Michael Hazell, Reesa Kassirer MSW, Dr. Pam Letts, Dr. Gordon Lithgow, Jan Lowenthal, Dr. Mortimer Mamelak, Rev. Peter Moore, Maye Musk RD, Dr. David Rapoport, Katherine Robins, Franz Schmidt, Lyn Sharratt, Arthur Soler, Rabbi Jerry Steinberg, Mara Swartz, Dr. Gordon Winocur, Dr. Maxine Gallander Wintre and Robin Woods.

Special thanks to Ruth Allen, John Borda, Paul Bruno, Al Denov, Lynn Irwin, Kevin Kassirer, Gillian Stoker-Lavelle, Marci Lipman, Ken McLachlan, Linda Montgomery, Barbara Mourin, Lesley Parrott, Robert Reilly, Debbie Rothstein, Arthur Scott, Joy Shepherd, Joseph Sorbara, Bernie Younder and Daniel Weinzweig, for sharing their personal stories with me.

My gratitude—for their help—to Peter Armstrong, Robert Beder, Carole Cook, Elaine Dewar, Bea Eisen, Wendy Eisen, Terry Finkel, Farley Flex, Rick Gossage, John Henderson, Harold Hillman, Marlene Hore, Gerry Morris, Pearl Richman, Robert Ross, Al Sokol, Susan Speirs, Gillian Tsintzaris, Charis Wahl, Irving Wortsman and Simon Zucker.

My appreciation to Yanka and Yolanda Van Der Kolk, whose photographic artistry are world class.

A special thank you to my publisher, Denise Schon of Macmillan Canada, for believing in me. And to my editor, Nicole de Montbrun, who delicately performed "liposuction" on what was a very fat manuscript. My appreciation to Robert Dees, Liza Algar, Elizabeth Crinion, Ann Nelles and Francine Hollands—also at Macmillan. As well, thanks to Jackie Rothstein for her help at the beginning of the project.

Thanks to my wonderful friends Linda Stork, Brenda Baker, Barbara Burrows, Wendy Cecil Cockwell, Julia Hidy, Sharon Holesh, Samena Jeffery, Andrea Kraus, Marlene Landa, Rona Maynard, Aileen McKenzie, Allan and Natalie Millman, Sharon Newman, Ann Rohmer, Tisa Starr and Ylva Van Buuren for their support.

And, especially, to my dear family Adam, Joel, Paul, Michael, Cheryl and Steven, for their love and encouragement.

*To the memory of my parents
Mary and Harry Dembe*

CONTENTS

INTRODUCTION

Let me describe a typical morning in my life as a chiropractor.

"I need a good treatment," said Joe Womersley, as he hopped up on my treatment table with an energetic bounce. "I'm a little stiff today. The forty-two kilometer run on Baffin Island was for wimps, so I ran eighty-four kilometers!" Joe is sixty-nine.

My next patient was Major-General Richard Rohmer. As I was checking his back, he told me he was very busy with his law practice, working on his nineteenth book and still playing tennis three times a week. "By the way," he added, "did I tell you that my wife and I are planning a trip to France for the fifty-year celebration of D-Day?" Richard is seventy.

I stood for several minutes at the entrance to Treatment Room 3, waiting patiently for Mrs. DA as she slowly pushed her walker towards me. "My back and legs are really sore today," she said hoarsely with her familiar, deep smoker's voice. As I gently helped her feeble legs onto the table, she announced hopefully, "My doctor is giving me some new pills for my heart." After her treatment, I helped her tie her shoelaces and guided her to her walker. Mrs. DA is sixty-four.

There were many more patients to see that morning—from five-year-old David who fell at school to Susan, forty-two, a healthy, fit triathlete nursing a sore knee. The last patient rushed in and flopped facedown on the table, his round belly hidden from view. "I'm parked illegally," Martin explained breathlessly, "so give me a quick crunch. My lower back is killing me!" Hearing my exasperated sigh, he continued, "You're about to give me another lecture on my weight and eating. I promise as soon as I get a little more time, I'll start exercising." As he raced out of the treatment room, he yelled to Deanna, my assistant, "I'll call to make another appointment," and disappeared. Martin is forty.

In seventeen years of private practice, I have treated thousands of patients from age one to ninety-two. My description of that particular morning is typical of my day. I often reflect on the people whose lives I've touched and the ones who've made a difference to me. I share a history with many of them, watching them journey through the stages of life, growing up and growing older. And they've watched me grow—from a fledgling grad of twenty-nine into an experienced forty-six-year-old. In my curious, observant way, I began to notice something fascinating: there is no one pattern for normal aging. There are huge differences in how people age—some old at sixty, some young at eighty—differences in appearance, in attitude, in health, in mobility, in spirit. "Why," I asked myself, "are there some seventy-year-olds in nursing homes and some seventy-year-olds running marathons, playing with grandchildren, traveling the world?" There is a personal reason behind the question. Three years ago, my mother, at age seventy-six, passed away in a nursing home after many years of ill health. Anyone who has experienced the agony of watching the deterioration of a loved one knows how I feel. I remember saying to myself, "I never want to end up like this." On the way to my mother's room, I passed dozens of wheelchair-bound seniors, some barely alert, most inert. The experience strengthened my resolve to understand the aging process.

I know how I want to age. I want to be like Judith Kazdan, running marathons at seventy-four, or like Rabbi Gunther Plaut, writing and lecturing at eighty-two. But how to get there? Is successful aging luck, genetics, attitude? Can we choose the way we age? These questions led me on a determined search for answers. My quest has focused on one key issue: loving life as opposed to just living long. My interest is not just longevity; rather, it is *passionate* living. *How* we live is more important than *how long*! I coined the phrase "passionate longevity" to describe the special joie de vivre, the zestful spirit and energy many people possess, regardless of age.

I know how I have lived the first forty-six years of my life. Now, what do I need to know, what must I do, to ensure that the next forty-six will be equally healthy, happy, productive, passionate? I reasoned that the only way to discover the answer is to ask those who are already living that way—those seniors who are healthy, happy, productive and passionate. What could be more inspirational than learning about life from those wise men and women who have a head start of forty or fifty years! All seniors weren't my target group. Instead, I wanted to interview exceptional, extraordinary, remarkable, outrageous role models who had loved and laughed for seventy, eighty or ninety years. I sent out an SOS. I announced to patients, friends and colleagues that I was looking for Stand-Out-Seniors. And I found them—everywhere. When I listened to *how* these people were described by their families and friends, I knew I was on the right track. Feelings of great love, admiration and reverence abounded. Unfortunately, we all know older people who are cranky and pessimistic, not much fun to be around. But my stand-out-seniors had fans, young and old alike.

In the past year, I have been privileged to meet many incredible people. I visited their homes, saw how they lived and listened to their life stories. They gladly shared their wisdom and philosophies of life with me. I noticed a common thread among their stories. I began to hear similar experiences, witness similar personality traits, notice similar courses of action for health, work and life in general. The same things were important to all of them. It soon became apparent to me that there were ten key characteristics that defined their lives, ten words that spoke volumes about their minds, bodies and spirits. The ten principles I believe are the secrets to passionate longevity are tenacity, sociability, productivity, unity, mobility, vitality, responsibility, creativity, flexibility and spirituality.

This book is an exploration of these ten concepts. In it, I examine issues surrounding the mind—our intellect and emotions, the relationships we form, the activities we love. Then I progress to concerns of the body—fitness, nutrition and holistic healing. I conclude with the triumphs of the human spirit—creativity, flexibility and spirituality. Every one of us is at a different place in our personal journey to passionate longevity, so begin reading wherever you are. You may be drawn to a word that resonates for you; explore that chapter first. Need to make changes in your life? Read the chapter on flexibility. Concerned about your diet? Check out

Vitality. I have also included some of my poems to enthuse and amuse. And throughout the book, you will find the wit and wisdom of some of my senior friends, distilled into their 10 Secrets to Growing Younger.

Words barely convey what this baby boomer learned in researching this book. The process of writing changed me. I realize that the older generation, our life mentors, have much to teach us. Their stories helped me to forgive and to explore my capacity for spiritual growth. I think my Type A personality has become more patient and accepting. This book contains sections on the importance of family and friendship, the value of optimism and the challenge of loss and change, as well as practical advice on taking responsibility for health, keeping mind and body active and dealing with adversity. For those at mid-life, the time to assess, evaluate and change is now. For that reason, this book is not a retrospective but a *prospective* look into the future, exploring the factors that enable us to lead long, happy, healthy, passionate lives.

When you finish this book, you will know what you need to do to age successfully. The choice is yours. So grab an imaginary suitcase, turn the page and get ready for the journey of the rest of your life.

1

TENACITY

Tenacity is the hallmark of the optimist—
someone who refuses to give up when faced
with adversity.

Picture this scene: it is a miserably cold, windy day, with a driving rain so strong that at times the lone runner can hardly see where she is going. Her shoes and socks are soaked from the puddles, a steady spray of water from cars pelts her legs, yet she plods along undaunted, determined to reach the finish line of this, her thirty-sixth marathon. Focus on the runner: seventy-four-year-old Judith Kazdan. "I wore a garbage bag over my shoulders with a makeshift hole for my head to attempt to stay dry. My hands were so cold and numb that I had to run practically the whole way rubbing my hands together. At the halfway point [thirteen miles] a policeman informed me that all lanes were now being opened to traffic; as a slower runner, I would have to run on the sidewalk. I looked around for other runners but couldn't see anyone. But I knew I wasn't last." With no runners in front to lead the way and no one behind her, Judith became anxious about the race route. "I couldn't remember whether I had to make a right or left turn to get to the bridge. Someone at a water station gave me a map but it was so wet I couldn't read the words," she recalled with a laugh. Winds were gusting up to fifty kilometers per hour, and sheets of heavy rain blew in her face, but Judith forged ahead alone, flatly refusing a ride from a motorist. "No, thanks, I said, and kept on going." And then she got lost after four and a half hours! She eventually got back on course and reached the finish line, after toughing it out for five hours and forty-five minutes. "This had to be my worst marathon ever. But these experiences make me strong. I refused to give in. There's no way I would quit!"

What an incredible woman. I, too, had participated in this marathon, and lasted only ninety minutes outside in that bone-chilling, steady rain—and I was just a spectator, *watching* the marathon, armed with umbrella, gloves and jacket. When Judith told me her story, I didn't have the heart to tell her I had retreated home to a hot, soothing bath.

From the story of one tenacious marathon runner to the extraordinary fighting spirit of a marathon walker. Eleanor Mills, eighty-one, has severe osteoporosis. In 1982, she suffered a fracture of her spine. "I could hardly move," she recalled, "but I decided I had no aptitude for being bedridden and disabled, so I got dressed. I knew I must keep going. I wasn't going to let a broken back stop me!" From teetering across a room unassisted, Eleanor found that with the help of a walker she was now able to walk eight miles. "When I first tried my walker, I felt airborne. I said, 'I could walk to Vancouver!' and the idea of the cross-Canada walk was born." Eleanor Mills and her "Boney Express," a team of women with osteoporosis, are now leading five-kilometer walks in eighty-five communities from Victoria to Toronto to raise money for and increase awareness of osteoporosis, a crippling disease. As I studied the face of this woman, the word "resilient" came to mind. She is a role model for us all when she states, "Never give up. Whatever happens to you in your life, *never give up!* You must keep going. You've got to get on with things."

Ruth Atkinson Hindmarsh knew the meaning of Eleanor's words. One week before her ninety-seventh birthday, as she was coming in from the greenhouse, she tripped on a rug. She fractured her hip and seven ribs; she needed forty stitches to sew up the gash on her arm. A spinal anesthetic left her conscious while surgeons repaired her hip with a metal plate, wire and a pin, so she chatted with the doctors while they worked on her. The next day she was sitting up, in great spirits, cheerfully enjoying visits with relatives. Her comeback amazed doctors. "I have no intention of retiring and I dare them to fire me!" she challenged, speaking of her twice-a-week job as director of *The Toronto Star* and president of the Atkinson Charitable Foundation. Seven weeks after her surgery, she was at the office, poring over requests from organizations for grants. She worked for four more years, until her death at one hundred and one years of age. Philosophical about life until the very end, she joked, "I hope I just drop dead. But not now. I'm having too much fun."

Tenacity is the hallmark of the optimist, a resilient individual who refuses to give up when faced with adversity. Major-General Richard Rohmer inscribed one of his books for me with his personal philosophy: "Influence the course of events!" During an interview, I asked him what the title would be if someone wrote a book about his life. Without hesitation he replied, "*On to the Next Windmill*. Remember Don Quixote? He went through life going up to windmills to challenge, attack and destroy them. You move, in life, from challenge to challenge. I've had many careers, many challenges. There's always something new . . . it's been great fun." Motivating words from an indomitable spirit.

Every senior I interviewed demonstrated tenacity and resilience, no matter what life handed them. Think of a hardy plant you'd forgotten to water that survived despite the odds. While pessimists are consumed with a feeling of helplessness, these senior optimists were feisty, tough and in control, possessing a passion for life that only optimists understand. Recent studies suggest that optimism offers life-enhancing benefits: personal and professional success, health, well-being and longevity. Are pessimists doomed to a miserable, shortened life, or can they learn to be optimists? Can optimism alter our immune system and our health? Is there a link between optimism, tenacity and longevity? Within the optimistic personality is the feeling of *hope*—the expectation that tomorrow will be better than today. Is there a relationship between hope and health? I will explore these questions, as well as the healing power of laughter—our sixth sense—which I call "inner jogging." Time for the next stage of our journey: on to the next windmill.

The Rainbow Connection

I see two types of patients in my chiropractic practice: those who get better and those who don't. Give me ten minutes and I can usually tell which patients will recover fairly quickly and which will suffer prolonged pain. Their feeling about their condition gives me their prognosis even before I begin any physical examination.

A patient who is a pessimist will often say to me, "I don't think I'm ever going to get better." Pessimists exude a feeling of helplessness that translates into, "Nothing I do really matters." Such people delay seeking help initially, and when they finally do, often fail to follow the doctor's advice on treatment, diet and exercise.

On the other hand, optimistic patients view their condition as temporary, a minor setback that will eventually heal. "What can I do to speed up the process?" they ask, eager to participate in their health care. This interest gives them a sense of personal control over their illness. The optimist's and pessimist's attitude to health is the approach they take to life in general.

Here is a case in point. Dennis, a forty-two-year-old lawyer, came to my office complaining of recurrent lower back pain that affected his marathon training. "It's my own fault for not stretching enough," he began, revealing his remorse for not taking better care of himself. During the course of treatments he admitted that he was unhappy not only about his back, he was unhappy with his life, yet he felt powerless to make a change. After two years of treatment, he is still complaining about his unfulfilled marriage ("Who else would want a retread like me?") and his boring job ("What's the point of looking during the recession?"). Dennis's pessimistic attitude prevents him from changing and keeps his back and his life stuck indefinitely in a painful groove.

I became intrigued with the power of optimism when I realized that all the seniors I interviewed were optimists. Imagine the positive feelings from a group of passionate men and women, aged sixty-eight to a hundred and one, healthy, happy and still making plans for the future! Not one asked, "What if I'm not here?" I began to wonder whether there was a link between optimism and longevity. These are some of the optimistic comments I have heard:

From Joe Womersley, sixty-nine, whose marathon running has helped him get through life's problems: "Even when I'm going through rough times, I keep saying it's just like a marathon. You're at the eleventh mile. Soon you'll see the finish line. A challenge in life can always be broken down like that."

From Ida Farber, eighty-five: "As a youngster I was always taught to look on the bright side. If you think negatively, you'll sink into a mud hole. So forget your troubles and put them in the wastepaper basket."

From Marjorie Rothstein, eighty-four: "I've always been an optimist. I feel about sixty-five. I'd like to live to be one hundred. All those things I can't do anything about I just dismiss. I don't worry about it."

From Jean Holland, who at eighty completed her thousandth mile in the YMCA pool: "I feel enthused about it. I still swim a mile a day and don't intend to give it up. I'm looking forward to the next thousand miles."

Allan Lamport, the ninety-two-year-old former Toronto mayor and a political legend, is another optimist. After his wife died in 1965, Lamport moved quickly to recover. "When you're in trouble, you've always got something to do," he said. "And that is to try to get out of it."

Optimism is an attitude that goes beyond hoping to live to be a hundred. It's an all-encompassing can-do philosophy that affects all aspects of life. Optimists possess what I call "the rainbow connection." Even when problems and difficulties arise, their optimistic attitudes and wonderful sense of humor transform these obstacles into a rainbow, that serendipitous moment when light and water conspire to bring us a brief but unparalleled beauty.

The Link Is What You Think

Many patients come to my office for stress reduction. Their unresolved emotions and repressed feelings start to affect their bodies, and they ache all over. In this weakened state, they often succumb to colds, flu or viruses. They feel tired all the time.

Psychological states affect physical health and wellness. Emotions trigger chemical events in the brain that can alter nervous system function, hormone levels and immune system response.

The immune system is a group of biochemicals, cells, tissues and organs; it acts as the body's cellular defense against illness. Using the language of biochemicals and nerves, the mind and body communicate constantly. Thoughts, attitudes, beliefs, values, memories and moods can change our body's chemicals and how we feel and function. Psychologist David Myers, in his book *The Pursuit of Happiness*, says: "Emotions are biological events. Our body's immune system fights disease more effectively when we are happy rather than depressed. When we are depressed, the number of certain disease-fighting cells declines, making us more vulnerable to various illnesses."

There is now much scientific evidence that equates optimism with good health. Optimists are always asking, "How can I change, fix or improve this situation?" Let's suppose an optimist discovers a lump in her breast. Her first thought will be, "It's probably just a cyst or enlarged lymph node, but I'll get it checked out anyway." She then seeks medical attention. If the lump is malignant, this optimist will summon all available support systems—therapy, meditation, visualization, diet and exercise programs, family and friends, books, prayer, drugs, natural healing—whatever it takes to combat the disease.

Optimists are classed as *hardy individuals*, a term used by behavioral scientists at the University of Chicago who were exploring patterns of sickness and health in society. They wondered *who* gets sick and *why*. The scientists discovered that hardy individuals view change as a challenge; they are committed to their work, their families and life in general; they have a strong belief system that gives them a sense of control over their lives. When faced with a situation they cannot change, these hardy souls are able to dig deep within themselves to deal with it. Think of people in your life who are optimists. Have you ever marveled at their upbeat attitude and good health?

We now know that a major determinant of good health is what we think. But where and how do we learn to think optimistically or pessimistically? Probably in childhood. Every time children receive an answer to those universal questions "Why?" and "How come?" they also receive insight into their parents' view of the world. The manner in which events are explained to children has a tremendous influence on their thinking. Children listen carefully to how and what adults say, especially when something goes wrong. A parent's explanatory style is the genesis of optimism and pessimism, according to Dr. Martin Seligman, author of *Learned Optimism*.

In one study, Dr. Seligman counted the disease-fighting cells in the blood of three hundred people whose average age was seventy-one. He found that those with an optimistic explanatory style had stronger immune systems. If pessimism can deplete your immune system, it is likely to impair your health over your whole life span.

In another study, Dr. Gordon Winocur, PhD, of the Rotman Research Institute at the renowned Baycrest Centre for Geriatric

Care, found a dramatic relationship between optimism and cognitive function (thinking, learning and memory). "We wanted to know why some people who were physically healthy, with normal IQs, thrive in institutions while others don't," he explained. "We discovered that people who are very active, optimistic and hopeful for the future, those who have a sense of meaning in their lives, with some control over decisions that affect them, function at a very high level cognitively. In other words, these people are aging successfully." He then described a typical situation to illustrate his findings. "Let's say someone moves into an institution with the optimistic attitude, 'What a great opportunity! I don't have to cut the grass anymore or pay rent. I'll have more time to do all kinds of new things.' Compare this to the pessimistic person who says, 'I don't have a home to take care of, no one to cook for. I have to eat when they tell me.' It's important for this individual to feel that he has choice and some control in his life. Otherwise, he will get discouraged, be less active and withdraw. And I believe that as a result the physical processes of aging would be accelerated."

Being optimistic doesn't mean we won't get sick or depressed or experience failure. What is crucial is what you think when you do fail or get sick. Furthermore, optimism doesn't stop us from getting old.

More research is needed in the area of longevity; science still cannot predict who will live to a ripe old age. While doing the research for this book, I realized that adversity doesn't necessarily mean poor health. On the contrary! The seniors I interviewed were an inspiration; they not only survived war, loss of family and economic reversals, they actually thrived on these challenges because of their hardy, optimistic attitudes. To learn a good technique for becoming an optimist, keep reading.

Sunny-Side Up

To become an optimist, a pessimist must challenge the deep-rooted thought patterns that are an inherent part of his or her belief system. We need to change the tape inside our heads, for the way in which we talk to ourselves determines whether we are optimists or pessimists. To begin this process, start listening to your inner voice, especially in unpleasant or unfortunate situations. When you experience rejection, do you automatically assume you are worthless

The 10 Secrets of Eleanor Mills, age eighty-one

1. While you've got brain and muscle and the possibility of activity, never feel sorry for yourself.
2. Be resourceful. If you can't get things right one way, find another way.
3. Be kind. Be nice to people.
4. Be patient. Let problems simmer in your mind; very often they sort themselves out.
5. Never give up. Whatever condition you've got or not got, never give up.
6. Take responsibility for your health.
7. Do things because you love people, not because you want to be a success.
8. See obstacles as challenges.
9. Stay physically active. There's nothing to be gained from sitting.
10. Fretting about the future is a waste of time.

and unlovable? Do you find yourself making sweeping generalizations, using words like *always* and *never?* Do you make comments such as, "I'll never meet anyone again!" or, "I'm always making dumb mistakes like that!"? Dr. Seligman recommends learning a strategy known as *disputation* to combat this tendency. Disputation teaches you to argue with your pessimistic thoughts. If someone unjustly accused you of being a bad person, you would vehemently disagree, pointing out all sorts of examples to make your case. In exactly the same way we must argue with our own distorted thoughts. Attack your beliefs head-on. How accurate are they? Check out the truth of habitually pessimistic thoughts.

Here is an example of disputation at work. Suppose you are on a diet. At a Christmas party, your willpower weakens and you eat everything that is not bolted down. Feeling awful, you return home and demolish the remains of a frozen chocolate cake. After all, you reason, you've blown the diet anyway. In your pessimism, you say: "What's the use? I'm a pig and that's that. I'll never lose weight!" To dispute this negative reasoning, try arguing with yourself this way: "Look how strong I've been in sticking with my diet during the last two weeks. I attended a fitness class this morning and danced for an hour at the party, so I worked off a few calories today. I've already lost some weight, and after my run tomorrow, I'll make that delicious vegetable soup for this week's lunches." In this manner, you emerge from your internal monologue with self-esteem intact. Pessimists commonly exaggerate their shortcomings; disputation trains us to question the factual accuracy of these negative beliefs.

There are other ways to change from hard-boiled into sunny-side up. Seek out optimistic companions. If a trusted friend is an optimist, start listening to his or her explanatory style. Then explain that your own negative beliefs repeatedly afflict you. As an exercise, take a typical situation and ask your friend to criticize you in the same manner in which you criticize yourself. Give the friend permission to be mean. Your role will be to dispute the unkind accusations out loud, summoning all the counterarguments you can. What great practice in learning to be positive!

If you find yourself slipping into negative thought patterns, start focusing on the parts of your life that are healthy, successful and encouraging, instead of highlighting the aspects that aren't working. If you don't have everything you want right now, that doesn't mean you won't have it someday. Take relationships, for example. You could meet the person of your dreams six months from now. So what is a six-month wait out of a whole lifetime?

Take personal credit for your successes. Perhaps you have found the perfect job. Don't tell yourself and others it was just luck or that you were in the right place at the right time. Acknowledge that you have the talent, qualifications and knowledge required. When negative situations do occur, ask yourself, "What lessons am I to learn from this? Have I been given an opportunity for growth, instead of merely the recipe for failure?" Rehearse success. Optimists always picture themselves accomplishing their goals. Visualization techniques allow you to imagine your dreams. With eyes closed, picture yourself getting a new job, losing weight, landing that important deal.

A meditation for turning the straw of life into gold is presented in Jack Kornfield's book *A Path With Heart*. He describes a technique that will change our relationship to life's difficulties. Imagine that this earth is filled with especially gifted souls, that every single person you encounter is as enlightened as Buddha, everyone except for one person—you. Pretend all the people you encounter on your life's journey are acting as they do solely for your benefit, to provide the teachings and challenges you need to awaken your greatest potential. Sense the lessons being offered to you. Inwardly thank your companions for their instruction. Throughout the week, continue to develop the image of enlightened teachers all around you. What a powerful shift this can create in our thinking! Meditations like this one will revolutionize your whole perspective on the negative events and setbacks that happen to all of us, optimists and pessimists alike.

With practice we can change our pessimistic patterns. Optimism is the healthiest, happiest route to passionate longevity, so order a sunny-side up life for yourself.

Try Hope

While making hospital rounds, Dr. Bernard Lown, a Harvard cardiologist, told his staff that a dozing patient had a "wholesome, very loud third-sound gallop." The other doctors understood the code: the patient's heart was straining and in danger of failing. In spite of this gloomy diagnosis, the patient surprised everyone by recovering. Months later at a checkup Dr. Lown asked the man if he could explain his astonishing recovery. "I certainly can," he said. "When I heard you say I had a wholesome gallop, my spirits lifted for the first time and I knew I'd get better!"

Hope is the coping mechanism that allows us to deal with the stress of a life crisis. It is the feeling that things will be better in the future. Two kinds of factors influence a person's ability to hope, personal factors and sociocultural factors. Personal factors include memories of fulfilled hopes in the past, our feelings of being needed and experiences of trust and faith. We are more likely to feel hope if we perceive that we have control over our destiny and can make our own choices in any situation. Sociocultural factors include the attitudes of family and friends who share and support our hopes. The process of hoping begins when a person discovers some reasons for feeling hopeful. Should the particular situation change, the hopeful person modifies expectations or substitutes new hopes. Suppose you are running a marathon and hope to win a medal in the over-thirty category; as you near the halfway point, six other runners about your age pass you, looking very fresh. You recognize them as your competition, and your hopes for a medal fade. You then modify your goal: instead of winning a medal, you'll settle for running a personal best time. Unfortunately, by the time you reach the twenty-mile mark, you are feeling fatigued and your right calf muscle is cramping. Once again, you modify your goal; you'll be happy just to finish the race.

When we find that our hopes are unsupported and unrealistic, we may decide to focus only on the immediate present. We may say at this point, "I'm taking each day as it comes." There are three stages in the process of hope. This first is *encouragement*, when there is some basis for hope and we are motivated to keep striving toward our goal. Following this is *worrying*, a time of uncertainty of achieving the goal. Finally we experience *mourning*, during which we give up or seriously alter the hope and eventually learn to grieve.

I am privileged to be able to give the gift of hope to my patients. Many of them, struggling with their first-ever back problems, bodies contorted with pain, search my face for a glimpse of hopefulness in my eyes. They want reassurance, encouragement and advice. I've always felt that a doctor's bedside manner is as important as the treatment, if not more important. I believe that what I say and how I say it help the healing process as much as what I do. Healing begins with caring. Caring means listening and communicating empathy and hope. I've never told a patient I can't help, because I am ever an optimist. I truly hope and trust that I can.

Laughter, the Sixth Sense

Laughter is cathartic; it helps us deal with both physical and emotional pain. When we laugh we massage all the internal organs in the body, an activity I call "inner jogging." Laughter can reduce depression, ease tension and help us communicate better. Researchers think that laughter releases endorphins, the body's natural painkillers, and gives us an elated feeling or natural high. Dr. William Fry, Jr., of the Department of Psychiatry at Stanford Medical School, compares laughter to a physical workout. It causes huffing and puffing, speeds up the heart rate, raises blood pressure, accelerates breathing, increases oxygen consumption, gives the muscles of the face and stomach a workout and relaxes other muscles not involved in laughing. Twenty seconds of laughter, he contends, can double the heart rate for three to five minutes. That is the equivalent of three minutes of strenuous rowing. Norman Cousins, in *Anatomy of an Illness*, describes how laughter helped him recover from ankylosing spondylitis, a progressive connective-tissue disease: "Ten minutes of solid belly laughter would give me two hours of pain-free sleep. I also tried to bring the full range of positive emotions into play—love, hope, faith, will to live, festivity, purpose and determination."

Other studies on the benefits of laughter have shown a connection between humor and our ability to adjust to major life stresses. Those who value humor are those most capable of coping with tensions and severe personal problems. A study at the Loma Linda University Medical Center in California demonstrated that laughter enhances the immune system. The scientists measured several stress hormones in healthy male subjects after they viewed a sixty-minute humorous film. There was a marked increase in immune-cell proliferation.

I love to laugh—it beats crying any day! For the past seventeen years, I have been collecting cartoons for my office. They're now organized into a large album for patients to read in my consultation room. Often I'll walk in and greet a patient who is obviously in pain but is also laughing out loud—thanks to my cartoon collection. The healing process has begun even before I've said hello. I love the dry humor of George Burns, age ninety-eight. He says, "You know what things are special to me being over ninety? Breathing and bran flakes! Every morning I read the obituary column. If my name is not in there, I have breakfast."

There is much to learn from the individuals I interviewed who have lived twice our years and more. Their lightness of spirit comes from the rainbow connection: the ability to see life in an optimistic, humorous way. So, as you pack your suitcase for the journey to passionate longevity, add this special prescription for your rainbow connection. Take two jokes and swallow them with a half-full glass of optimism. Watch out! This formula is highly addictive and may cause permanent side effects: laugh lines around the eyes and frequent stomachaches from laughter.

The 10 Secrets of Frank Shuster, age seventy-eight

1. The key to life is a sense of humor.
2. Everything in moderation, including moderation.
3. Have fun.
4. Follow the Golden Rule.
5. The key to life is a sense of humor.
6. Do what you love.
7. When it comes to loss and adversity, do the best you can.
8. Never retire.
9. Keep busy doing the things you love, and you won't have time to think about growing old.
10. *Live* life, and of course, the key to life is a sense of humor.

2

SOCIABILITY

Family, friends and community

The Christmas season is a fitting symbol of all that is special for humanity because it is a time to share with family and to reconnect with old friends. Although I come from a Jewish background, I have celebrated many Christmases and treasure the rituals. In my mind I can see happy faces around a large dining room table, the room alive with color, each place set in anticipation of a feast, all the family silverware on display, and the good dishes, the golden-brown turkey on a platter, casseroles filled with a garden's delight of orange and green vegetables, a mound of cranberry sauce, wineglasses for toasting togetherness, red and green decorations on the wooden mantelpiece and a crackling fire in the fireplace.

Christmas is about home, coming home to family and friends, having a place where we belong, where we feel a connection to our past. Christmas is also about remembering those less fortunate. Yet for some people, Christmas can be a very lonely time, when we are reminded of all the things we don't have, perhaps a family, a place to call home. Maybe we're far away, continents or wars separating families and friends. Christmas seems to highlight all that's best and worst in our relationships; perhaps that's why it's so important.

Whenever I spoke to seniors, asking what sustained them, what gave them strength, the answer was always the same: family and friends. I was touched by the inspirational stories of unconditional love and reciprocal nurturing from their children and grand-children. I left their homes with a clear understanding of the values that are really important in life: relationships, home, tradition, family stability, community. These are the things that last. If our goal is passionate longevity, we want to bring with us on our journey the things that make life worth living into our later years: family, friends and community. I call this *sociability*.

Roots

Do you remember the fires that ravaged thousands of homes in southern California in the fall of 1993? Many people lost everything they had. Smoldering ashes and skeletal shells outlined the walls that had once enclosed a family and its history. While watching the newscasts of this disaster, I thought about my own home. What possessions would I take with me if fire threatened? Furniture, china, clothing—all the things we present to the outside world—could remain behind. These store-bought items can all be replaced. What I value most would probably fit into one large carton. After I rescued Napoleon, the cat, I would choose to save the treasures that my mom left me—simple things like her recipes, her yellow bowl (home to hundreds of cake mixes), her never-fail jar opener, the frying pan with blackened bottom for perfect blintzes. I would find room to save family photographs, the love letters my dad wrote to her during the war, a few trinkets of jewelry, the antique thesaurus Dad used when he was stuck for a word, our old family Scrabble set. All these items in my treasure chest would not fetch five dollars in a garage sale, but they are symbols that connect me to my past; these are the ties that bind me to my family history.

Do we ever leave home? Even when no one lives there any more, we always retain our need for the idea of "home," that loving place in our hearts, the distant memory of how things used to be when we were all together as a family. For me, home will always be the house on Scenic Drive in Hamilton, where I lived from grade three until my high-school graduation.

I know that I am blessed by happy memories of my childhood home; sure, we had our problems, but the images that remain for me are positive. Some adults, however, are not as fortunate. Many, in fact, are inspired—even driven—to create in their own world the childhood home they never had. One of my dear friends is a passionate gardener; in her north Toronto home she has nurtured the garden that didn't exist during her wartime childhood in Europe. Every tree or rosebush she plants today is a loving gesture to the scared and insecure child who grew up in a town scarred by bombs and explosions. Other adults are determined to ensure their children experience a loving and secure home that contrasts with the doubts and uncertainties of their childhood. And some unfortunate adults deal with their childhood disappointments by denying their current need for home, never ready or willing to put down roots, afraid to admit they missed something in the past and unaware that they can create a comfortable and secure home today.

Change is part of life. But while the physical home may change, the meaning of home never does. The home for which we all yearn means safety, roots, memories, individuality, comfort. There are people who can be happy in two hundred square feet of space, even in a nursing home, and people who are miserable surrounded by ten thousand square feet of luxury.

When my mother's health began to decline, my brother and I helped her move into an independent seniors' residence attached to a newly constructed nursing home. Medical care was available as required. Mom had a pleasant bachelor apartment with sliding glass doors opening onto a small balcony. She was a widow who had moved frequently after my brother and I left home, and many of our possessions from the big house in Hamilton were long gone. Nevertheless, the last remnants of furniture from the family home filled that small space: a turquoise reclining chair, the antique coffee table, one bookcase, her kitchen table, a few knickknacks, several plants. One of Mom's favorite hobbies was collecting and polishing driftwood; several precious pieces that had survived all the moves were displayed in various corners. Family photographs were everywhere. Mom enjoyed the friendship of the other residents and participated regularly in the social activities. She especially looked forward to the group dinners every evening at five o'clock. One day she asked me if I had seen the "other building," her way of referring to the nursing home. I never dared ask, "You mean the nursing home?" I knew she could never bring herself to use or hear those two words. The "other building" symbolized her very last home; for her it represented the beginning of the end.

When her health deteriorated, Steven and I were with her when she announced, "I think it's time for me to go to the other building." We cried together that afternoon, recognizing what her decision meant for her and for us. She passed away several months later in the "other building."

Chicken Soup for the Soul

"Would you like to come for Friday night dinner?" asked the Rothsteins. "We always have room for one more." The promise of homemade chicken soup with plump matzo balls stirred up remembrances of joyous family dinners we used to have when my parents were still alive. I accepted with delight. The Rothsteins' Sabbath table was crowded with family and friends. Everyone recited prayers, sipped wine, devoured food and exchanged lively conversation.

Every senior I interviewed stressed the importance of maintaining family unity through rituals.

Rituals such as family dinners, birthdays and holiday celebrations symbolically link the members of a family; they create a sense of belonging and reinforce our personal identity. They also sustain us in difficult times, when we are in ill health or dealing with loss. Even rituals like the nightly bedtime story can help maintain strong family connections. Eating dinner together, the most basic of family rituals, is considered to be a barometer of family stability. Sociologist John R. Kelly of the University of Illinois believes, "Dinner together is one of the absolute critical symbols in the cohesion of the family." Unfortunately, with the increase in two-career couples, single-parent households and overcommitted lives, mealtime often results in the grab-and-gulp approach. The dinner hour is shrinking to standard microwave time. Sitting at a dinner table for a relaxed meal means more than merely sharing food; it gives family members the opportunity to share thoughts and feelings.

Family rituals and shared meals are perfect opportunities to nurture our relationships, heal past hurts, express our love and commitment and experience the acceptance of others. Sure, Christmas dinner and Passover seder suppers are wonderful. What about the rest of the year? Some tips on making meals more memorable three hundred and sixty-five days of the year:

- Turn off the TV during dinner.
- If you know your mother's or grandmother's recipes for chicken soup or cabbage rolls, serve them to your family along with stories and remembrances that link you to your past.
- Start new family traditions. Grab a calendar and see what days you can celebrate. For example, one family has a special dinner to mark the first day of summer.
- Recreate family rituals that may have been lost or forgotten. Did your parents always celebrate a special anniversary? Find out what they did and try it with your family.
- Involve the whole family in the planning, preparation and clean-up of every meal.

And what about single people or individuals who have no relatives? There are many positive and imaginative ways in which we can still create a family setting. Perhaps we should be more open to shared and cooperative living arrangements with friends. Remember the ideals behind the commune or kibbutz movements? A growing number of individuals who are separated from relatives make a new family out of their friends and neighbors. Such extended families can bring together old, young, single, divorced and married in a relationship with the same close ties as a more traditional family. Whatever our situation, one thing is clear: we all need to feel part of a family. I have a suggestion for Dave Nichol, the former marketing whiz at Loblaws supermarkets: he should create a product called "Memories of Chicken Soup." A daily sniff would trigger all the remembrances of home and those wonderful family dinners that we all need.

The Fifth Commandment

Here's a riddle. We are allotted only two; we never know how long we will have them; once they're gone, we don't get any more; we may try to substitute others, but they will never be the same; often we don't appreciate them until they are gone. The answer: parents. They've been idealized and criticized. God knows, in therapy they've been analyzed! For every positive loving childhood experience, there is a painful, traumatic one. Did one of your parents have a condition—alcoholism, mental illness or physical disability? Did you suffer from APS (absent parent syndrome)? Was there abuse in your childhood, either physical or emotional? Were there times when you felt belittled or ignored? Did you have an overbearing mother or a tyrannical father? The possibilities are many, and everyone has a story.

Many of those stories have been told in the books found in the self-help section of your local bookstore. If all these stories could be rolled into one, the title could be *All I Really Learned About Life I Can Blame on My Dysfunctional Parents*. But is growing up in an unhappy family really the cause of all our troubles? Stephanie Coontz, author of *The Way We Never Were: American Families and the Nostalgia Trap*, describes a long-term study that tracked individuals from infancy to adolescence. Researchers then tried to predict which youngsters were more likely to lead successful, happy lives and which would turn into troubled adults, all based on family histories and childhood experiences. When the researchers revisited the subjects at age thirty, they were shocked to find that their predictions were wrong in two-thirds of the cases. As the author observes, "The researchers had consistently overestimated both the damaging effects of early family stresses and the positive effects of having a smooth, successful, non-challenging childhood and adolescence. They had failed to anticipate that depth, complexity, problem-solving abilities, and maturity might derive from painful experiences rather than easy successes. Boys and girls who had been happy and popular as athletes or beauties in high school had no incentive for innovation and struggle." When I look back on the difficult times of my childhood with my aged, old-fashioned dad and a sick mom, followed by my high school years as a wallflower, I know there is no single right path for parents to follow, no one *normal* pattern of family experiences that will ensure well-adjusted children.

As we approach mid-life, there is a shift in the way we interact with our parents. We become parents to our parents. It begins in almost imperceptible ways, perhaps with remarks like, "Mom, I think you should take your umbrella." Then we progress to advice, opinions and action on legal, family and health concerns. One of my patients helps her widowed mother with modern dating etiquette. She told me about one conversation they had: "I'm so delighted that she is dating a nice man and I suggested to her that maybe she should pick up the restaurant check next time." As we age, parents become less "magically omnipotent," a phrase coined by Dr. John Oldham, a psychoanalyst at the Columbia University College of Physicians and Surgeons. We see them as real people, almost as peers. To help individuals understand their particular family dynamics, social worker Reesa Kassirer puts parents' first names on a blackboard. "I'll write John and Mary, not Mommy and Daddy. I want clients to see their parents as human beings, so they will better understand how their parents evolved." During an interview, Kassirer emphasized a point that I, too, would like to emphasize. "Stop blaming your parents," she said. "They did the best they could at the time they were teaching you about life." It is vital to forgive our parents, to let go of any anger and resentment in our hearts so we may move forward emotionally. "At mid-life we ask ourselves, 'How do I want to spend the next half of my life?'" says Maxine Gallander Wintre, PhD, associate professor of psychology at York University. "It is necessary to reconcile with the past so that we may move into the next stage of our life without regret."

I agree completely. Whatever you need to do to understand and make peace with your parents, do it.

- Join a therapy group or go for individual counseling.
- Keep a journal.
- Read up on your particular issues. For those who need to reconnect with distant dads, try *Absent Fathers, Lost Sons* by Guy Corneau. If your relationship with your mother is problematic, try *The Dance of Intimacy* or *The Dance of Anger* by Harriet Lerner. Bookstores are full of excellent resources.
- Write a letter to an absent parent expressing your long-buried feelings. You don't have to mail it!
- Change *your* attitude. Try looking at your parents in a loving light.
- Accept that you may have to be angry and hurt before you can forgive.
- For those of you who are close to one or both parents, you are blessed. Nurture that relationship.

Your heart can't fill with love when the veins and arteries are clogged with negative feelings from the past.

Husbands and Wives—Relationships that Work

"Above all, you've got to be friends," advised Nick, a handsome gray-haired man of eighty as he helped his attractive wife, Katie, seventy-five, with her coat. When I became acquainted with this happily married couple ten years ago, their friendship was the first thing I noticed. These two people really like each other! I sometimes have the opportunity to watch unhappy couples interact in my office; their behavior reveals some of what goes on at home. Some typical scenes: George is explaining his back pain, and Martha keeps interjecting little details he forgot. Or says in a critical tone, "Well, if you lost that beer belly this wouldn't have happened" or "You? Exercise? That's a laugh!" Katie and Nick, on the other hand, consistently demonstrate a great deal of respect for each other; if either one has something to suggest on behalf of the other, it is done with the gentlest of voices, the softest of touches, the kindest of words. Nick always accompanies Katie to my office, regardless of whether he has an appointment. In his words, "We've got to look after each other in sickness and in health." The best part of their visits are the jokes. Nick is an incredible comedian, and even if Katie has heard his stories before, she laughs as hard as I do. They love to poke fun at each other but always in a loving, caring way. Curious why their relationship works so well, I asked if I could interview them for my book. They agreed and laughed together.

"Are you going to ask us about our sex life?" Nick inquired with a chuckle.

"Absolutely!" I replied. "So, is love better the second time around?" I asked with hope in my voice, hope for myself and the millions of other divorced baby boomers.

"It is more relaxed and fun," said Katie, who was sixty when Nick popped the question. "By the time you are sixty, you've learned so much about yourself and relationships, you hope you'll make the right choice in a mate. Neither one of us is perfect and we accept that in each other. The two most important qualities of a good marriage are compassion for each other and a great sense of humor. With a little bit of luck thrown in you'll be all set."

Nick believes one of the keys to a good marriage is shared interests. He and Katie both love gardening, croquet, walking the dog, entertaining family and friends at home. How do they deal with the small stuff in a marriage that drives people crazy?

"Nick is a diplomat," Kate confided. "He talks to me through the dog."

The dog?

Katie explained, "He'll say, 'Sigfried'—that's the dog—'why the hell does she put that black bathmat in the bathroom?' Then we laugh and talk about it."

And what about life's bigger problems?

"We look to each other for support, comfort and guidance," Nick answered. "We are just there for each other. We follow a basic code of ethics called the Golden Rule. Whenever problems come up, we deal with them right away and don't let anything fester. Life is too short for that."

"I read somewhere," added Katie, "that the ultimate test of a relationship is the ability to hold hands while you're having a disagreement. We can do that."

What about sex after seventy?

"Ask the dog!" joked Nick.

Katie answered, "We are playful, affectionate and caring, and that is what making love is all about."

It is inspiring to meet older couples who are committed to their relationships and still very much in love. Too often we hear about the marriages that aren't working out. I spoke again with Reesa Kassirer, a social worker in private practice who specializes in individual and couples counseling; I wanted her expert views on relationships.

Reesa began with some cheery facts: "Out of every twelve marriages, three are fantastic; three are just okay; three are like that Peggy Lee song, 'Is That All There Is?'; and three are lousy, but they still stay together."

I thought about the mediocre marriages and wondered, do all troubled marriages need therapy or can unhappy couples solve their difficulties themselves? Reesa gave me some interesting insights into the therapy process. Therapy helps many couples, but not all troubled spouses find themselves able to choose this option for healing. Why? "Some couples are either not ready to do the work required or they're uncomfortable with the very concept of talking to an outsider," she replied.

Therapy can help us understand our patterns of behavior—the stuff we do to each other that is rooted in our family histories.

What are these patterns from our family?

"Our very first school is our family of origin. That's where we learn to function. How we were treated, what we heard or didn't hear, what messages we got from our parents either consciously or unconsciously: these are familiar to us, and the familiar is powerful. For example, a common message that children receive is 'You don't count' or 'You never listen to me.' Or perhaps you lived in a family where the father was the boss and the mother was subservient, in other words an unequal relationship. We take these patterns with us and repeat them with our mates. So we might pick a mate who has struggled with the same basic issues as we have; our unconscious radar zooms in, we sense the familiar and we fall in love."

Does every couple do this? Reesa replied, "The two people in a relationship are like two identical peas in the pod; each may react differently—one may withdraw and the other becomes hysterical—but they will both have the same basic issues. The person who grew up in an unequal family situation will not marry a person who learned the pattern of equality; they wouldn't be able to relate to each other. We choose a mate who is at the same level of emotional maturity and awareness as we are. A needy person will not fit with someone who has a good sense of self and healthy communication skills. He or she will pick another needy person.

"We choose a mate who fits for us, given our needs at that moment in time. After a marriage failure, people often ponder the question, 'What did I ever see in him or her?' They forget about where they were at that moment in time."

"How do we break away from our destructive patterns, or are we doomed to fail?" I asked. I knew that since the divorce rate among remarried couples is fifty-seven percent in the United States, a grim statistic, it's vital that couples learn to work on their relationships if marriages are going to be saved.

Reesa had some good advice: "Knowing your triggers is one of the keys. Maybe when you were a child no one took much notice of the things you said or felt; you were never really heard. Then as an adult, when your mate ignores your opinion about something, you lash out and blame him for never listening to you. That sense of being ignored is your trigger, your stuff from childhood. With therapy, we learn to identify these issues and how to deal with them when the buttons are pushed. Another key is to have realistic expectations about any relationship. Our partners can't heal the wounded parts of us and make us feel whole again. Such healing is emotional growth work we have to do ourselves.

"A fantastic marriage doesn't just happen with the words 'I do.' It is a process of growth that begins with the self. In a nutshell, great marriages involve knowing, accepting and being honest with yourself. If I can look at the not okay parts of me and not be ashamed of them, then I can accept you. So unless you can forgive yourself for the parts that aren't perfect, you can't forgive anyone else. Once I can do that, then I don't have to clutch you or overpower you or want to own you.

"In a fantastic marriage there is a willingness to work on issues, resolve them and then move on. There was a study done on what makes a family emotionally healthy or unhealthy. The author found that emotionally healthy families dealt with the same number of painful issues as the unhealthy families; however, when a painful issue came up, the emotionally healthy family dealt with it, resolved it and then moved on. By contrast, in the unhealthy family, nothing was ever resolved; anger and resentment kept building up.

"Finally, a fantastic marriage works toward unconditional acceptance for each other. If you accept yourself unconditionally, then you can accept your mate unconditionally."

On the query whether fantastic couples communicate in a special way, Reesa had a positive answer: "Yes, they do. They learn to say 'I,' not 'you,' as in, 'I feel upset when you . . .' Compare this to the accusatory 'you never' or 'you always.' Each partner can stop blaming the other and instead acknowledge their own stuff. They say what they feel and admit what they want; they don't assume anything, and finally they check out what their mate is saying so that they really hear what he or she is asking."

Is there any hope for the millions of us who are divorced and willing to enter into a second marriage?

"Yes, of course. Nature plays a funny trick on us when we're teenagers. During the period when our bodies, our hormones and the clock tell us it's time to develop a relationship, we may not be ready emotionally. There are many successful second marriages; but whether it is a first or second marriage, there has to be emotional maturity, honesty with self, and the couple must be willing to work on the relationship. Remember, no one can be happy all the time; you have to be willing to accept the bumps that are a normal part of life and deal with them."

The "Passion" in Passionate Longevity

Whenever I mention the title of this book, many people brashly inquire, "From your research, will I still be 'doing it' when I'm ninety?" I reply, "If you are 'doing it' in your forties and fifties, it's likely you'll be 'doing it' in your eighties and nineties, providing you maintain general good health!" Considering health from strictly a physical point of view, all research indicates that sexual activity need not diminish with aging. In fact, approximately seventy percent of healthy seventy-year-olds continue to have regular sexual intercourse. More than one quarter of healthy men and women older than eighty are still sexually active; their average frequency of intercourse is four times monthly, according to a report by Dr. Stephen Holzapfel in the *Canadian Family Physician Journal* (April 1994). The key word here is *healthy*, for the greatest barrier to sexual activity in our senior years is lack of a healthy sexual partner. Dr. Holzapfel cites a study that found that seventy-four percent of married men and fifty-six percent of married women older than sixty maintained an active sex life, whereas only thirty-one percent of unmarried men and just five percent of unmarried women were sexually active. It is an unfortunate reality that while the desire may still be there, sometimes the partner isn't. Most healthy women older than eighty have no partners, and even those with partners often have to deal with impotence.

It is important to debunk the myth that sex among those older than sixty is infrequent or nonexistent. Yes, parents and grandparents can still be found in the bedroom, and they are not just having a nap. The real issue is not the aging process; the issue again is *health*. Medical illness is often the culprit in sexual dysfunction, rather than aging alone. Family physicians are the best resources for those who need to address these sexual concerns. For men, impotence may be due to diseases such as arteriosclerosis (hardening of the arteries), diabetes, hypertension, thyroid and renal disorders; impotence may follow prostatic cancer surgery. Not surprising, however, is the effect of medications, the most common doctor-induced cause of sexual dysfunction. Drugs prescribed for hypertension and gastrointestinal conditions are the most frequent villains. Male potency is also negatively affected by alcohol, tobacco and narcotics. In addition, psychological and relationship factors play a major role in sexual problems.

With the subject of menopause finally out of the closet, so is the issue of sexuality and the postmenopausal woman. According to a study quoted by Dr. Holzapfel, "There is no clear upper limit of when women cannot be sexually active, with some still enjoying intercourse past the age of one hundred." A decrease in estrogenic stimulation, however, can lead to failure of lubrication and diminished labial response. Such atrophy may make intercourse painful. Estrogen replacement therapy can be beneficial. Hormonal changes associated with menopause, whether natural or surgical (from hysterectomy), can also affect desire, arousal and orgasm. As with men, sexual expression is a function of psychological and relationship factors combined with biology, so those issues must be addressed, as well. During my interviews with seniors, many of them, particularly the women, often single or widowed, complained that lack of opportunity, rather than lack of interest, limited their sex lives. Then there is energetic Ginger Eisen, seventy-seven, recently married to a charming man of eighty-six, who implied, with a look, that there is still lots of life left in both of them.

So if there was ever a reason for baby boomers to stay healthy and fit, sexual longevity is it. There is a strong connection between being physically active and being sexually active. Research studies have shown that people who are physically active report greater frequency of sexual activity and more satisfying sexual relations. We know that exercise makes the body work better, and sexuality is part of the whole body. Furthermore, the penis is totally dependent on the pressure and volume of the blood supply for adequate function. If the arteries are clogged or the veins incompetent, the organ stays flaccid. So, men, get out those running shoes for peak cardiovascular fitness. A regular aerobic program keeps the muscles, blood vessels and nerves in optimum condition. Furthermore, although more difficult to quantify, the psychological effects of fitness on sexuality should not be underestimated. Feeling good about your body raises your self-esteem, which in turn can lead to increased interest in sex.

By the year 2025, one in five people will be seniors—the bulk of them baby-boomer seniors—many of whom will be healthier, fitter and no doubt sexier than we ever thought possible. The sports slogan *Just do it* will be taking on a whole new meaning.

Friendship—Reciprocal Nurturing

On a rainy day thirty-six years ago, a brown-haired girl named Barbara, with friendly face and caring eyes, listened intently to my complaints during recess. After I described how strict my father was, she offered support and advice. Even though Barbara was only nine years old, she already displayed the empathy that would find its expression in later years through her career in counseling and parent education. Now whenever I introduce Barbara, I always say, "This is my oldest friend: we've been friends since grade four!" Of course I couldn't have known then how precious friendships are, but looking back I realize that Barbara helped me through the difficult periods in my childhood. Different cities and crowded schedules have reduced the frequency of our visits; nevertheless we see each other for a marathon catch-up session two to three times every year.

Friends are as vital as a pulse to the body. A good friend nourishes the heart. Friends sustain, entertain, reduce pain and remain. An old Arabian proverb says: "A friend is one to whom one may pour out all the contents of one's heart, chaff and grain together, knowing that the gentlest of hands will take and sift it, keep what is worth keeping and with the breath of kindness blow the rest away."

One month before my fortieth birthday, I did a quick assessment of my personal life.

Status: Separated
Score: Men 0
Girlfriends 22

Since I had temporarily struck out with men, I decided to celebrate my new decade with the women who have made a difference in my life, the ones who have always been there "through fat and thin," as I wrote in a song called "Girlfriends." I threw my very own fortieth birthday party with the girls, all twenty-two of them. We giggled, gossiped and gobbled up a delicious assortment of potluck dishes. Then a precedent-setting action occurred. I asked a question of the women, and in turn each one stood up to share her story. This gathering and its question format have now become my annual summer garden party to celebrate girlfriends. In the first year, the question seemed straightforward: How did we meet each other? What I heard from my friends touched my heart, for I learned the ways in which my friendship had made a difference in their lives. Another year the question was, "What lessons have you learned in the past year?" The question triggered a flood of shared confidences, laughter and tears, as lessons of trust, friendship, patience, betrayal, courage, hope, love, grief, missed opportunity and satisfying achievement were openly discussed. One woman shared the story of her son, diagnosed with a psychotic disorder; another had recently lost a parent. Others were going through the "slings and arrows of outrageous fortune" thanks to the recession; still others were dealing with marital discord. My party was a microcosm of life itself! The last verse in my song is a tribute to girlfriends:

> We've got wrinkles and gray hair,
> Sagging thighs, flannel underwear,
> Now we're widows, but it's all right,
> 'Cuz you're my date on Saturday night.

One truth is clear: men may come and go, but my girlfriends are forever! Those summer garden parties help us keep our faith in each other alive.

While a friendship can be a source of strength, it can also be as fragile as a sheet of glass, fracturing when exposed to a thoughtless word or an insensitive act. One of my patients described the pain she felt when her girlfriend finally discovered Mr. Right and she was shown the exit sign. Then, when the hot romance ended, her friend wanted comfort and tried to restore their previous friendship, a common problem for girlfriends. No one is happy if a relationship becomes a one-way street; for friendships to work there has to be mutual giving and getting, reciprocal nurturing and mutual benefit.

Over the course of a lifetime, many of us will experience friendships that must end. Friendships cannot exist with betrayal—those close encounters of the worst kind. Imagine the hurt, pain and grief of discovering that a friend you shopped with, traveled with, shared secrets with, had lunch with, exercised with, shared birthdays with is also having an affair with your husband! Most women agree on this: they are more devastated and hurt by their friend's betrayal than by their husband's infidelity. A husband having an affair is terrible enough, but when it is with your girlfriend . . . Such an outrage is unthinkable and unconscionable. It takes a long time to forgive.

I recently heard some wonderful definitions of a best friend. One was, "One who understands our silence." And my favorite: "A best friend is the one who comes in when the whole world has gone out." About twenty-four years ago I met one of my best friends, Linda Stork, at George Brown College. We have been through every life situation together—marriages, divorces, going back to school, boyfriends, loss of family and pets. I am so glad she is in my life! I am also blessed with a long-distance best friend, Sharon Newman in California. We were bunk mates at Esalen in Big Sur. Meeting her was the miracle that helped me through the low point in my life, the end of my marriage. She helped me to open a door to my inner child and to discover a more spiritual me.

Although the dynamics of friendship among men are changing, many are still unable to discuss personal matters openly, especially thorny topics such as sexuality, marital conflict, feelings of inadequacy and mid-life upheaval. Daniel Weinzweig, forty-six, joined a men's group after he recognized a need to redefine his masculinity and his male place in the world. He believes that men need to release themselves from the straitjacket of the masculine image. He described his group to me. "Within our group there was a level of trust, intimacy and safety. No one cared what your profession was; we were all human beings with feelings." Topics such as, what is a man? relationships with fathers, friendships and sexuality were discussed openly in the group. "Men have never felt comfortable discussing their sexuality and they still don't—even if it is the nineties," Daniel continued. "It's a shame-based subject. But in our men's group there was a commonality of feeling, a recognition that none of us was alone. Having a common human experience with people of the same gender is powerful. Women and men are and will always be fundamentally different." One area in which this difference is evident is in building friendship. Women find it easier to share confidences, and they develop closer, more meaningful friendships than those shared between males. I remember meeting a new group of women at a dinner party. After five minutes, we were cheerfully chatting away about our divorces, celibacy, blind dates and menopausal symptoms. There was an immediate feeling of trust, acceptance and caring; it was okay to be vulnerable in front of each other. Several women exchanged telephone numbers, and new friendships blossomed as a result.

Samuel Johnson wrote: "We cannot tell the precise moment when friendship is formed. As in filling a vessel drop by drop, there is at last a drop which makes it run over; so in a series of kindnesses there is at last one which makes the heart run over." We will take these heartfelt feelings with us on our journey to passionate longevity, making life worth living into our twilight years.

Grandchildren—God's Reward for Growing Older

I will always remember the expression of joy, love and passion in Anne Blair's eyes when I interviewed her. Anne's voice bubbled with delight as she described how busy she stays visiting her fifteen grandchildren and ten great-grandchildren. "The children keep me going. I have to be well and stay well for them. My greatest pleasure is going to the flea market in Florida, buying presents and bringing them home for my grandchildren. I make a point of remembering everyone's birthday and anniversary with this," she said, reaching into her purse to show me her bible, a birthday book full of names and dates. She continued, "I check this book every day to make sure I haven't forgotten anyone. My calendar is filled with family occasions—weddings, bar mitzvahs, graduations and birthday parties. I'll be eighty in February, but I'm too busy living to worry about my age. I'm the luckiest person in the world to have such a wonderful family. My grandchildren always end their telephone conversations with these beautiful words, 'Love you, Bubbie.' " Her story touched my heart with its message of love across the generations.

Many of my other senior friends tell similar stories. "I have two children, eight grandchildren and three great-grandchildren," said Bernard Herman, eighty-two, beaming and pointing to a family photograph. "I consider them all precious, so I tell people I have thirteen children. When I hold the little ones in my lap, hugging and kissing them, it's the most wonderful feeling in the whole world."

Grandchildren. Just saying that word to the seniors I interviewed elicited indescribable feelings of euphoria. Questions about fitness, great personal achievements and philosophy of life were answered with enthusiasm, but when I inquired about grandchildren, faces radiated with an extra special joy, eyes twinkled, posture was reduced to a mushy softness, hearts gushed with love. In most of the homes I visited I saw living room walls covered with photographs of smiling children at every age and stage of growth. What couldn't fit on the walls were displayed on dressers, coffee tables and fridge doors.

I believe the grandparent–grandchild relationship is a powerful bond of loving acceptance and unconditional love. This relationship encompasses the parenting role but without the depth of responsibility and level of expectation parents often have. "Grandparents are different from parents," believes Joy Shepherd, the thirty-seven-year-old granddaughter of Max Sharp, ninety-two. "No matter what I do in my life, it's okay with them. I know they'll still love me one hundred percent, and there is total acceptance. I can call them up, day or night, and go over there. There is never a time that is not good for me to call them." Between the generations, there is reciprocal nurturing. Grandparents feel needed; grandchildren feel loved. Grandparents have time to listen; grandchildren find their voice. Grandparents, through play, grow younger; grandchildren, through play, grow up. Grandparents can offer an emotional sanctuary for the grandchild; they act as mentors, care givers, advisers, historians. On the other hand, grandchildren can provide an emotional boost when times are difficult for the grandparent. "My four-year-old grandson was my savior during my business crisis," admitted Robert, fifty-five. After his family automotive company went bankrupt, Robert faced nine months of unemployment. During this time, he and his grandson played games for hours, went to children's movies and treated themselves to dinner together. Robert explained, "He took my mind off my troubles. An afternoon with him lifted my spirits. He remains the joy in my life. I tell him he's my best boyfriend."

Sometimes the wise, gentle counsel of a gray-haired grandparent can have a powerful effect on a young child. Kevin Kassirer, thirty-five, vividly recalls an incident that changed his life when he was six years old. "I was in my bedroom crying after it was discovered that I had a learning disability. My grandfather came into my room, sat down on the bed and told me two stories. One was the fable about the tortoise and the hare; the other was about a boy named Jimmy, his difficulty climbing over a wall and the obstacles he overcame to succeed. When Grandpa finished he said, 'I want you to promise me one thing. No matter what you do, always do your best.' His words really affected me. He was willing to accept me as long as I did my best. My grandfather's advice became my watchword in life."

There are many different styles of grandparents to suit every family situation. Grace Lawrence, seventy-six, became a long-distance grandmother when her son and his family moved to Australia. She really missed her two granddaughters, now eleven and eight. She describes their strategy to strengthen their bond: "We began writing letters, then progressed to tapes. I would read the girls a story on tape so they could listen to it at bedtime. Then my husband and my son became ham operators, so for the last six years we've been talking to each other over the airwaves. Now we use faxes to keep in touch. I always give the girls some money for Christmas, and later on they send me pictures of the items they bought." A little imagination and the wonders of modern technology have kept this family together.

Max Sharp has nineteen grandchildren and thirty-four great-grandchildren. Joy Shepherd especially loves his maxim, "It's nice to be important, but more important to be nice." Joy has many reasons to treasure her grandfather. She explains, "When my grandmother passed away three years ago, it was like losing a mother. Since that time, a regular group of grandchildren and great-grandchildren meets Papa Max for lunch every week. We don't go out of a sense of duty; we just love being with this kind, gentle, loving man. Papa and I are kindred spirits. I can't explain it; the feelings are just there."

What significance does this vital intergenerational relationship have in terms of passionate longevity? No scientific studies have yet explored the link between having grandchildren and living a long, happy life. But the feelings expressed by the many seniors I interviewed cannot be underestimated, and these feelings are life-enhancing. For some, grandchildren are their reason for existence; the new generation gives meaning to their lives. Max Sharp promised his granddaughter that he would still be around for her seven-year-old son's future wedding. That should be enough to motivate Max to hang on for many more years.

But not everyone can be like Max, blessed with his extensive family. If grandchildren are important for quality of life, where does that leave individuals like me who will never become parents, let alone grandparents? What about the grandparents who are estranged from their grandchildren? Or parents whose children are childless for whatever reason? There are many possibilities. The Baycrest Centre for Geriatric Care is one group that has recognized the need for intergenerational programs. Through their child-care program, young and old are brought together to learn from each other. As Mara Swartz, the center's recreational therapist, explains, "There is life in children. Older people sense that they are still worthy; they still have something to give to the little ones. Wonderful friendships develop, and for some seniors without grandchildren, that bond gives them back a family connection." Some of the activities that young and old can share include exercise and arts and crafts; there is even an adopt-a-grandparent program where local high school girls are assigned to seniors for once-a-week visits. One exceptional project was called "At My Age." Eight seniors were paired with eight children, ages three to five, to learn photography. Before the ten-week program began, Swartz conducted an orientation session scaled down to a four-year-old's level of understanding. She wanted to show the youngsters how some older people with disabilities see, hear and move. She told the children that the seniors wouldn't be able to run as fast as they could, so they would have to walk slowly; then she also explained that a wheelchair is just like a bike. The kids listened to her with cotton in their ears to mimic hearing loss, and walked around for a few minutes with one eye covered. After learning how to use the most basic point-and-shoot cameras, and with the help of a volunteer, the junior and senior photographers found the experience memorable. Swartz summarized the program: "The kids really provided their partners with some motivation. The seniors had a chance to look at life from a child's perspective, and the children were fully accepting of people with disabilities." One youngster commented, "My favorite thing was taking the pictures," then added, "and holding my partner's hand." What a poignant story.

Even though I do not have children, my life is blessed with four wonderful nephews; the two oldest, Michael, twenty-four, and

Paul, twenty-three, lived with me while I wrote this book. The two youngest, Joel, ten, and Adam, eight, have confirmed my status as Aunt Elaine; we have a playful and close relationship that fills that gap for nurturing. I am hopeful that my next permanent relationship will include the bonus of his children and possible grandchildren. I rather fancy being a step-grandparent.

The 10 Secrets of Max Sharp, age ninety-two

1. It's nice to be important, but it's more important to be nice.
2. To help someone in life is a good deed.
3. If you have the health, you have the wealth.
4. Worry makes you sick. If you have something to overcome, you have to try to do it.
5. The greatest accomplishment in life is to make your body healthy.
6. On regrets: this is water under the bridge. Look forward to the future.
7. You have to help yourself. If you're not going to do it, who will?
8. Walking is the best exercise.
9. Do the best you can *today*.
10. There is nothing more important than family.

The Power of One

In an old Hasidic story, a curious rabbi asked the Lord to teach him the difference between heaven and hell. "I will show you hell," said the Lord, and led the rabbi into a room with a big round table. In the middle of the table was an enormous pot of stew, but nevertheless the people sitting around the table were starving and desperate. Everyone at the table was holding a spoon with a very long handle. It was possible for each person to reach the pot to take a spoonful of stew, but because the handle of the spoon was longer than anyone's arm, no one could get the food into his or her mouth. The rabbi saw that their suffering was indeed terrible; this really was hell. "Now I will show you heaven," said the Lord, and they went into another room that looked exactly the same as the first. There was the same round table and the same pot of stew. The people as before were equipped with the awkward long-handled spoons, but the people in heaven were well nourished, laughing and talking. At first the rabbi could not understand. The Lord explained: "You see, they have learned to feed each other."

I was touched by the compassionate attitudes of the many seniors I interviewed. Altruism was an important part of their lives. Most had been involved in volunteer work for years, as had their parents. Ida Farber, eighty-five, a patient at Baycrest Hospital, recalls as a child tagging along while her mother canvassed homes for donations; the money raised bought the building that became the first Jewish Home for the Aged. "There are so many organizations that need help," says Ida. "Just look around and you'll find them. Even if all you have is an hour a week, volunteer somewhere to help those in need. Helping those not as fortunate gives you such a marvelous feeling inside. You'll feel like you're on this earth for a good purpose!"

The feeling of wanting to do good and help others is often experienced at mid-life. At this stage in our life we are motivated to pay back society for the support it has given us. We begin to realize that the world we live in (family, school, churches) has helped in our growth and development; it is now time for us to contribute, to help others. In 1963, psychoanalyst Erik H. Erikson called the years between forty and sixty-five "middle adulthood." He described this stage as a time of "generativity," the term he coined to explain our desire to contribute to the world through family and work, and the development of our concern for future generations.

How do we express generativity? One way is through parenting, by showing our love and support for the valuable members of the next generation, our children. Or generativity may be demonstrated through volunteer work or through one's occupation. By providing services or quality product, we contribute to the well-being of those who need them. This gives us a feeling of returning something of real value to society.

There is also a life-enhancing dimension to volunteerism. People who take an active role in their community tend to be healthier than those who live in social isolation. One woman who has spent years doing community work is Elsie Palter, eighty-four. She says, "It's important to be involved in various fields of interest to you. We have a responsibility to give something back." The late Audrey Hepburn, a glamorous star noted for her elegant beauty, helped children in underprivileged countries for many years. Her words are an encouragement to all of us: "If you ever need a helping hand, you'll find one at the end of your arm. As you get older, remember you have a second hand. The first hand is to help yourself; the second hand is to help others."

Have you noticed people wearing buttons that read: "Practice random kindness and senseless acts of beauty"? A random kindness can be as small a gesture as letting someone pull in front of you in traffic; it also includes larger acts such as volunteering to distribute food to the homeless at Thanksgiving. A senseless act of beauty may involve picking up someone else's discarded pop can from the sidewalk. This altruistic movement is spreading, and so are the positive feelings it generates.

Here are some suggestions to practice your own random kindness:

- baby-sit for someone who is housebound
- shovel your neighbor's walkway
- put a dime in a stranger's parking meter
- buy someone flowers
- smile at the supermarket cashier
- when you are finished with your magazines and paperbacks donate them to a hospital
- clean out your clothes closet and give the discards to charity
- give that restaurant doggie bag to a homeless person
- buy a Christmas present for a child from a needy family
- cook a hot meal for a senior

Think of the times in your life when someone surprised you with a completely selfless act of kindness. Weren't you inspired to do something for someone as a result? All it takes is one person— you—to start the ball rolling. As more and more people get involved, imagine the momentum. Giving, whether it is a gift of one's time or a gift of money, embodies a love for humanity.

The 10 Secrets of the
Honorable Pauline McGibbon, age eighty-four

1. Be a volunteer.
2. An education is essential.
3. Whatever you're doing in life, do the best you can.
4. Find a hobby that you enjoy, for example, reading, music.
5. It's very important to have things in common with your mate, such as love of reading, golf, theater.
6. With personal conflicts, look at the situation in someone else's shoes.
7. Be tactful. Remember, other people have feelings, too.
8. Find something that you enjoy doing outside the home.
9. "Old" is in the mind. Keep yourself busy.
10. Patience and a sense of humor will get you through most everything.

3

PRODUCTIVITY

Working with a passion at something
you love.

C an you imagine having to make an appointment with a one-hundred-and-one-year-old? In fact, Ruth Atkinson Hindmarsh was so busy that her grandson, who was making all the arrangements for my interview, could only offer me two possible times during the whole week when she would be available! Ruth laughed at the thought of retirement: "I want to go on until I can't." And she did, working two days a week as director of the Atkinson Charitable Foundation until her death.

Ask ninety-seven-year-old Rhoda Bennett what she's been doing three times each week for the past twenty years. Rhoda volunteers her time at a home for disabled children. Honored in a newspaper article as one of the unsung heroes in her community, she feeds children who are developmentally and physically challenged. Rhoda lovingly communicates with each child, many of whom are in wheelchairs or bedridden. Her eighty-year-old niece, Pearl Zucker, remarked, "Rhoda's dedication to those children has given her an incentive, a reason for getting up in the morning." Pearl and her eighty-six-year-old husband, Sol, also have an important reason for getting up in the morning. For the past ten years, Monday through Friday, these sales representatives can be found in local supermarkets checking the shelves for products distributed by their son's food brokerage business. "We even attend the sales meeting every Monday morning at eight."

You won't find energetic eighty-year-old entrepreneur Ed Mirvish sleeping at eight o'clock, either. He'll be where he always is—working at his office in Honest Ed's, a Toronto shopping landmark, until noon each day, including Saturday. Then he visits his many restaurants until 2:30 p.m. Later on, the theater business pulls him away from the food business, where he works until dinner. "I don't stop," he explained enthusiastically. "When you find that *something* that excites you, then it's not work, it's your passion. I am living my passion. Work is fun. Every day is a holiday when you love what you do!" Ed's attitude is the very essence of what I call productivity—working with a passion at something you love.

When scientists studied a large number of healthy, happy centenarians found in the Caucasus Mountains of Georgia in the former Soviet Union, they found one key factor: these people had never retired. Even though they were more than one hundred years old, there was always a need for their services—weeding in the fields, tending animals, cleaning house, caring for grandchildren. I am convinced that keeping busy doing the things you love will jet-propel you on the road to passionate longevity. Grace Lawrence, now seventy-six, has never had to cope with the stress of retirement; she just never stopped working. This amazing woman still teaches four aqua-fit classes a week to seniors at York University; when she's not teaching, she plans exercise programs and coordinates the music for her classes. She told me about her students' enthusiasm: "The girls are expecting I'll be there until I'm ninety. As long as I'm physically and mentally able, I'll keep teaching. Everyone has to be needed and wanted; you have to feel you're helping humanity somewhere, no matter what your age. That's the feeling I get from my work."

Through my research I've gleaned three important facts:

1. Most people do not love their work.
2. Those who want to make a change often wait for circumstances to motivate them.
3. Most people do not know what their passion is or how to find it.

Through interviews, I discovered that many of my baby-boomer patients are struggling to find their passion. They want something they really care about, something that closely matches their interests and values—a life path as opposed to another job.

To help you in your search to find that passion, I've outlined strategies that include visualization, the love list, career counseling and support groups.

A Cheerleader for Life

My father had a profound influence on my life. I remember his voice: loud, emphatic, articulate. His manner was persuasive and authoritative. When he spoke, I listened and obeyed. He was an entrepreneur and an inventor. "All you need is one good idea, Elaine!" he would lecture, pounding his fist on the nearest table for emphasis. I was not about to question the wisdom of a man who had lived fifty-four years longer than I had. I was nineteen at the time; he was seventy-three.

I had my first good idea at age twenty, thanks to my mother's help. She introduced me to the latest fashion fad from Florida: crocheted jewelry. I saw the potential market in Canada for these colorful beaded rings and chokers. With enough start-up capital from my dad—who was thrilled with my enterprise—I bought supplies, hired twenty skilled artisans and enthusiastically sold the jewelry to boutiques and department stores across the country.

My father's other favorite fist-pounding line was, "Elaine, be your own boss; don't work for anyone." In the jewelry business I was my own boss for two years. I loved the feeling of directing my own one-woman show. Unfortunately, the fad ended, and so did my business. At twenty-two, I was unemployed, depressed and fatherless; my dad had died that year from cancer.

Soon after, a new mentor came on the scene in the form of a love interest. Michael was forty-one, nineteen years older than I; his voice was emphatic and articulate, his manner persuasive and authoritative. When he spoke, I listened. Does any of this sound familiar? Michael's favorite line was, "Get a profession, make your own money, don't depend on any man." His pupil was ambitious yet very stuck. I had no idea what I wanted to be. I resisted any suggestion that I return to school. My last memory of school was of dropping out of second-year university to start my jewelry business. Michael was logical and practical: "You're not going to discover your passion in the classified section of the newspaper. Go for career counseling. Find out your strengths and weaknesses." I found out everything I needed to know at the YMCA career development center. After a full day of tests—aptitude, psychological and personal preference—my responses were assessed. Then the results were tabulated and compared with others in my age group who wrote the same tests.

The lengthy evaluation by a psychologist confirmed what I already knew in my heart.

- I need to be in control; that translates into self-employed.
- I love to persuade and motivate people to do something.
- I have to be in the limelight.
- I am very creative and innovative.
- I lead by energizing people.
- I am a risk taker.

A profession was not spelled out for me, but the psychologist and I brainstormed to generate ideas. I was excited by all the new options.

By chance (does anything ever happen by chance?) I bumped into an old friend who was studying to be a chiropractor. "A chiropractor?" I mused. Both my parents had been helped by chiropractors. My heart danced with the possibilities. I could motivate patients to be healthy, help those in pain and I'd even be self-employed! There was just one enormous obstacle. "You'll need first-year-university chemistry," the registrar at the chiropractic college announced. "You have all the other prerequisites." Chemistry? The only chemistry I understood was that magic *je ne sais quoi* between a man and a woman. Not one to be daunted (my other traits are tenacity and persistence), I earned that university credit in chemistry with the help of a patient tutor.

I admit I had one grave concern: my age. Several years had passed. I'd be starting my four-year chiropractic program at age twenty-five. "I'll be twenty-nine by the time I graduate," I moaned. Michael straightened me out in short order. "Elaine, you're going to be twenty-nine anyway; at least as a chiropractor you'll have what you want, instead of drifting into endless stopgap jobs." The four years flew by; in June 1978 I opened my office.

For the past seventeen years I have been living my passion. Not only have I been able to help patients in my clinic, but I've also rekindled a talent from childhood: public speaking. I won numerous speaking awards in public school, then branched out into

acting in high school musicals. Now I regularly address corporations and organizations on health, wellness and longevity.

My creative urges have found an outlet. I've been writing poems
and rap songs about everything from men to menopause, and I
perform them during my motivational seminars. Recently I
received what I consider the ultimate compliment: I was called a
"cheerleader for life." My joie de vivre comes from loving what I
do. It gives me energy. I am alive with a purpose.

The Flow—Kenny G and Me

Five years ago I approached CPI, one of the world's successful concert booking agencies. I wanted to add my name to their
roster of doctors who treat visiting entertainers performing in
Toronto. At the time they were looking for a reliable chiropractor and
massage therapist who could make "house calls" on short notice.

Thanks to my phone call to CPI, I've had the opportunity to treat
some famous spines—those belonging to Phil Collins, Paula Abdul,
Bryan Adams and most recently Kenny G, the talented soprano
saxophone player. His haunting music is passion itself. Kenny's life
story is also about passion.

Kenny, who grew up in Seattle, started piano lessons at age six,
like many other kids. He was constantly prodded by his mother to
practice but he hated the piano. His life changed four years later. On
the *Ed Sullivan Show* he watched a musician play the saxophone.
He was mesmerized! He begged his mother to let him try this new
instrument. She decided to rent one in case he lost interest. "It was
magic," he said. "I couldn't put it down. I'd play day and night. I
never really needed lessons, I found it so easy to play." He joined
the school band in grade four and soon was the best musician in
the school.

In high school he was asked to do some gigs so after class he
would play in local clubs. At the University of Seattle he studied to
be an accountant by day and played in clubs at night. He joined a
band and was soon signed by a record company. His latest release
has sold ten million copies. His advice to those who are searching
for their passion? "Be a risk taker. Sometimes you have to get out of
your comfort zone to find your way. Fear of failure often stops us
from taking that first new step. If you find that you don't enjoy
what you're doing, try something else."

Kenny G has what University of Chicago psychology professor Mihaly Csikszentmihalyi calls "flow". This is the zone where we are so absorbed with what we are doing that we lose consciousness of time. Flow is a state of total concentration and absorption; it's the ability to be completely engaged in a project. Flow involves every one of our senses; it takes us to a place far removed from the clock-watching, boring, restless stereotype of work.

In your life, what are you doing when you flow? Are you working or exercising? Are you involved in a hobby that absorbs you so totally you forget to eat? As Kenny G found out when he got that first saxophone, when you click with that special something it really is magic.

How can you learn how to flow? Start by writing down all the activities you really love. Visualize yourself doing all the activities you love full time. Do you want to do any of them full time? Are any of these activities financially feasible? If you love to read and frequently stay awake until dawn to finish the last chapter, have you considered a career involving books or editing? Would you like to work in a library? Let your mind go on a fantasy trip. Think of related areas where you could incorporate reading, for example the publishing field. Stretch your mind to explore the unthinkable, the unknowable, the untouchable. Is there someone who has your dream job? Send them a letter. Call them. Take them to lunch. If you can't get through to this person on the telephone, befriend the secretary. Tell him or her why you're calling. Don't be obnoxious, but be persistent and tenacious.

As Kenny G encourages, "Get out of your comfort zone to find your way."

Thank God It's Monday

You can't keep unhappiness a secret, especially unhappiness at work. Your body always knows about it long before you're ready to express your feelings out loud. Some telltale signs and symptoms:

1. It's Sunday night and you're getting that miserable headache again—the one that feels like a tight band around your head. The Sunday Night Syndrome is triggered by anxiety and fear directly related to work. The body doesn't know the difference between a rehearsal (just thinking about being at work) and actually being there. The reaction is the same. If you are in this

condition, it's time to look at the cause, rather than patching up the headache with pills, potions and lotions!

2. It's Monday morning, seven o'clock. You've just heard that familiar wake-up call from your clock radio. How many songs, traffic and weather reports do you hear before you finally crawl to the bathroom? The ease or difficulty of getting out of bed in the morning indicates your level of excitement and enthusiasm for the day ahead. When it comes to work, "Many people are just going through the motions," observes Michael Hazell, a career consultant with Robin T. Hazell & Associates. "Most can't remember the last time they felt excited about their careers. The world is full of people who do not enjoy their jobs. These people work during the week so that they can do what they really enjoy during their time off." Now picture this scene: you are leaving with your friends early in the morning for your favorite ski resort. Do you tear out of bed before the alarm? That's enthusiasm!

3. It's Monday morning, nine o'clock. You've just returned from a short vacation. You stare at those dreaded client files piled up on your desk. Suddenly you feel a squeezing pressure in your chest, and a sharp pain shoots down your left arm. Beads of sweat drip down your chin as you dial 911. More fatal heart attacks occur on Monday around nine o'clock than on any other day of the week. This bizarre fact was documented in medical literature as far back as 1980. "How could our heart know what day it is?" you might ask. Physical reasons have been proposed to explain the phenomenon known as the Black Monday Syndrome, but so far none of these physical possibilities has been proven. "Could the *meaning* of Monday be the difference? It might be that human beings, creatures who are uniquely sensitive to the symbols and inner meanings in life, are paying a terrible price by returning to jobs and work situations they despise," says Larry Dossey, an expert on mind-body medicine and the author of *Meaning and Medicine*.

The health risk of being chronically unhappy at work has been known for some time. In 1972 a study done for the Massachusetts Department of Health found that the best predictor for heart disease was not any of the usual physical risk factors (smoking, high blood pressure, elevated cholesterol) but rather job satisfaction.

Will working long hours erode your health? A study presented at a meeting of the American Psychological Association found no relation between long work hours and symptoms of ill health among nine hundred Canadian workers surveyed. Indeed, the healthiest were those who worked long hours because they were absorbed in their work and loved it. It's not devotion to work that harms your health, but a job that makes you feel powerless and insecure. So, the ability to put in long hours at a task you like may actually promote good health.

When I suggest ways to make changes in their work lives, some patients resist my solutions. They offer excuses: "I'll wait until the recession is over," "I can't afford career counseling," "I haven't a clue what I would do instead," "I'm lucky to have a job." Some unfulfilled individuals prefer comfort over challenge, safety over growth. Risk taking is scary for some, motivating for others.

What about your body? Is your heart telling you to make a change? Are your muscles tightening to grab your attention? You, too, can own the Thank God It's Monday attitude. It's not luck; it will happen if you make it happen.

The 10 Secrets of Ed Mirvish, age eighty

1. Get an education—it won't guarantee success but it will give you tools to work with.
2. A sense of humor gets you through the rough spots.
3. When you find something you love to do, then it's not work. It's your passion.
4. In business: keep it simple, go against the trend, fulfill a need.
5. Keep breathing.
6. Everyone is good at something, but no one is good at everything.
7. Trust your gut feeling.
8. Life's main purpose is to be of service.
9. You don't grow old if you persist in staying young.
10. Whatever you do in life, it's important to have a reason for getting up every morning.

A Dream Strategy to Find Your Passion

On March 21, 1992, I took a trip into the twilight zone. My navigator on this trip was David Talbot. David asks clients to dream out loud, then coaches them on how to make their dream come true. "I want you to choose a time in the future," he said, "when you are happier than you ever thought you could be. You are completely fulfilled and love all the things you're doing." I chose March 21, 1995. David continued, "It is now March 25, 1995. A life plan that you created three years ago has been implemented. You are a quantum leap ahead of where you thought you could be. Describe your life." With the help of a special computer that projected every word I spoke onto a large screen, that dream world started to become real.

I was readily able to describe every aspect of my dream life—work, creative endeavors, finances, leisure, relationships, life-style. I talked about the book I had written, my flourishing chiropractic practice, my committed relationship with a special someone, even the make and model of the new car I was driving.

When I finished, David said, "Now I want you to come back to the present and pretend you are a pessimist. Tell me all the reasons your dream won't work. These are called the hurdles." I began in this way: "I'm afraid of failing . . . I don't have a plan . . . I resist change . . . I worry a lot . . . I push myself." The fears and anxieties spilled out very easily.

The next and final step on my odyssey was the action plan. David instructed me, "For each hurdle think of a positive action plan." Under his expert coaching, I attacked each one like a sprinter exploding out of the starting blocks. "Make a list of . . . assemble a team to . . . update my . . . complete a . . . create a detailed . . . write . . ."

After this four-hour voyage, I left with a typed copy of my computerized dream strategy, along with the action plan that would turn potential into reality. It is not surprising to me that my dream is now unfolding as I had hoped. I had a plan for my dream.

How does this system work? As a management consultant, David Talbot found that people have difficulty stating their goals and objectives. His method allows his clients to visualize their life as if it has already happened. "I am really asking people to dream," he explained. "When clients describe their happy life they are really talking about their goals and objectives."

His philosophy is that within every one of us there exist many hidden talents and passions; we are probably not even aware of our many inner resources and abilities. We may discover some of the talents through our hobbies and leisure activities, not necessarily through our work. Children commonly become totally absorbed in their play, able to forget time, ignore hunger pangs and resist a parent's repeated plea to come inside now! David believes that in an ideal world these are the very feelings adults should experience at work. Such enthusiasm and involvement is what he calls being engaged in life.

Clients who are stuck at various stages of life seek David out. A change in a work or personal situation may trigger the feeling that there's a gap between where they are and where they'd like to be. Some clients are unable to articulate where they'd like to be but they do recognize their unhappiness. With David's method, clients understand that an enriched life is not about finding another job but about finding their passion. As a life coach, David can motivate them to begin the process of realizing their dream.

Visualization
Sometimes we get an answer when we least expect it, often before we've even formulated the question.

Normally I am supercharged with unbridled energy. One day not long ago, I found myself sitting very still, my mind empty of thoughts, eyes closed. It was a glorious fresh summer morning in Algonquin Park; seated on the beach in front of our group was Linda Montgomery, an artist. She was reading to us, from Shakti Gawain's book on visualization, a selection called "Contacting Your Inner Guide."

I listened attentively and tried to follow the suggestions she read to us. I'm a very visual person, so I had no difficulty imagining a path in the woods that led to a clearing. In front of me was my inner sanctuary. I would see or sense my inner guide in this peaceful place. My inner guide appeared. I was startled to visualize a giant pen with legs walking toward me. My inner guide had given me the answer: write! That afternoon, with cries of encouragement from the loons, I composed my first poem.

Visualization does not require special skills. Anyone can use this method. Visualization is the technique by which we use the imagination to create what we really want in life. In her book, Shakti

Gawain explained the process: "We always attract into our lives whatever we think about the most, believe in most strongly and/or imagine most vividly. If we are basically positive in attitude, expecting and envisioning pleasure, satisfaction and happiness, we will attract and create people, situations and events which conform to our positive expectations."

The ability to visualize is an important tool; it can help us get what we want and need out of life. David Gershon and Gail Straub, in their book *Empowerment*, make this observation: "Until you can visualize something as possible, that thing cannot begin to manifest. You must see the possibility clearly in order to move toward it." Many athletes use mental imagery or visualization for a quick rehearsal before an event. A diver, for example, might perform a double somersault with a half twist one final time in his mind as he readies himself on the board. Psychologists suggest that people develop an image bank of various scenarios they can call on to help relax, to get motivated or to revisit a finest hour to help build confidence.

In 1982, after many months of consistent marathon training, I felt physically ready to break three hours. At bedtime, I would close my eyes and visualize the time on the finish-line clock. The time I imagined was always less than three hours. I often saw 2:59 or 2:58 in my mind. Not once did I see a time of more than three hours. I actually ran 2:57:57 in my marathon. I succeeded because I believed I would. Researchers at the University of Texas have monitored brain activity as patients performed various body motions; then they tested the brain as the patients *imagined* performing the same motions. The researchers found that the same areas of the brain were activated whether the patients were doing the physical movement or merely imagining it. So a mental rehearsal of an action puts the mind through a workout that is not unlike the real thing.

Whether you are attempting to pole-vault to new heights or trying to find your passion in life, imagery can mentally walk you through it to discover your full potential.

Visualize Your Dream
I would like to take you through a visualization exercise. Before you begin it's important to relax and clear your mind. The most receptive times for visualization are just before sleeping or in the

morning just after awakening. Now close your eyes and consider the following questions.

- What great thing would you achieve if you knew you could not fail?
- If you could imagine your work to be any way you wanted, what would it look like?
- If you could do any kind of work on earth, regardless of training or experience, what would it be?
- What does your ideal work environment look like? Are you inside or outside?
- Do you work in an office or at home?
- What field are you in—sports, arts, health, leisure, industry, education, media, travel, science?
- Are you self-employed or working for someone?
- What talents and gifts are you expressing?
- How much money are you receiving?

Were you able to let your heart and passion speak to you during this exercise? What images sprang into your mind? Does the work you visualized express the authentic you—the person you really are?

This exercise will confirm one of three possibilities. First, you may already be doing what you love. Second, you may need to act on the visual images you received to make your passion a reality. Or finally, you may need to practice visualization techniques regularly to open up your mind to new dreams.

Some of us may have an inner critic who spins endless reasons why our dreams won't materialize. We hear a cold, negative voice that says, "I'm unqualified; it's too complicated to change my life; there's a recession; I don't have the money." We have to learn to shut out that negative voice.

Shakti Gawain has a method to replace negative mind chatter. She recommends using an affirmation—a strong, positive statement about something in your life, as if that situation or condition already exists. She explains, "Even ten minutes a day of reciting affirmations can counterbalance years of old mental habits." Affirmations should be stated in the present tense and can be any positive statement. For example, "I now have a wonderful job," or, "I am now attracting loving, satisfying, happy relationships into my life." One affirmation that I found to be freeing, expansive and supportive is: "I am willing to risk all I have been for what I can become."

The Love List

"You want me to write a love list?" I asked David Talbot, my dream strategy coach. "How would a list of my past romances help me with my dream? Most of them were nightmares!" "Not *that* kind of list," David explained. "I mean a list as described by Robin Woods in his book *What You Are Is What You Love*."

Here's how to start your love list: write down everything you love in the whole world: sights, sounds, smells, tastes, feelings; the things that make you laugh; your values; the people and places you treasure; your favorite art, music and hobbies; your special leisure, sports and fitness activities; the qualities you love about yourself and others.

Your love list will give you valuable insights into your passions. Once the list is completed, group together the items that have similar characteristics; for example, those that relate to creativity, work situations, social settings, hobbies. If the key to happiness is doing what you love and loving what you do, then you'll find the answer in your love list. Your vocation should ideally incorporate many of the items in your list.

I began my list by jotting down dozens of my favorite sensual delights: the smell of fresh-cut grass, a banana Popsicle on a hot day, warm feet in bed, the smell of fresh-ground coffee beans, eating chocolate, laughing, rainbows, popcorn at the movies, the soft fur of Napoleon (my cat). My thoughts flowed with ease. I discovered 512 things I absolutely love. I am constantly adding new items to my love list, as joyful things happen to me all the time. One recent addition to the list has been, "The satisfaction I feel when I finish a chapter of this book."

Some of my career or vocation items are:

- being the center of attention
- speaking in public
- being my own boss
- meeting new people
- having a routine
- solving problems
- motivating people
- being healthy

Obviously with a list like this I would not be happy pushing a pencil behind a desk or being a computer programmer!

Many people have discovered their passion through a love list. Carol, for example, hoped the rumors of layoffs in her department were true. At age forty-six and after nineteen years of work, she was ready to quit her government job anyway. But what would she do? Some items on Carol's love list:

- walking in the woods
- gardening and flower arranging
- getting out of the city
- cooking
- baking pies
- driving in the country
- intimate dinner parties
- bird-watching

Carol is now the proprietor of a small country inn east of Toronto. She has never been happier.

Lynn, an honors English graduate, was working as a telephone service representative until corporate restructuring eliminated her position.

Her love list included:

- live theater
- watercolors
- sewing
- classical music
- *My Fair Lady*
- *Gone With the Wind*
- the Academy Awards
- traveling

Lynn is now designing costumes for a major repertory company.

Jan Lowenthal, a career management consultant, related this story about one of her clients: "An insurance executive was dismissed as a result of a company merger. During our interview I sensed that he had no passion for the industry; his job was just a means to an end. But when he spoke about his bird-watching hobby his eyes would light up. His entire body language changed. He told me he had taken small groups on bird-watching tours. I encouraged him to investigate the potential of turning this hobby into a business. He is now conducting nature tours worldwide for a travel agent. I had dinner with him a few months ago. He is a changed man; he's enthusiastic and just loves what he is doing with his life."

Why not create your own love list? Here's how to begin: at random, start jotting down your thoughts. You might also make a separate list of the things you dislike. Share your list with someone you trust, then brainstorm together to sort your lists into specific groupings or categories. Your personal love list is more effective than a tranquilizer for the relief of sadness or depression. When you read all the hundreds of wonderful memories, people, places and things you love in the whole world, you'll realize how blessed you really are. Too often we focus on what's wrong in our lives. The love list gives you a megadose of everything in your life that is special.

The late Malcolm Forbes, former owner and editor-in-chief of the business publication *Forbes*, summed up my feelings when he said, "Whatever you like to do, just find a way to do it. The biggest mistake people make in life is not trying to make a living at doing what they most enjoy. There's no job that's all joy. But to work at a job you hate is probably the biggest waste in life . . . Success follows doing what you love to do."

Dream Team

I've always believed that if I can't solve a problem myself, I should share it with others who might be able to offer a solution. Sometimes I'll ask three or four friends for help with the same challenge, people like my longtime girlfriend Linda; Bertha, my bookkeeper, born with common sense; David, a close friend; and Steven, my brother and best friend.

Besides problems, I share my dreams. Dreams need more than wishing to come true. The love list and visualization techniques help define our dreams, but they alone won't make anything happen no matter how positive our attitudes or how many affirmations we recite. We each need a team to support and motivate us. In order to make our dream a reality, we need many resources and every offer of assistance that comes our way.

Barbara Sher, author of *Teamworks* and *Wishcraft*, explains the process of forming a success team, a small group of people whose

"Blue-Skying It" at the YMCA

The YMCA career planning centre was, for me, the lost-and-found department. Twenty-two years ago, I arrived on their doorstep, lost, hoping to find myself. I did! I returned there recently to speak with Franz Schmidt, the director of the program. Schmidt explained how the program works: "Very few people do career or life planning in a rational, logical way. Many come here wounded by some change in their life; they're unemployed as a result of a layoff, bored at work or home, or looking for new challenges. Some start to show physical and psychological symptoms, which are often the way their inner voice tries to get some attention. Something inside cries out, 'Wake up—your life is not working!'" After extensive testing, a psychologist discusses the results with each client. Clients also receive ongoing help for five years, as the YMCA recognizes that career development is a process.

Schmidt describes the possibilities: "Our tests are a tool, a stimulus for ideas, for themes, for patterns. We do not put people into boxes; instead the test results can be very freeing. Clients will say, 'Gee, here I was stuck in this accounting job and I didn't know that I resemble people in the creative field.' That's the stimulus they need to explore their creativity. A career has to have meaning; work gives purpose to our lives. I ask each client about their future fantasies: If you *blue-sky it*—that is, describe your ideal life—how do you want life to be? They'll often say, 'Well, it isn't practical but my dream is living in the country, doing something creative, running my own business . . .' There's excitement in their voices when they share these dreams."

Of the four thousand clients Schmidt has counseled, most are baby boomers. "Mid-life is an important shift time. Distortions become clear. People realize that their job in life is not to please their mom or become the businessman Dad wanted them to be. We are committed to helping our clients find their own meaning, their truth. When you find it, joy will propel you through the last half of your life."

only goal is to help each member of the team get what he or she wants. "This support group will help you develop plans for any goal, give you information and contacts, phone numbers, addresses and how-to-do-anything directions. This team will be involved and interested in your progress, applaud you when you've accomplished an objective and, when you need them, help you find alternative ways to reach your goals. They'll help you stick to your projects—and they'll do it all for free. Why? Because some-day you're going to return the favor!"

Success teams are based on Sher's principles that, first, people have better ideas for others than they have for themselves; and second, people have more courage for others than they have for themselves. She starts her seminars with two questions: "What do you want?" and "What's the problem?" Our teams can help us find the answers to both questions.

Jan Lowenthal believes in the networking principle for career change. "Talk to people. Start with your best friend or someone you trust. Tell them you're unhappy. Brainstorm with them. If there is someone working in a field that interests you, call them. Rather than making a cold call it's easier if you have a referral to help you in the door. You might be able to say, 'John Smith recommended that I talk to you about your industry.' While you're out there network-ing, you'll hear about opportunities; they don't just happen."

Get out of your cocoon. Take the initiative. Don't let fear of the unknown stop you from finding your passion. Sometimes it's pain-ful to ask yourself: what is the truth? Who am I? Where do I want to go? What do I want to do? There are many self-help and career planning books. Read them.

Patients regularly share their dreams with me; they know that I am interested in the challenges standing in their way. I love prob-lem solving, and after a few minutes my brain starts oozing with ideas: "Call my friend . . . have you read . . . there's a seminar at . . . take a course on . . . I had the same problems—here's what I did . . ." By the time they leave my office they have found some motivation and direction to pursue their dream.

Going Back to School—At Forty-five

Sometimes life follows a convoluted course on purpose. We may not understand it at the time; impatience makes us wish we were "there" already. But "there" keeps changing as we change. Often when you're "there" for a while, you'll feel a tug or a pull toward "here."

Such was the meandering path Al Denov followed, from urban planner to naturopathic healer. At forty-four he chose to leave a secure job with the provincial government, a staff of ten people and a steady paycheck every two weeks. He remembers those days: "But I wasn't happy. After seventeen years I needed a change. I wasn't being stimulated. Everyone thought I was crazy when I quit, but I had to do it." After a two-month mental break visiting friends in Europe, he returned home hopeful but unemployed.

A tiny advertisement from the Ontario College of Naturopathic Medicine changed his life. Al continues his story: "I've always been interested in preventive health care so I called to request some information." Excited by the course descriptions, he made an appointment to see the dean. "They would admit me to the four-year program with the proviso that I would obtain a university credit in organic chemistry. I had all the other science prerequisites." Al enrolled in organic chemistry at the University of Toronto. "I said to myself, 'If I can get through this after a twenty-three year absence from school I'll be ready for the intense four-year naturopathic program.'" He passed and began what he calls the hardest four years of his life. "I was in class for a full eight hours each day, then the real work started when I got home." His studies culminated in grueling exams: the final board tests consisted of seventeen exams plus orals and practical testing.

Is Al Denov happy now? "From day one it has felt right. I smile every day because I've found my passion." Now in his fifties, Al is a naturopathic doctor in Toronto helping patients stay naturally healthy. Does he have any advice for those who are contemplating a return to school? "Don't let age stand in your way. It's never too late to go back. There are always obstacles in life—leap over them to achieve your goals."

The traditional framework of life, with youth the time for learning, is not true anymore. Many individuals are exploring new career options that may require additional education or new skills. If, as some experts believe, we will have six or seven careers in our lifetime, then lifelong learning will be the norm, and so it should be. I dropped out of university to start a business; maybe my meandering path will take me back to school at age seventy-five to finish my degree. Who knows?

Life After Work

For people who have been vital, active, creative and successful, retirement can be the kiss of death. Society sends us a message when we retire: "Move over; we want someone younger and more productive." For many, after a lifetime of hard work, such a message is a shock to the system. But there is *life* after work; we don't need remuneration to prove our usefulness to ourselves and others. Hobbies, volunteer work, travel, education—all these options can provide some of the same satisfaction as the old nine-to-five job, and often more!

As the economy has changed, there is now a new dimension to the meaning of the word retirement. Many of my baby-boomer patients are announcing their forced early retirement long before the traditional age of sixty-five. Some haven't even reached age fifty yet. Once again, attitude is the most important component in the retirement business. Bob Reilly was ecstatic when his company's reorganization allowed him to take an early exit. Five minutes after he left, he started a new consulting business, drawing on his lifetime of experience. Here was a second chance for him, an opportunity to realize a lifelong dream of self-employment. Bob prepared for his departure for six months before his official last day on the job, so he suffered none of the depression and anxiety such change often brings.

There are positive ways to look at the experience of retirement, regardless of your age. First, delete the word *retirement* from your vocabulary. Keep only the first two letters, *re*, and create some new words: renew, rejuvenate, reward, rebuild, recreation. We have to realize that in all life's situations there is change and the potential for growth. Here are some suggestions if you're feeling stuck for an answer to the question, "What should I do now that I don't have to go to work?" Start with research. Read what those who study the future have to recommend; study current and projected trends. Begin with Faith Popcorn's book *The Popcorn Report*, or John Naisbitt's *Megatrends*. Be open to new business ideas, such as franchising or home-based consulting firms. Think of the explosion in computer careers, ranging from software design to hardware repair. Since we are going to be the next wave of seniors, are there possibilities for new health-care and recreation products for us? Ginger Eisen, age seventy-seven, has launched a new business specializing in bathroom renovations and accessories for the physi-cally challenged. Still stuck? Don't forget all the techniques I've outlined to help you find your dream. If your first career kept you in a ho-hum job, occupied but not passionately involved, now you have the time to reflect on what really matters in your life. Now, maybe for the first time, you can do what you love.

Time Out: Life Between Dreams

Mid-life is often a time *between* dreams—the dreams you thought you wanted (or someone else wanted for you) and the dreams you haven't articulated yet. Just like the great middle ground between the end and the beginning, the place between dreams is really an important space. William Bridges, author of *Transitions*, calls this space "the neutral zone." It is where self-renewal occurs.

After my marriage ended several years ago, I traveled to Esalen and found my neutral zone: the famous retreat center in Big Sur, California. Built high atop a cliff with the Pacific Ocean crashing on rocks below, this magical place allowed me to be truly alone, per-haps for the first time in years. When people say, "I need to get away," they really mean that they want to reconnect with them-selves. I returned home reconnected, refreshed, recharged and restored.

If you are between places and spaces, don't struggle to fix your inner turmoil; allow yourself to recognize and honor it. Here are some ways to explore the meaning between your dreams.

Find time to be alone. Unplug yourself from the treadmill of life. Go for a walk in the woods alone, sit beside a lake or an ocean.

Keep a journal. Words that could not readily be expressed even to my therapist spilled out easily when I began writing about my life in poems and rap songs. Writing is cathartic for most people.

Read. Much wisdom can be found in books such as *The Precious Present* by Spencer Johnson, *The Velveteen Rabbit* by Margery Williams and *Hope for the Flowers* by Trina Paulus. The simple yet profound messages contained in these books are inspiring.

In *Hope for the Flowers*, two caterpillars have a conversation about the process of becoming a butterfly. One caterpillar says to the other, "Watch me. I'm making a cocoon. It looks like I'm hiding but a cocoon is no escape. It's an in-between house where the change takes place." The time between dreams is that cocoon where change takes place, that halfway house where we can snuggle up with ourselves, alone, in a dark safe space.

Beware of family and friends who may attempt to sabotage your trip to the neutral zone. You may hear comments such as, "Quitting your job in a recession? Are you crazy? You're just being selfish." Sometimes negative comments hide the real truth, which may be, "I wish I had the courage you have!"

What Calls You Here?

Part of mid-life is coming to terms with the dreams other people placed on us. What was your dream before you stopped dreaming? The soul-searching process will uncover those lost parts we need to reclaim. Mid-life is a transition time on our journey. There arises from within a deep call for reflection, evaluation and reorientation. Life is like a train that has stopped at a station. Will you stay on and continue in the same direction or get off and explore a new destination? Maybe you need to sit there for a while, not sure yet what to do. What suitcases will you take with you? Is there anything in your baggage you need to discard as you continue on your journey? Something new you need to learn for the rest of the trip?

On the first morning of a workshop at the Hollyhock Retreat Centre in British Columbia, workshop leader Atum O'Kane asked us, "What calls you here?" One by one we explained the reasons for attending a seminar on mid-life passage.

Some of the reasons were:

"I've spent my whole life doing for others, now it's my turn to find out what I want."

"I'm not sure where I fit in this life. I was widowed three and a half years ago."

"I want to change careers and I'm scared."

"My business went bankrupt and I don't know what to do next."

"A relationship ended after twenty-three years and I'm feeling lost."

"This is my fiftieth birthday present to myself."

"I feel completely stuck in my career and hope to get some direction here."

"This is my time out to refocus my energy and discover what lies ahead."

I want you to imagine being in a wonderful relationship. The anticipation of seeing this special person excites you; you are challenged to grow, mentally and physically, whenever you are together. Time passes and you don't notice it. Friends comment on the great passion that is between you. Everyone recognizes this description of romantic love; most of us don't realize that we can experience the same feeling at work. Work is love made visible, wrote Kahlil Gibran in *The Prophet*. Does anyone ever feel "in love" with work? Yes, those who are engaged in life. These individuals might not use the term *work*; to them it's play, a calling, a mission, a purpose, a raison d'être. Does Wayne Gretzky work at hockey? Is Barbra Streisand's singing work? These people, and countless others, have discovered their passion.

Is there a link between passion and longevity? A testament to this connection is described in a wonderful passage in Norman Cousins's book *Anatomy of an Illness*. Cousins recalls a visit to the late Pablo Casals, the renowned Spanish cellist and composer. Casals, an octogenarian, had such severe arthritis it was difficult for him to walk and dress himself. His back was bent over, his hands swollen and clenched, and he had difficulty breathing. Nevertheless, each morning Casals played the piano. Cousins wrote about the transformation that began as Casals started to play: "I was not prepared for the miracle that was about to happen. The fingers slowly unlocked and reached toward the keys like the buds of a plant toward the sunlight. His back straightened. He seemed to breathe more freely. Now his fingers settled on the keys. Then came the opening bars of Bach . . . He hummed as he played, then said that Bach spoke to him here—and he placed his hand over his heart. Then he plunged into a Brahms concerto and his fingers, now agile and powerful, raced across the keyboard with dazzling speed. His body was no longer stiff and shrunken but supple and graceful and completely freed of its arthritic coils."

Cousins observed that Casals was completely caught up in his creativity, goals and life's purpose; the effects on his body chemistry were amazing. Casals lived a remarkable ninety-seven years!

I believe that doing what you love is life-enhancing. We know the immune system is affected by our emotions. As Dr. Deepak Chopra wrote in his book *Ageless Body, Timeless Mind*, "Our cells are constantly eavesdropping on our thoughts and being changed by them. A bout of depression can wreak havoc with the immune system, falling in love can boost it. Joy and fulfilment keep us healthy and extend life." Remember, the goal is not just living long, it's loving life. When you find your passion, life will be *loved* to the fullest.

4

UNITY

*Thoughts, beliefs and emotions have an
impact on health.*

Here's one new word that won't fit on a Scrabble board: Psychoneuroimmunology. Simply defined, it means the study of how thoughts and feelings (psycho) interact with the nervous system (neuro) to promote healing (immunology). Exciting research in the past decade has shown that emotions, which trigger chemical events in the brain, can also affect nervous system function, hormone levels and immune system responses.

Just what is the immune system? The immune system protects us from disease; it defends the body against cancerous cells and invaders such as bacteria, viruses, fungi, parasites and allergens. Ready for all conditions, this military force has no single main headquarters or chief organ. Instead, the immune system is a cooperative network of biochemicals, white blood cells (leukocytes), tissues and organs (thymus gland, spleen, tonsils) distributed throughout the body in various locations. Until recently, scientists believed that the immune system functioned as an entity separate from the brain, neither one able to influence the other; however, a discovery has been made indicating that there are lines of communication between them. Neuroscientist David Felton, MD, PhD, professor of neurobiology and anatomy at the University of Rochester School of Medicine, found that nerve fibers between the nervous system and the immune system "talk to one another. A constant flow of information goes back and forth between the brain and the immune system suggesting that every time we have a thought or a feeling, hormones are released that send a message to the immune system."

Just think of the ramifications of Felton's statement. Thoughts, beliefs and emotions can have a major effect on physical health; there is a unity between mind and body, a continuous, unbroken flow. According to Margaret Kemeny, psychologist and researcher at UCLA, "When we feel happy, sad, angry or fearful there are very clear changes taking place in the brain which cascade down through the body." And research is showing that relaxation, meditation, biofeedback, support groups and optimism may affect the course of physical illness. Here are some fascinating studies on this unity, the mind–body connection.

- At the Ohio State University College of Medicine, scientists have shown declines in the activity of immune-system cells in several groups of people under stress: medical students taking final exams, people caring for loved ones with Alzheimer's disease, women who have recently gone through a difficult divorce.
- Scientists at Ohio State University also tested the effects of loneliness on the immune system. Two groups of people were given psychological tests to determine how lonely they were. In the group that was lonelier, there were lower levels of natural killer cells, a type of white blood cell believed to be important in the control of viruses and cancers.
- Laughter, love and optimism seem to have a positive effect on both preventing and curing disease. Students at Western New England College in Springfield, Massachusetts, were found to have dramatically higher levels of a virus-fighting component known as immunoglobulin A after watching a comedian on videotape. No changes were found when the students watched a serious documentary.
- Dr. Kiecolt-Glaser of Ohio State University found that when forty-five geriatric residents in an independent-living facility were taught relaxation and guided-imagery techniques three times a week for a month, they showed a significant increase in disease-fighting natural killer cells.
- Optimists are healthier than pessimists. Of a group of ninety-nine Harvard University graduates followed for thirty-five

years, those who explained their misfortunes and disappointments in an optimistic way tended to have better health than their pessimistic classmates, according to a report in the *Journal of Personality and Social Psychology*.

• Tests done at the Menninger Clinic in Topeka, Kansas, showed that people in love suffer fewer colds than those who are not in love, and have more of the white blood cells that actively fight infections.

• At Stanford University School of Medicine, the emotional support derived from group therapy has been shown to lengthen significantly the lives of women with advanced breast cancer.

There are still many unanswered questions about the mind-body connection. Margaret Kemeny points out that the popular idea that happiness is good for our health while sadness is harmful for us has no scientific basis as yet. Also, the link between stress, immune-system function and illness is still unproven. Not everyone who has a lowered immune system gets sick. Much depends on an individual's coping style and personality.

Dr. Ken Pelletier, associate clinical professor in the departments of medicine and psychiatry at the University of California, feels that the key factor necessary for good health is social support, even more important than feeling in control of your health. He says, "Supportive interaction among people may affect our ability to resist illness." Dr. Blair Justice, professor of psychology at the University of Texas and author of *Who Gets Sick,* cautions, "Illness isn't all from the mind. There are three areas that control our health: the mind, the environment and genetic predispositions. No matter how positive a person is, if there is an overpowering environmental or genetic reason for a person to get sick, they will." Dr. Bernie Siegel, assistant clinical professor of surgery at Yale University School of Medicine and author of *Love, Medicine and Miracles*, has his own theory: "I am convinced that unconditional love is the most powerful stimulant of the immune system. If I told patients to raise their blood levels of killer cells, no one would know how. But if I can teach them to love themselves and others fully, the same changes happen automatically. The truth is, love heals."

Ultimately, the unity between mind and body is really about quality of life.

Genetics—Prophetic or Theoretic?

Imagine an individual who is happy, productive and optimistic, passionate about work, fulfilled in his or her relationships, loving and well-loved. Can these positive factors make up for lousy genes? I posed this question to two scientists.

From Dr. Gordon Winocur, of the Rotman Research Institute at the Baycrest Centre for Geriatric Care: "We can't deny that inheritability is a significant factor in disease and the aging process. However, our genetic expression interacts with many other factors; for example, emotional stress may hasten the appearance of a genetic factor, whereas a healthy diet and a satisfying life-style may delay a genetic predisposition. There is much more to aging than the mere passage of time. Our concern should be about successful aging, not longevity or genetics. The objective is not to live to ninety-seven if you're incapacitated; the idea is to lead a happy and full life right up until the end."

From Dr. Gordon Lithgow, a geneticist with the Institute of Behavioral Genetics at the University of Colorado: "It doesn't matter how deliriously happy you are, you are not going to live to a hundred and fifty. Generally, if you are happy, you are healthy. If you want to reach *your* potential of your natural life span, never stop learning, remain alert and keep physically active; this behavior allows you to compensate for lousy genes, but it does not halt or reverse the aging process. There is still so much that we don't know about longevity and aging. Scientists have not yet found the answer to the question, 'Why are there genes in us that determine life span?' We don't even know how many genes there are!"

The views held by Winocur and Lithgow are called the "evolutionary theory of aging." According to this theory, there is indeed a genetic factor, but it can be influenced by our particular environment, so that healthy life-style choices and personal fulfillment can slow the aging process. I've always suspected that longevity was more complex than picking the right parents or having good genes. The views of Winocur and Lithgow suggest that longevity has much to do with our happiness quotient, optimism and hope, with keeping our brains and bodies active. Medical journals are filled with reports of how an individual's will and tenacity to fight off disease can marshal the body's defences in ways technology cannot equal.

And how does one explain why members of the same family, with the same parents and upbringing, have different life spans? A ninety-two-year-old patient of mine, Mrs. P, is the eldest of sixteen children. At least half of her brothers and sisters are already dead. Why? Here is Mrs. P's story: she married early (seventeen) and had a very fulfilling family life, with many hobbies and outside interests to keep her busy. She loved her work and had many friends. She never smoked or drank, ate a low-fat diet and walked everywhere. Many of her siblings smoked and drank; some were unemployed; many had unresolved issues. In essence, their lives were less happy, less fulfilling. I believe Mrs. P's happy life slowed down the ticking of the genetic clock.

Why we age and what we can do to slow down the process has baffled scientists for decades. By studying fruit flies, nematodes and rodents, molecular biologists hope to find the answers. The nematodes, or roundworms, contain many basic structures also found in humans: nerves, muscles, blood vessels, digestive tract, reproductive system. This lowly creature dies, as if on schedule, in twenty days, making it ideal for research. Molecular gerontologist Dr. Tom Johnson and his team at the University of Colorado have discovered and mapped a gene that begins to age nematodes when they are only three days old. When this gene is inactivated, the worm lives one hundred and ten percent longer. In a recent *Life* magazine article, Dr. Johnson speculated, "Within a few years we could nail the aging mechanism in mice. After that, research in humans should go rapidly. We hope to find the genes that shorten life, and one by one, knock them out." Another team of biologists has identified a genetic mechanism that measures, and possibly determines, the rate at which human beings age. This discovery of a clock of aging is a victory for the genetic theory of aging. However, we still don't know exactly where it is located in humans, or how it works.

Regardless of theories, molecules or experiments, this much is clear: aging is not a disease. It is a very specific, individual process for all of us. Each person has a unique biological life span that can be influenced by more factors than scientists have yet discovered. But because inheritability is a major factor, it is prudent to learn as much as you can about your family history. If heart disease or breast cancer runs in your family, you can then ask yourself, "What can I do to minimize the risk? Change my diet, exercise, reduce my stress level?" Much evidence points to the importance of the "passionate" part of "passionate longevity." When we pursue passionate longevity, we are living and loving life. And *how* we live life then becomes more important than *how long*.

The 10 Secrets of Sigga Moore, age eighty-two

1. Meet friends halfway. To have a friend, be a friend.
2. Slough off criticism—worrying won't cure the problem.
3. Be a good listener; don't jump in with advice.
4. Be kind, generous and not overbearing.
5. Have sympathy—a lot of people need it.
6. Hospitality wins all.
7. The body is the temple of the soul; don't abuse it.
8. Be content to be a follower. There are too many leaders already.
9. Be neighborly, but don't thrust yourself on the lady next door.
10. Doing the work you like, married to the person you like and having children because you really want children—that's a successful life.

Stress—From SOS to Success

A man in a supermarket was pushing a screaming child in his buggy. Other shoppers could hear the man's voice saying, "Just relax, Edgar, calm down." The cashier watched as they turned the corner and went down the next aisle. The wailing child, in defiance of his dad, flung his arm out and knocked down a display of crackers. Again, everyone heard the man's voice say calmly, "Edgar, take some deep breaths; cool it; relax. We'll be out of here in no time." Finally, someone went up to this man and said, "I am amazed at how well you handle Edgar's tantrum." He turned to the shopper and said, "Lady, *I'm* Edgar."

Well! That's one way to cope—talk to yourself. According to the late Hans Selye, the world's foremost authority on stress, life without stress is death. Stress is the spice of life; in just the right amount it energizes and motivates. Stress in itself doesn't cause disease; however, the manner in which we react to what happens to us can and does cause illness.

The amount of stress we feel, and whether it is good or bad stress, depends not on the situations we face in life, but on how we perceive and react to them. Joan Borysenko, author and psychologist, believes the way we react to stress depends on two factors. The first is our innate core of resilience, which has not yet been described scientifically; second is the manner in which we were nurtured as children. "Children who aren't resilient, who don't have whatever this special extra something is, grow up to find that they don't trust; they feel a tremendous sense of isolation. To me the best definition of stress is the sense of isolation—from oneself, from others and from the universe."

Selye coined the word *eustress* for positive stress, the stressors we view as challenges rather than threats. We feel in control, and thus we believe we can influence the course of events. Negative stress, what he calls *distress*, occurs when we view a demand as threatening. We feel a sense of helplessness and are powerless to change the events in life. Chronic negative stress has destructive consequences on the body. In one person, prolonged resentment and anger may stimulate an excess of digestive acids that eat away parts of the lining of the stomach or small intestine, creating ulcers. Another person may suffer from high blood pressure, leading to chronic hypertension, a risk factor for heart attack, stroke or kidney failure. Most importantly, the immune system—the body's mechanism for fighting disease—is influenced by stress. The immune system communicates with the brain; the brain regulates the stress hormones. During periods of prolonged stress, elevated levels of adrenal hormones appear to have a destructive effect on the disease-fighting T lymphocytes, which are small, circulating white blood cells that attack cancer cells, viruses and foreign substances. Several studies have shown that a depression or bereavement is sometimes followed a year or so later by the appearance of cancer.

The buildup of small but constant stressors seems to inflict the most bodily harm. Frequent interruptions, traffic jams, lost keys, broken appointments—all these take a terrible toll. Too many changes—moving, a divorce, a new job—can also signal the onslaught of physical symptoms. Incidentally, the body doesn't know the difference between actually being in a stressful situation and just thinking about it. Thinking about firing your employee while driving to work is the same as actually being in the office doing it. The body begins to release those hormones active in the stress response.

Similarly, people who perceive a loss of control over their lives are more likely to suffer ill health. A 1986 study showed that elderly people placed in nursing homes without their consent tend to decline more rapidly and die sooner than those who help decide where they will live.

Fortunately, we each have a stress threshold—a tolerance level— beyond which we begin to experience physical or psychological symptoms. The following are some early warning symptoms that too much stress is accumulating:

- frequent colds and sore throats
- restless sleep or insomnia
- sudden emotional outbursts
- headaches, backaches
- nagging fatigue that lingers from day to day
- stomach and gastrointestinal upset
- frequent use of pills or alcohol to help you sleep or relax

By learning to listen to your body when it speaks to you, stress can be kept to a manageable level.

Reality check: if you are alive and breathing, there will always be stress in your life. Love relationships won't always be perfect, the weather will be as fickle as ever, you'll never have enough money. The key to survival is stress management.

Why Does the Other Line Always Move Faster?

"My husband says I have two speeds—full or off," said one of my Type A patients as she grabbed for the telephone ringing in her purse. I waited for her to finish the call before resuming my treatment. "You'd better plug me into your electronic diary for regular visits," I suggested, as I kneaded her chronically tense neck muscles. She was typical of my Type A patients who epitomize the philosophy, "Make me well so I can continue doing the things that make me sick."

Type A's are everywhere. Type A's are the people who finish your sentences for you, pound on the door when the elevator is slow in coming, argue with the strangers in the express line who have slightly more than the designated number of items in their baskets, blast you with the horn from the car behind. Type A's have an intense sense of urgency; they rule their lives by their watches. They walk fast, talk fast, eat fast. Take them to an art gallery and they rush through in order to see every single painting, rather than pausing to appreciate the individual expression and beauty of each one.

Scientists have long conjectured that certain personality traits and illnesses might be linked, for example, anxiety and ulcers, depression and cancer. In 1969, two cardiologists, Drs. Meyer Friedman and Ray Rosenman, established the concept of the Type A personality. They theorized that the person who is aggressive, hard-driving, hostile, impatient, competitive and tense is at risk for chronic chest pain (angina) and heart attacks. Follow-up studies, however, failed to confirm the link between Type A behavior and heart disease. Investigators then found that not all aspects of Type A behavior are harmful—the positive sides to Type A's are their ability to seek out challenge, the value they place on productivity and success and their need to know how well they are doing.

According to Dr. Leonard Syme of the University of California, it is the lack of control over the anger-causing situations, rather than the hostility itself, that determines the long-term health effects. James Billings, a psychologist and epidemiologist, agrees: "Beneath the Type A behavior lies a tremendous need to be in control." Other researchers are finding a link between heart disease, cancer and suppressed anger. Dr. Mara Julius of the University of Michigan found that women who suppressed their anger in confrontations with their spouses had twice the mortality rate of other women, even when other factors such as high blood pressure and smoking were considered. Ultimately, a variety of psychological factors—including personality characteristics, mood and coping style—can affect the way a person deals with stress, and this in turn affects physical health.

Anger is a normal, useful emotion when based on honest, realistic convictions and expressed assertively and respectfully. What is destructive, however, is the waiting-for-a-fight hostility some

Type A's possess. Learning to deal effectively with situations that are out of our control or cause us to be angry is a skill that can be learned. Here are some suggestions.

- Caught in a traffic jam? Airline lost your luggage? Power failure wiped out your computer? Repeat to yourself: How important will this seem six months from now? The answer to this question will put today's annoyance or frustration in the proper perspective.
- Always have Plan B ready. Meeting someone after work, after a concert, after a snowstorm? Assuming neither one of you has a portable telephone, your arrangements should be, "If I'm not at your place by seven, I'll meet you at the restaurant." When you leave room for unanticipated stress such as delays, you short-circuit potential anger-filled situations.
- Exercise, exercise, exercise! It is a well-documented fact that exercise releases that pressure-cooker feeling in the body, channeling repressed anger and frustration into physical activity. Individuals who are fit are better able to withstand the physical and psychological challenges of stress than those who are out of shape.
- If you regularly bite off more than you can chew—and then chew like crazy—it may be time for some serious stress management. Do you have frequent outbursts of uncontrollable anger? Write down your feelings and the situations that trigger your responses in a journal, then consider appropriate therapy to learn to cope with your behavior.
- One Type A patient of mine changed the way he routinely overreacted to stress. He described his new approach: "I've learned to love my enemies. If I allow someone's behavior to infuriate me, then I empower that person. I give that person the power to make my heart beat faster and raise my blood pressure. Why should I let anybody do that to me? So now if someone cuts me off in traffic, I throw him a kiss."
- Learn to keep your mouth shut. We've been given one mouth and two ears for a reason. Listen before you open your mouth to attack or jump to conclusions. Have you ever wrongly assumed that someone was out to get you before you heard all the facts?

- Avoid situations that you know in your heart drive you crazy. An impatient Type A should not go to the supermarket on Saturday at noon and expect to breeze through. If you detest traffic jams, don't leave for the cottage late Friday afternoon. Wait until rush hour is over, or leave early the next morning. If you have an important appointment, allow extra time to get there, especially if weather conditions or parking availability are problems. If something unforeseen occurs, practice deep breathing and count to ten. Breath-holding is common in tension-filled situations.

Dr. Dean Ornish, MD, assistant clinical professor of medicine at the University of California, helps Type A personalities deal with their emotions in a positive way. He believes our biggest battles are waged in the mind, so that is where healing must begin. Many people, he feels, are socially isolated; that is, they lack a real sense of intimate connection with other people. "When you relate to the world from a position of isolation, it may lead to chronic stress and ultimately to illness," he says. Several times a year, he offers an "Open Your Heart" retreat, which includes diet, stress management and psychological programs for heart patients. The most powerful healing tool is the group support sessions where patients open up and share their feelings. Dr. Ornish describes this process: "By addressing the underlying emotional issues and recreating a sense of connection and community, we can transform anger to contentment. We show them how to regain control over their lives in a life-enhancing rather than destructive way."

Admitting you're a Type A is no excuse for remaining one. Perhaps mid-life is the time for some personal assessment, an opportunity to look for answers to hard questions.

Owning Our Stuff

The new patient leaned toward me with a puzzled look on her face as she said, "I can't understand why this injury hasn't healed. The accident happened more than seven years ago!" KS easily recalled the details of the traumatic rear-end collision that created a chronic syndrome of pain and stiffness in her neck extending right down to her shoulder. "Show me where you feel the pain," I asked, watching her place the flat of her hand in the groove between her neck and shoulder. Good—the first major clue, I thought, like a defence lawyer about to trap an unsuspecting witness. KS outlined the various treatments that had been prescribed and the success of each one. "At first, I improved a lot; then I seemed to reach a plateau. In the last year and a half in particular, the pain has been almost constant. I feel like there's an elephant sitting on my right shoulder." Clue number two, I noted. I then proceeded to examine her muscles. Concrete would have felt softer. "Did anything major happen in your life a year and a half ago?" I inquired. KS hesitated, then said, "That's when my mother died." With very little urging from me, out spilled the story about her cold, distant mother; not once did my patient ever hear her mother say, "I love you." "She would turn her cheek whenever I attempted to kiss her." KS's eyes filled with tears. "Then, after she died, I never had time to grieve, as my daughter got engaged one month after the funeral. Instead I had to plan a wedding." Obviously, deep feelings of anger and guilt still burdened her. I gently explained the connection between the emotional pain she was repressing and the physical pain in her neck and shoulder. "The car accident caused the initial injury; however, your unresolved feelings of anger and guilt add fuel to the fire. You've heard the expression, 'I'm carrying the weight of the world on my shoulders.' Well, that's the elephant you described." KS heard me out, but I sensed her unwillingness to look at the deeper issues. I respected her request that I just fix her neck and shoulder. We never talked about her mother again.

On another day, EL grimaced as she shifted her weight from one hip to the other. "I have trouble sitting because of sciatic nerve pain in my leg," she explained. "The pain starts in my buttock and shoots down the leg." This sixty-one-year-old woman had made the rounds of doctors' offices, from orthopedic surgeon to neurologist, without much relief. Following my gut instincts, I asked her a question she didn't expect. "Tell me. What is going on at home? Any stress?"

She answered in a serious voice, "Actually, ever since my husband retired, he's been a pain in the ass and gets on my nerves."

I laughed and pointed to her buttock: "This is your husband!"

"But I really do have a pain," EL protested.

"I believe you," I assured her, "but we must treat the cause, not just the symptom. I can treat your pain but you are the one who has to deal with the stress from home that is triggering this condition."

I never saw her after that first visit. She wasn't ready to work with me and do her half of the healing.

Sometimes patients are willing to probe a little more deeply into their emotional pasts. Another story from a patient: "I'm sure it was the golf. Plus I've been super busy packing the kids off to camp," explained the thirty-five-year-old woman who could not move her head. She called our office after waking up that morning with torticollis, a complete spasm of the muscles of the neck. "Are you sure you can't recall anything specific, even something stressful, that might have caused this?" I asked her. She sat on my treatment table searching her mind for an answer. Her face suddenly turned pale. "I doubt whether this has anything to do with it, but I just remembered that today is the first anniversary of an operation I had to remove a tumor from my thyroid." I could easily believe what I was hearing. How many times had she consciously or subconsciously thought of that date? Remembering any day that is significant in your life—the anniversary of a parent's death, your ex-husband's birthday, the day the doctor diagnosed your cancer—opens a floodgate of emotions, sadness, anger, fear. The woman was relieved when I reassured her it was completely natural and normal to experience the same feelings of fear one year, or even ten years, later. Her neck improved dramatically after that first visit.

My chiropractic office is a microcosm of life itself. Pain may be the ticket that admits the patients through the door, but once they're inside, I need to find out what is really going on in their bodies. Is the patient suffering from a strictly mechanical, musculoskeletal condition, or is there a deeper issue that needs to be addressed? Pain is often the only way the body can grab our attention.

Hands-on therapy is powerful healing. Sometimes my hands feel like ears that listen to what the patients are saying and how they are breathing whenever I touch a painful muscle. At times, a chiropractor can work on one painful area, and buried emotions will surface. Tears well up, and the patient may talk about an incident in his or her life that had been forgotten on a conscious level. As I help my patients acknowledge their feelings, I may motivate them to explore the issues further in psychotherapy. As well, there are many different therapies available to help individuals deal with emotional problems using a physical method known as bodywork. Gestalt, bioenergetics, Reiki, Feldenkrais and Rolfing are just a few examples.

Being a doctor is a privilege. If I can be a catalyst for patients to resolve issues that need healing, that is also my reward. Once we begin to honor ourselves—own our stuff—and listen to our hearts, our physical pain can at last diminish.

The 10 Secrets of Bill McMullen, age eighty

1. Relax.
2. Most people are decent and honorable, so enjoy them.
3. Don't bear grudges.
4. *Never* let the sun go down on your anger.
5. Practice moderation in everything.
6. Enjoy your family.
7. Enjoy and practice religion.
8. Be thrifty, *not* stingy.
9. Accept that life can be tough.
10. Live one day at a time.

The Gift of Illness

Somewhere between puberty and mid-life, usually around the age of thirty, we learn the truth. We are mortal! That realization may be precipitated by the loss of a parent or grandparent. In our forties and fifties, we all have had the startling experience of hearing about someone, perhaps a friend or acquaintance around our own age, who has a serious illness. We shake our heads in disbelief. Maybe the bad news is about us. Those who walk that painful path are often changed forever, usually for the better. Here is how one woman, Priscilla Welch, described the lessons she learned from cancer: "It made me aware of time and priorities. And I hope it's made me a better person—that I'm a bit more compassionate, that I listen to people and that I appreciate life more."

One of my patients found an unexpected opportunity to reexamine her life while she recovered from a serious illness. She described the experience. "All I could think at first was, why me? as I lay in bed looking out the window. Then as the days passed, I began to wonder if this illness happened for a reason. I then asked myself, 'What's the deadwood in my life that I don't need? What can I change in order to live my life fully, with as much love as I can?' As a result, I decided to end the relationship I was in. I also became much closer to my parents. Before, I was always running in and out of their life. With their daily visits, I was able to really listen to their concerns; now we have a new understanding of each other. It took pain to change my relationships."

Pain—the great motivator. Do we ever learn from pleasure, the easy stuff? Looking back over my life, I see that the important lessons grew from my experience of hardship, loss and pain. With a softer, more compassionate heart, I was then able to feel the pain of others. People often ask me what I learned from the seniors who were interviewed for this book. The most important lesson had nothing to do with their exercise regimes or what they ate for breakfast. Without exception they exuded a spirit, a passion, a joy that was obvious as soon as I met them. They were enveloped in joie de vivre. Yet their lives had not been without tragedy and loss. They had lived through pain and through troubles, and they realized that passion *and* sorrow, joy *and* trouble are what life is all about. As one ninety-two-year-old woman philosophized, "No one goes through life scot-free!" Once you accept that we are all going to die, you can choose how you want to live. Bernie Siegel, a physician known for his work with cancer patients, summed up these feelings when he said, "Some people need a death sentence proclaimed before they let go of all their restraints and start to really live. When you know you have a limited amount of time here then you start to think about how you want to use that time. Your illness gives you permission to say, 'No, I don't want to do that today, because I won't have this day back again.' If you allow your inner voice to remind you that you could die tomorrow or on the way home, it allows you to live in the moment, appreciate it and make use of it."

Inner change is not restricted to lessons learned in a life-threatening illness; even a painful lower back strain can be the catalyst for personal growth. Some patients who consult me for their first-ever back pain think my office is really Dembe's Garage and Body Shop. They say, "Just fix up my body, Doc, and I'll pick it up in the morning." They are often surprised to learn that pain is the body's way of getting their attention. When I ask them what or who they have been neglecting lately, the answers tumble out—

home, family, friendships, sleep, fitness. Saying these words out loud is the first step, the shock they need to get their life back on track. And most do.

Some people can focus only on the way their illness is manifested; they are not interested or emotionally able to see any positive aspects. Then there are people like Priscilla Welch, with incredible attitudes. "While I'm recovering from my cancer, I can take a course. I can learn something new. Breast cancer forced me to stop and rest instead of going hell-for-leather like I've been doing for ten years. This is an opportunity. It's a friend."

5

MOBILITY

*Exercise is fundamental to increasing your
health span.*

Imagine sitting in your doctor's office. The doctor says, "I'm
going to write out a prescription that will make you feel better,
help you lose weight, eliminate insomnia and constipation,
reduce stress and anxiety, curb your appetite, improve muscle
tone, increase your energy level and self-image, protect your heart,
slow down the aging process and, regardless of how you feel right
now, make you feel better tomorrow." You'd say, "Wow! Give me a
lifetime supply!" What do you think is in that prescription? The
recipe for a magic elixir? The answer: fitness.

Joe Womersley started taking the "fitness pill" at age fifty-two.
Business problems created great stress in his life; he was unable to
sleep at night as he pondered his escalating debts. At a friend's
suggestion he joined the Fitness Institute. "That was my turnaround," Joe says. "I went from two-hundred-pound slob to fitness
freak." He quit smoking and eight months later ran the Boston
Marathon in three hours and forty minutes. Since then, he has
completed more than a hundred marathons.

Since discovering fitness, Joe has celebrated each passing birthday in a very unusual way: every year he runs his age in kilometers.
For his sixty-ninth birthday, he ran sixty-nine kilometers, around
the perimeter of Metropolitan Toronto. Sixty-nine kilometers
might seem an impossible dream to most people, but it was rela-
tively easy compared to Joe's ultimate challenge. At age sixty he

tackled the Ironman Triathlon in Hawaii, completing the 2.4 mile swim, the 112 mile cycle and the 26.2 mile run in fifteen and one-half hours. Joe wants to motivate others to choose health and fitness. "If you haven't got your health, you have nothing," he believes. What would be a perfect day for Joe? "A great run, a bottle of wine, dinner with a friend, music and then some damn good sex!" Joe Womersley exudes a passion for life.

I met another senior who was serious about fitness. The late Dr. Paul Spangler, who took up running at age sixty-seven, ran seven miles three times a week and swam or lifted weights on the other days. In 1993 he completed the New York City Marathon in 9:23:25. "Running helps me experience the full joy of living," he said. "I've never enjoyed life more than I do now. I expect to be running competitively when I'm one hundred." He almost made it. On March 29, 1994, he died in the middle of a seven-mile training run. He was ninety-five.

In fact, seniors emphatically state that exercise and movement are fundamental for people who want to increase their health span (that is, the number of disability-free years). According to Jack Goodman, PhD, associate professor at the school of physical and health education at the University of Toronto, society has "widened the gap between health span and life span. We live longer than we did a hundred years ago but the key is to extend your health span. Fitness is a vital component in allowing us to do that."

Energetic George Richards, eighty, knows the meaning of health span. This lifelong athlete teaches fitness classes to an enthusiastic group of men aged sixty to seventy-five. "If you don't use your body, it's not generating any power. The body is like a machine, you've got to work it regularly," he says.

The three main components to fitness are cardiovascular endurance (or aerobics), muscular strength and endurance, and flexibility. I'll help you fit fitness into your life, give you some strategies for improving your exercise habits and motivate you to become the athlete you really are. So grab your running shoes: you'll need them for the journey to passionate longevity.

Cardiovascular Endurance—Aerobics

Cardiovascular endurance is the most important aspect of fitness because it forms the foundation for whole-body health. It is the ability of the heart, lungs and blood vessels to process and transport the oxygen required by exercising muscle cells to function for a prolonged period. The aerobic energy system is the body's primary method of energy production: it produces virtually all the energy that maintains the body at rest and more than ninety percent of the energy needed during aerobic exercise. The exception is the short burst of intense exertion, like sprinting, called anaerobic exercise, which uses energy produced by the anaerobic system, "in the absence of oxygen." Our aerobic energy system is dependent on an adequate supply of oxygen, which is limited by the efficiency of the cardiovascular system. When the anaerobic system kicks in, increased energy is produced but it also generates the waste products that cause muscle fatigue.

Because of the way the body produces energy, it's important to warm up before exercise and cool down afterwards. During the first few minutes of exercise, there is a delay in the delivery of oxygen from the blood to the working muscles. To minimize the use of the anaerobic energy system at this time—which produces lactic acid and muscle fatigue—a gradual warm-up period is required. The best warm-up is one that mimics your sport at a gentle, easy pace, such as a slow jog before a run. Stretching cold muscles before exercise is not recommended, as it could lead to injury. However, stretching (flexibility exercises) can be performed in the cool-down period when muscles and tendons are pliable; furthermore, stretching helps rid the body of waste products accumulated during exercise.

Guidelines for Aerobic Fitness

How frequently, how long and how intensely should I exercise? The answer can be summarized using the FIT formula.

F–Frequency: three to five times per week
I–Intensity: sixty to eighty percent of maximum heart rate
T–Time: thirty to sixty minutes

Frequency
Recent research indicates that to achieve a training effect, that is, an improvement in your fitness, exercise has to be regular and consistent. Cycling twice a week is fun, but don't expect to see significant improvements in your fitness level at this rate of exercise. The

general rule for beginners is to exercise every other day. This schedule gives the body a chance to recover thoroughly between workouts.

Intensity

Intensity refers to the effort put out. Exercise should be intense enough to reach and maintain your target heart rate zone (THRZ), giving you maximum aerobic benefits for your efforts. This rate is the minimum number of times the heart needs to beat each minute to have a positive effect on heart, lungs and blood vessels.

To calculate your THRZ, follow these simple steps:

1. Determine your predicted maximum heart rate. Subtract your age from 220 (the maximum heart rate). If you are forty, for example, your predicted maximum heart rate is 180 beats per minute ($220 - 40 = 180$).
2. Multiply your maximum heart rate by the percentage you intend to use for your workout. An out-of-shape forty-year-old might start an exercise program with a target of 65 percent to 75 percent of his or her maximum predicted heart rate. If that rate is 180, then the target heart rate zone for a starting workout would be 117 to 135 beats per minute ($180 \times .65 = 117$; $180 \times .75 = 135$).

To monitor your heart rate, take your pulse either at the wrist or the neck using the fingertips. Count your pulse for fifteen seconds (the first beat is zero, not one) and then multiply by four to arrive at your heart rate per minute.

Once you get used to listening to your body, it will not be necessary to take your pulse as often. Your body will tell you whether you need to speed up or slow down. One good rule of thumb: you should be able to carry on a normal conversation while exercising without sounding out of breath; this is called the talk test.

Time

To achieve a training effect, an exercise session should last a minimum of thirty minutes. At this point, it is important to identify your fitness goals. Are you training for the Olympics or recovering from a heart attack? If your goal is to reduce excess body fat, try to schedule thirty to sixty minutes of exercise four or five times per week. An easy number to remember is two—that is, two hours per week (thirty minutes times four workout sessions) should be set aside for fitness. This modest schedule still leaves one hundred and sixty-six hours of the week for the rest of life!

Types of Activity

The fitness activity you choose has to be fun and should suit your personality and life-style. What does personality have to do with choosing a fitness activity? Lots! I'm an outdoors person; I love to be outside in the fresh air, feeling the wind and the sun on my body. I need to be in close touch with nature all the time. As a result, running suits me perfectly. I could not stick with a fitness program if it meant being stuck inside a walled-in squash court. If you're a people person and like company, try an aerobics class. Choose something that moves your spirit and soul, that makes your heart sing emotionally as well as physiologically. Other aerobic activities to keep your heart happy are cycling, brisk walking, swimming, rollerblading or cross-country skiing, to name a few. Just remember the FIT principle: whatever you choose has to be intense enough to maintain your target heart rate zone. Let's say you choose cycling. Coasting through a residential neighborhood on your bike or stopping for traffic lights at every intersection will do little to improve fitness. The same is true for walking. When I say brisk walking I don't mean window-shopping!

And speaking of walking, did you know you're only two feet away from the world's greatest exercise? Walking may not seem as exciting as rollerblading, running or cycling, but it is an excellent aerobic conditioner if done properly, not to mention a great calorie burner with low risk of injuries. Walking a mile uses approximately one hundred calories. People are often surprised to learn that if they take a brisk forty-five minute walk four times a week for one year, while eating the same amount, they will burn enough calories to lose eighteen pounds! Furthermore, all the weight lost will be fat, because regular exercise preserves lean muscle mass.

For maximum results in a walking program, work up to walking three miles in forty-five minutes, four to five times per week. For additional benefits, you might add some hill training: find as many hills as you can and march up them, swinging your arms and breathing deeply with your diaphragm. Power walking (walking with hand weights) also increases the intensity; start with small hand-held dumbbells, pumping and pulling them as you walk. When you reach the twelve-minute-per-mile level of walking, you may switch to a walk-jog program: walk ten minutes, jog one to two minutes, then walk some more. Be creative. Visit new neighborhoods, explore the local parks, hike through the woods. Get out three subway stops early and walk the rest of the way to work. Forget elevators; try the stairs instead. Buy a dog, do errands on foot, leave the car at home.

Proper footwear is a must. There are many excellent walking shoes available. I recommend a supportive running shoe for walking, especially if you have flat feet, if your arches roll in or if you are overweight. A few words on breathing: most of us assume we are taking in plenty of oxygen. However, shallow chest breathing, a common breathing method, leaves the body underoxygenated. Diaphragmatic, or belly, breathing increases the amount of oxygen in the blood, which helps to reduce stitches.

Perhaps you're already a fitness buff. Want a refreshing change of pace from your favorite fitness activity? Try cross training, the use of more than one aerobic activity to attain cardiovascular endurance. Runners might try swimming, cycling or rowing to replace one or two workouts in their training routines. Not only does cross training add variety to fitness, it also creates a more balanced state in the body by exercising different muscles. The use of different training methods helps to reduce injury and prevent boredom.

Muscular Strength and Endurance

If you asked your body to shovel snow, move furniture or carry a heavy bag of cat litter from the trunk of the car into the house, would there be a major protest from your muscles? We are constantly making demands of our muscles. Standing and walking are activities that need only a minimum amount of muscle strength, but whenever we do more than that—climbing, lifting, pushing or pulling—we experience our weaknesses first-hand, through fatigue and sore muscles. An overall strengthening program can change all that, and then if there is something you'd like to do that is out of the ordinary, like hiking in the mountains in Arizona, your body will be ready, willing and able to cooperate.

Furthermore, many people assume that muscles deteriorate with age. Ask eighty-one-year-old Helen Zechmaster if she's gotten weaker as she's gotten older. Helen holds eight national age-group power-lifting records (dead lift 245 pounds, bench press 94 1/2 pounds, squat 148 pounds). She once competed in a men's thirty-five-years-and-older bracket because there were no other women entrants. She won. There's hope for all of us, regardless of our age or current physical condition.

Muscular strength is defined as the greatest force muscles can produce in one single, complete effort. Muscular endurance is a muscle's ability to perform continued repetitions of the same movement. Our muscles achieve this through coordination between the respiratory system (which delivers oxygen to and removes carbon dioxide from the blood) and the circulatory system (which delivers oxygen and nutrients while removing waste products from the cells.)

Maintaining muscle strength as we age is crucial for balance, coordination and mobility. Watch a frail, elderly person getting out of a chair, using hands for assistance because of weak, wobbly legs and ankles. Weak, inefficient muscles ask the body to work harder, resulting in low energy, fatigue, an unstable gait and the possibility of falls. Falls and their resultant fractures are the leading cause of death in people seventy-five and older. Unfortunately, twenty percent of the elderly who fracture a hip will die in the first year after the injury, usually from blood clots and other complications following surgery. Of the eighty percent of people who do survive, half will require long-term care, never regaining their previous level of independence and mobility. Another reason falls are so common in the elderly is lack of agility. Agility is muscular strength, endurance and flexibility combined with speed and coordination. Individuals who can move quickly, with frequent changes in direction, are agile. Dancing, walking on ice-covered sidewalks, stepping on and off an escalator—all these common activities require a good level of agility. While we don't need the agility of a professional basketball player, we do need to be agile enough to cope with the challenges of daily living in safety.

To improve your agility, try jumping rope, trampolining or t'ai chi, an ancient Chinese system of meditative movements that involve the entire body. These exercises improve balance, agility and coordination.

Getting Started

The most common type of strengthening exercises are those using progressive resistance training. This type of exercise builds strength by working your muscles against resistance. The resistance can come from your own body weight, rubber tubing or free weights (barbells and dumbbells). By gradually increasing the weight your muscles must move, you will improve your muscular strength.

Two other types of exercises also improve muscular strength: isokinetic and isometric exercises. Isokinetic exercises use machines to stress a muscle at a constant load throughout the entire range of that muscle's motion. Most of us are familiar with the Nautilus equipment found in most commercial fitness centers and health clubs, a fine example of isokinetic exercise. Some of us also remember pressing both hands together to increase bust size. That's an example of an isometric exercise. Isometric exercises use resistance against immovable objects, like walls; the resistance is so great that the contracting muscles cannot move the resistance object at all. Because of the difficulty of precisely evaluating the training effects, isometric exercises are not used as primary developers of muscular strength; on the other hand, a balanced programme of isokinetic exercise can be an effective, safe and enjoyable way to improve total body strength.

Use It or Lose It

Alex Beder, eighty-eight, has been weight training at the same gym for seventy-one years. When I interviewed him, he proudly took off his shirt to display musculature many forty-year-olds would envy. "I'm never tired," he says. A typical workout for Alex is twenty minutes of calisthenics, followed by one hour of weight training, then time on the stationary bike. He also walks a couple of miles per day. This lifelong athlete comments on the aging process: "Fitness has done more for me than anything money could buy. This is the most important thing in my life. I do as much in my workout as men fifty years younger than I am."

Alex has discovered one of the secrets to passionate longevity: fitness can redefine the so-called aging process. Let's look at what this really means.

Is the loss of strength inevitable with advancing age, or is it the result of disuse? One recent study found that resistance training reduces much of the loss of muscle mass and strength normally associated with aging. Through biopsies, scientists learned that the muscles of older men who did lifelong strength training looked the same as those of twenty-five-year-olds! On the other hand, biopsies performed on sedentary men and on those who did only endurance or aerobic training showed typical age-related changes. There is a clear message here: although some aerobic exercises do build strength (the legs in cycling; the arms, shoulders, back and legs in cross-county skiing), we still need an overall strengthening program to ensure continued muscle strength as we age.

You'd better grab a weight and hang on: this next study will blow you away! A Boston study of a group of ten *frail* nursing home residents illustrates the maxim, "It's never too late to start getting fit." Eight of the participants had a history of falls; seven used a cane or walker. In 1990, Maria Fiatarone, a doctor at Tufts University, recruited men and women aged eighty-six to ninety-six for an experiment in high-intensity resistance training. These weak old people lifted weights to determine if it was feasible to improve their strength. The muscle group tested was the quadricep at the front thigh. The quad is a very important muscle. In my seminars, I point to my quadricep and announce: "This muscle can make the difference between independence and dependence. Why? Because this is the muscle that allows you to get up out of a chair and to climb stairs. Imagine how humiliating it would be to have to ring for assistance whenever you had to get up from the toilet."

The subjects lifted light weights three times a week for ten to twenty minutes. In just eight weeks, the seniors more than doubled their strength; two of the ninety-year-olds tossed away their canes, and one man rose unaided from a chair!

This study certainly dispels the myth that past a certain age, your muscles can't grow anymore, that muscles inevitably waste with age. The positive results should motivate the seventeen percent of people older than sixty-five who are unable to perform major activities such as walking without assistance. Other American surveys have shown that after age seventy-four, twenty-eight percent of men and sixty percent of women cannot lift objects weighing more than ten pounds, the weight of a bag of flour. So if all that is standing between you and an independent, satisfying life-style is a weight, don't step over it. Pick it up and start using it.

Why Weight?

If you want to grow old successfully, the time to begin a strengthening program is in your thirties and forties, when you can still have an influence on the aging process. Why wait until age sixty when the effects of disuse have already begun? The greatest loss in muscle and muscle strength occurs later in life, after fifty or sixty years of age. This underscores the value of weight training. As Jack Goodman suggests, "You don't want to just walk to the grocery store, you want to walk home carrying your groceries." Of course, no matter what you do, you can't permanently forestall certain musculoskeletal effects of age: decreased flexibility, some loss of muscle mass, stiffening of connective tissue. However, even these signs can be greatly delayed and reduced through a regular strengthening program. Whenever my patients say, "I guess I should expect this at my age," I advise them to begin progressive resistance training and watch the results. They'll develop a spring in their steps!

So where do you begin?

- Before starting any exercise, get medical clearance from your doctor.
- Join a health club that features weight-training facilities.
- Check the local bookstore for books and magazines on weight training.
- Consider hiring a personal trainer to teach you a safe, effective workout.

Rules to Follow

1. Before you begin any resistance exercises, at home or in the gym, warm up the muscles through a light aerobic workout. Bike or jog for ten minutes. Follow this with gentle stretching exercises.
2. Proper breathing is important. Inhale before lifting, exhale while lifting, then inhale again while lowering the weight.

3. A weight workout can be completed in twenty minutes. Try to exercise every other day, as the muscles need adequate rest between workouts. It takes approximately forty-eight hours of rest to maximize fitness gains.

4. You don't have to lift heavy iron barbells for results. To strengthen muscles all you have to do is contract them smoothly and slowly eight to ten times against the resistance of your own body weight. That's enough to stimulate the growth of muscle fibers, nerves and blood vessels.

5. Listen to your body. It will talk to you often, especially when you are beginning any new fitness activity. Learn to distinguish the getting-into-shape soreness from the pain of overuse or overtraining. During the getting-into-shape phase, you might be stiff and sore for a day or two afterward or tired right after the exercise. With overuse or overtraining, you experience sharp twinges of pain *during* the exercises. My rule: it's better to underdo than overdo, especially in the initial stages of strength training. The first few workouts will show if you are doing too many repetitions of an exercise or using weights that are too heavy.

6. If you need further direction, advice is available from a variety of sources: chiropractors and other health professionals, as well as trainers and fitness consultants.

Don't be a slave to a training program; if your schedule doesn't fit with your life, modify the program. Fitness should be fun, not a punishment or a duty, so play with it and see what works best for you.

Get Strong, Feel Strong

Exercise in general reduces the effects of stress, anxiety and depression, but weight training has a very direct effect on self-esteem and body image, mainly because of the noticeable physical changes that result from regular training. When you see muscles sprouting or thighs trimming, you start feeling better about yourself, in control of your body. The experience of feeling stronger affects your psyche, and with new strength comes confidence. Those who are strong are no longer dependent on other people to lift, carry, push or pull anything.

Forty-six-year-old Barbara Mourin began a weight-training program three years ago. "I was concerned about osteoporosis and how I could prevent that. I wanted more than aerobics were giving me. Now I'm stronger, physically and mentally; my posture has improved and so has my confidence. I don't have to worry about not having strength to try new activities like rock climbing." Barbara is contemplating entering a weight-lifting competition.

I have been doing weight training twice a week, in addition to my regular running. Initially I struggled with squats and lunges even when I was using a fairly light weight; however, over the past year my body has adapted to the workouts and I'm feeling stronger. I can see and feel the difference! Have you noticed how tight lids are on jars? Now I can open them myself.

The 10 Secrets of George Richards, age eighty

1. If you don't love yourself, how do you expect anyone else to?
2. Try to look your personal best.
3. Be helpful, caring and sharing with all kinds of people.
4. Laugh a lot.
5. Do not take relationships for granted—work at them.
6. Never completely retire.
7. Forget yesterday's prices because you'll stop living and eating.
8. Be spontaneous and enthusiastic in everything.
9. Mix with all age groups—young and old.
10. Exercise. Dance. Keep your body moving.

Loose Living—The Benefits of Flexibility

We were designed to move. When joints move, we move. Flexibility is the ability of the joints to move through their natural range of motion. Flexibility reduces the risk of sports injury and improves balance, posture and athletic performance. Not every joint in your body is equally flexible, by design, and over the course of time, use or disuse will change the flexibility of a given joint. Nevertheless, we can do a great deal to retain, and even improve, our flexibility.

The natural aging process and inactivity are the enemies of flexibility. A sedentary life-style causes a loss of elasticity in the connective tissue and shortening of the muscles associated with the joints. People often don't realize that, while regular exercise builds muscle strength, at the same time there's a tendency for the muscles to get stiffer. So a regular stretching routine is absolutely necessary to maintain a normal range of motion. What if you wait until you're sixty-four to begin stretching? That's when Foofie Harlan started. Now seventy-eight, she is a member of the Sun City, Arizona, Cheerleaders. Harlan does a sixty-minute stretching routine twice a week, as well as two three-hour weekly rehearsals. She can still do splits, handstands, front flips and cartwheels. But why wait? Let's do it now.

Stretching
There are several ways to stretch to maintain and improve flexibility. The two basic types of stretches are dynamic flexibility exercises and static tighten-relax exercises. Dynamic flexibility exercises are smooth, easy movements that increase the range of motion for the joints of the body. Tighten-relax stretch exercises tense a muscle (or group of muscles) for ten to thirty seconds, followed by two to three seconds of relaxation, and then continue with gentle stretching for another ten to thirty seconds.

How often should you stretch? Even five minutes of stretching done three to four times per week will keep you loose. A daily five-minute stretch is ideal. If you stretch after an aerobic workout, when muscles and tendons are warm, you'll get the greatest benefit of all!

If you're new to stretching, here are some tips:

- Buy Bob Anderson's book *Stretching*, a great reference work, with excellent illustrations.
- Try a yoga class.
- Take a stretch and strength class at your fitness club.
- Look for stretching videos, which are now available.

Reality Check
Many of my active patients don't stretch at all; they're too busy pursuing the fitness activity they love best. When I ask them if they

stretch, they reply with embarrassment, "Sometimes." Or they show me one or two half-hearted two-second stretches. If you don't want to make time to stretch before and after your favorite sport, let me suggest a compromise. Before bed, lie on the floor and stretch all major muscle groups; I do this while watching the news. A good, long stretch will relax you before bed. You'll sleep better, and I can make one promise: you won't be as stiff getting out of bed in the morning. Try it tonight.

Exercise Myths

Here are some typical myths and excuses I hear from patients who don't want to exercise.

Myth 1. I don't need any exercise. I get plenty running after the kids, going up and down stairs and doing laundry.

Truth. Your active life-style is very good but not enough. Stop-and-start activities like housework elevate your heart rate for a few minutes, but not for the recommended thirty continuous minutes. Remember: you need sustained, intense cardiovascular activity to reap fitness benefits.

Myth 2. If I exercise, I might not have enough energy left for sex.

Truth. Wow, have I got good news for you! Exercise enhances sexuality, because when you exercise, you have more energy over-all. Physically fit people report less fatigue and more stamina during sexual activity. They also have greater self-esteem and thus feel more comfortable with their own bodies.

Myth 3. I'm too tired to exercise when I come home from work.

Truth. You are confusing mental fatigue with physical fatigue. Your brain may be tired from thinking all day, but your body still has a lot of life in it. Lack of oxygen is one major cause of fatigue. A brisk walk in the fresh air reduces that dragged-out feeling and gives you more energy to enjoy the evening.

Myth 4. I only have so many heart beats left and I don't want to waste them on exercise.

Truth. Regular, moderate exercise strengthens the heart and lowers the resting heart rate. People who are fit often have heart rates as low as forty-five to fifty beats per minute. A sedentary person's heart will beat seventy-five to eighty times per minute. The result? In just one day, an unfit person's heart must beat fifty thousand times more than a conditioned person's heart. In one year, that's a workload of seventeen million extra beats!

Myth 5. Aren't people who exercise more prone to injuries?

Truth. Injuries occur from not using your head when you use your body. Doing too much too soon, before muscles and joints have a chance to adapt to new stresses placed on them, will cause injuries. The key to safe exercise is to start slowly, warm up the muscles and build up fitness gradually.

Myth 6. I'm too stressed out to add any more activities to my life.

Truth. Regular exercise increases self-esteem and overall well-being, decreases depression and relieves negative stress. It's a lot better than pills, potions or lotions to help you sleep or relax.

Myth 7. I'm only twenty-five. I'll worry about exercise when I'm older.

Truth. Studies show that from age twenty-five, people who don't exercise at all can lose as much as two percent of their aerobic power per year. In contrast, fit subjects who biked or ran lost less than one percent per year.

Fitting in Fitness

Sometimes when I begin to explain the need for regular exercise, a patient will reply, "I haven't got time to exercise." And in fact, many people do face major challenges juggling family and career responsibilities. Nevertheless, I still believe that *everyone*, no matter how busy, should make time for fitness. Sometimes accepting the why for fitness makes it easier to find out how. We've all been given the same twenty-four hours in every day; what you choose to do with that time makes the difference. Those who make quality of life a priority don't struggle to fit in fitness; it just happens. Unfortunately, some of my patients always put other people's needs first. They postpone fitness until a project is finished or until the kids are in school. Some major event has to happen before we can begin taking care of ourselves.

If fitness is synonymous with work or drudgery or boredom, you haven't found the activity that expresses the real you. When patients say to me, "How can you run? I find it boring," I know that running is not the answer for them. Fitness is, but maybe through cycling, walking or aerobics classes, instead. We all have to find that special activity or sport we would choose to do, regardless of the measurable fitness benefits we might get. For long-term success, fitness has to be fun.

Fitness is the best way to reduce the everyday buildup of stress; even ten minutes of exercise will decrease that pressure-cooker feeling inside.

Remember: the longer the session, the greater the cardiovascular benefits, so if you have more time, use it. And if you're out of shape, it doesn't matter whether you get fit in eight weeks, thirty weeks or fifty-two weeks. The most important thing is to get out and move that body!

Strategies for Improving Exercise Habits

Sometimes the toughest part of a workout is getting dressed, that is, making the decision to exercise. I know someone who goes to bed and sleeps wearing her fitness gear (minus the running shoes, of course) so she won't talk herself out of it in the morning. Whatever it takes! Just do it. Here are some strategies that may help.

1. Develop a regular routine of exercising at the same time each day. Morning exercisers tend to stick with their fitness programs more easily; by setting aside time first thing in the morning, before the workday begins, they guarantee that little can come between them and their workouts. When patients tell me they're tired all the time, I advise, "Get up twenty minutes earlier and take a brisk walk before breakfast." Inevitably, those who try it come back and say they feel great and have much more energy.

2. Find friends who exercise and join them; socializing makes fitness fun. Fit friends motivate each other to stay on course. Instead of doing lunch, why not walk and talk at the same time? Breakfast meetings with active-minded clients could be held on a squash or tennis court.

3. Make an appointment with yourself: write "exercise" in your daily planner. In a busy life, it's too tempting to eliminate fitness entirely. When you see it written as an appointment in your book, you acknowledge a commitment to yourself. Remember: you always have time for the things you put first.

4. Join the Y or any other reputable fitness club. Paying for a

membership in a health club often motivates you to go. Surrounded by people having fun doing fit things, you'll want to join in. There are also many activities to choose from at a club.

5. Hang shoes or equipment on the doorknob. When you're just beginning a fitness program, you may need an extra push. Seeing your equipment on the door will remind you to use it.

6. Set out your goal in writing; specify the type of activity, frequency and duration. Fitness levels improve through regular, consistent workouts. If your goal is to run your first five-kilometer race by the end of the summer, and in April you're barely covering one kilometer regularly, writing out your goal will commit you to getting there.

7. If you can't run or walk because of inclement weather, swim or ski instead. Be flexible in your choice of activities. Go to a club or community center with a pool or weight-training facilities.

8. Reward yourself whenever you reach one of your goals. New clothes in a smaller size or a fitness-oriented vacation, such as a trip to a health spa, would be a suitable carrot to help you maintain your program.

9. Get involved in leisure activities with physical content, such as hiking or gardening. If you have an aversion to exercise, develop an active life-style. Try Ping-Pong, horseback riding, dancing, biking. Get active any way you can.

10. Keep a fitness journal and note your improved sense of well-being. As you record your experiences, you'll be able to see yourself progress. Initially you might write, "Had to stop after two minutes of jogging," or, "Out of breath, legs tired." Further on in your journal you'll be saying, "Felt good," and, "Ran four minutes without stopping, increased energy afterward." Rereading your entries is terrific motivation.

11. Have a periodic treadmill test for fitness assessment. This can be done at a health club or Y. A fitness test is a benchmark of your fitness level *today*. When you are retested some months later, you'll see how much you've improved, an instant motivator.

12. Proudly proclaim your fitness intentions to supportive family and friends. By announcing your intentions publicly, you'll be more likely to stick with your program. Make fitness a family affair—get everyone involved in an active life-style. Pack a lunch and go on a nature hike.

Movement Improvement

Did you know that sitting around too much can be as dangerous to your health as smoking? The latest word from the Canadian Heart and Stroke Foundation identifies "lack of exercise" as the fourth major risk factor for heart disease and stroke, behind smoking, high blood pressure and high cholesterol. Cardiovascular disease, which includes all forms of heart disease and stroke, is Canada's top killer, accounting for seventy-five thousand deaths a year—more than the combined total from cancer, AIDS and accidents. According to recent surveys, about forty percent of Canadians get no regular physical exercise. Such statistics inspired the Mount Sinai medical center to come up with this gem: "There is no such thing as a sudden heart attack. It requires years of preparation."

If you need further motivation, remember that regular exercise also helps the following:

- Sleeping
  A study showed that sedentary individuals had more periods of lighter sleep, and fewer periods of deep sleep, compared to fit individuals. On average, it took the inactive group twice as long to fall asleep, and they were awake for more of the night, as well.

- Cancer Prevention
  Researchers at the Harvard University School of Public Health found that people who exercised enough to burn one thousand calories or more per week had half the risk of developing colon cancer as less active people. You'll burn one thousand calories per week by walking ten miles, jogging or running for two hours or playing several hours of tennis. It seems that digestive wastes flow through the colon faster in fit people, so potential cancer-causing elements have less chance to make contact. Those who work out regularly also produce higher levels of natural killer cells, the white blood cells believed to be one of the immune system's defences against cancer.

- Recovery from Illness
  Fit people seem to bounce back more easily from bouts of ill health. In 1980, Judith Kazdan, a marathon runner, had surgery. Three weeks later, she started training again. Three months after the operation, she ran a marathon. Now seventy-four, she attributes her speedy recovery to her high level of fitness.

- Osteoporosis Prevention
  Osteoporosis is characterized by a thinning of the bones, and leaves many postmenopausal women fragile and susceptible to fractures. Physical activity plays a significant role in increasing bone mass when you're young and maintaining it when you're older. Exercises that involve the weight-bearing muscles of the legs, such as aerobics, jogging and walking, coupled with calcium supplementation and, for many women, hormone replacement therapy, will protect against serious bone loss. Remember, bone density can be increased with exercise in the premenopausal state, but is very difficult to replace once menopause begins. In addition, by focusing on strengthening the muscles of the spine, you will maintain good posture and decrease the curved back problem common in osteoporosis. Even without osteoporosis, poor posture plus the normal aging process can cause strain on the spinal joints, resulting in chronic back pain and stiffness. So it's essential to develop a strengthening program for the back and hips to ensure that your back stays healthy and strong.

- Diet and Body Fat Control
  My approach to the body-fat dilemma is this: get a thirty-to forty-five-minute aerobic workout four to five times a week. Combine with a varied, healthy, low-fat diet. We gain weight when our caloric input from food exceeds our caloric output. Vigorous exercise does more than just burn calories; it also revs up the body engine by raising the rate at which calories are used when the body is at rest. The effect of exercise lasts for up to twenty-four hours, so you continue to burn calories long after you've finished each exercise session.

- Longevity
  A landmark study of almost seventeen thousand Harvard alumni by Dr. Ralph Paffenbarger, Jr., found that longevity is positively influenced by exercise. Remember, everything that gets worse as you get older gets better as you exercise. And active people live longer, as much as two years longer than those with sedentary life-styles. Dr. Paffenbarger discovered that every hour spent exercising buys another two to three hours of life.

I can almost hear some skeptic say, "Is that all? All that work for only two more years of life?" My belief in exercise boils down to an appreciation of the *quality* of life. I'm prepared to exercise today, hoping to be an active, vibrant, mobile, independent, healthy eighty-two-year-old rather than an immobile eighty-year-old who requires care from family and nursing homes.

Making Your Body a Younger Place to Live

How old would you think yourself to be if you didn't know your age? The answer to this question can be very revealing, because it takes into account how you really feel about your overall level of wellness. I feel about twenty years younger than my chronological age, making me about twenty-six in terms of health and wellness. I attribute my youthful vigor and high energy levels to my longtime commitment to fitness. We seem to have a physiological age related to our level of physical fitness. How old are *your* arteries, kidneys, heart? When new patients come in, I always check their birth dates against how they look, move and communicate. Often I'll be face-to-face with a patient free of serious disease who nevertheless looks much older than her years; it doesn't take long to figure out what she hasn't been doing.

Did you know that an active sixty-year-old and an inactive thirty-year-old are equal in endurance and stamina? Joe Womersley, sixty-nine, says he can walk as fast and carry as much as any twenty-five-year-old. Just watch him beat many of the twenty-five-year-olds in the local marathon! The clock at the finish line doesn't lie, and neither does your body. However, you can slow down your inner clock with the right attitude, an attitude that says, "Everything I do with and to my body is important." Run, swim, walk or cycle and you'll maintain aerobic power. Work your muscles and you'll stay strong and build bone mass. Stretch and you'll stay flexible.

Twenty-five-year-olds think they're immortal; at forty-five, we know we're not. Looking around at some friends and patients my own age, I see health problems surfacing, like icebergs poking through the water. The difference between us is the choices we have made over a lifetime. So make fitness a priority in your life. Put fitness first and you'll change the way you grow old.

Fit—But Not Healthy

In spite of all the very positive benefits of fitness, exercise alone will not make anyone healthy. Fitness is only one link in the health chain. Other essential components are a low-fat, semi-vegetarian diet, a tobacco-free life-style, adequate sleep, satisfying relationships, stress management, a safe environment and meaningful work.

According to the World Health Organization, "Health is the extent to which an individual or group is able, on the one hand, to realize aspirations and satisfy needs; and, on the other hand, to change or cope with the environment. Health is seen as a resource for everyday life, not the objective of living; it is a positive concept emphasizing social and personal resources, as well as physical capacity." Health goes beyond the structure and function of the physical body to include feelings, values and reasoning. In this broad perspective, health can exist in the presence of disease; one does not have to be in perfect health to have a productive, meaningful and healthy life. In fact, the late Dr. George Sheehan, cardiologist and runner, believed that there is a healthy way to be ill. He continued running despite a longtime battle with prostatic cancer. "I may die from cancer," he said, "but my body is not going to die from anything else." What a great attitude!

On the other hand, some extremely fit people live unhealthy lives. I know competitive amateur cyclists who smoke and marathon runners with serious drinking problems. Other exercise fanatics are so addicted to working out that they are willing to neglect family and career in pursuit of negligible fitness gains. And what about the professional athletes who abuse their bodies with steroids and other illegal drugs? Those who hate exercise are quick to pounce on these examples of abuse, especially when tragedy strikes.

Best-selling fitness author Jim Fixx, who died while running at the age of fifty-two, is a case in point. He mistakenly believed that exercise alone would protect him from his high level of blood cholesterol. Up to age thirty-five, Fixx was an overweight smoker and no doubt had advanced arteriosclerosis. Because of his weight loss and exercise program, it is likely that he survived longer than might have been expected. But it is a mistake to believe that running or aerobic classes will permit any of us to eat whatever and whenever we want. Even a person who exercises daily may have to contend with high blood pressure, high cholesterol levels or weight problems. Exercise is *not* a substitute for common sense, regular checkups and sensible diets.

Nevertheless, it is my experience that most exercise enthusiasts live healthy lives. It seems that exercise often kick-starts us to eliminate all sorts of unhealthy habits. Sandy was a thirty-two-year-old man who came to see me because of acute lower back pain. He smoked and sported a typical bulging gut from years of inactivity. When he also complained of low energy, I suggested that he start exercising. For Sandy, the key to success was finding something he liked to do. He said he used to enjoy cross-country running in high school, so we began with a walk-run program. Now Sandy runs regularly; he's quit smoking, lost weight and can't believe how good his back feels!

Exercise can be a powerful catalyst for change. When you exercise, your social life may change as you start associating with healthy, active people. Your diet changes, and you choose high-energy foods, like pasta, over high-fat items like French fries. When you start taking pride in your body, you won't want to ruin it with cigarettes or excessive alcohol. For this reason, I tell patients to begin exercising instead of nagging them to quit smoking and lower their fat intake; the rest follows naturally. Don't be discouraged if you take a few detours; no one becomes fit overnight. Once you experience how good feeling good is, you won't want to stray too far from the healthy road to passionate longevity.

Fitness—My Story

The late Dr. George Sheehan, cardiologist, runner and author, said, "All of us are athletes, some of us are in training, some of us aren't." I began my athletic training at twenty-nine years of age. Given my running career, most people today assume that I was active in high school. Nothing could be further from the truth. My hormones were active; I could have won awards for running after the boys! But I begged my mother to write notes to excuse me from gym class, and the only outdoor activity that mildly interested me was baseball. Sports were not encouraged in my family, but we were major hikers, hitting the Bruce Trail on most weekends to commune with nature, pick wild berries and bird-watch. I never suspected I had any athletic ability whatsoever; I was in for a major surprise.

When I moved from Hamilton to Toronto at age twenty-two, I was into my third year of smoking. I played the occasional game of tennis, and in the summer I splashed around in a pool to cool off between long stretches of suntanning. I wasn't interested in being active or getting fit, although I did quit smoking in 1972, two years before I began my studies to become a chiropractor.

Two major events in April, 1978, forced me to rethink my sedentary life-style. I was about to graduate as a chiropractor and wanted to be a positive role model for my patients. How could I possibly motivate them to choose health and fitness when I barely knew the meaning of these words? In addition, four years of sitting too close to the fridge had produced a gluteus that was maximus. I did not like the lower half of my body, since the sands had shifted to the bottom of my hourglass figure. Diets galore—the water diet, the grapefruit diet, Dr. Atkins's diet revolution—had all failed. I didn't need fat calipers to convince me that my body needed an overhaul.

I was serious about changing my life and very impatient; I wanted the fastest, most direct route to lean and mean. As a typical Type A personality, I decided to run off my excess baggage. What I didn't know at the time was the profound way running would change my life. I found some shorts that barely fit, bought some basic running shoes and tackled one block, one *long* block. Day after day I persisted, until my breathing became less laboured, and then I began to add more blocks. My body felt great *after* each workout! At my level of fitness, the emphasis was definitely on *work*; running was not fun, yet I persevered. Soon my adventurous spirit set a new goal; one mile without stopping. I did it. How about one and a half miles? Then two?

As time passed, my body seemed to be complaining less and enjoying itself more. I liked how I felt; I liked how I looked. My gluteus was becoming minimus. Four months later, I entered my first ten-kilometer race; it was like climbing Mount Everest, but at last I was a runner, an athlete! Runners join running clubs, so I did, too. The members were busy discussing their fall marathon plans; I listened to them, intrigued and amazed that anyone could run 26.2 miles. After a while, I thought, "Why not?" So, a few months later, I, too, ran a marathon—the Skylon, from Buffalo to Niagara Falls. I had to alternate walking and running for the last ten kilometers, but

I did it! Just before they were closing the race, I limped to the finish line, with only six people left to cheer me on, the marathon volunteers. The clock read 4:51:09. Elated by my accomplishment, but determined to get faster, I hired a coach, trained consistently and did speed work on the track. Four years later, I ran a personal best time of 2:53:53, making me the eleventh-fastest Canadian female in 1982!

What has kept me running has nothing to do with body fat, heart rates or race times. Rather, I discovered something I truly love to do. Thus, my life story is divided into two halves: before and after running. Running and sport have become models for life, teaching me lessons on setting goals and reaching them. Sometimes I have felt disappointment, too. I have discovered determination, creativity, perseverance and patience because of running. My inner strength has been challenged and tested with each marathon. With reflection, I now know that the marathon experience spills over into everyday life: since I have pushed my body to the finish line, I believe I can survive whatever obstacles life places in my path. Running has made me strong. Says Max Goldhar, seventy-six, whose high school memories revolve around athletics—football, basketball, fencing, swimming, skiing, tennis and sailing, "Sports train you for life. You learn about teamwork, give and take and friendship—everything you need to know in the business world."

Your personal marathon finish line may involve going back to school, writing a book, quitting smoking. Small, progressive, consistent steps will get you there; set a goal and go for it. I did it. So can you.

The 10 Secrets of Max Goldhar, age seventy-six

1. Have a sense of humor; it will help you cope with adversity.
2. Identify the question, and the answer will usually follow. Many people sit around and talk about the problem without identifying what the essence of it is.
3. Try to develop as wide a range of interests as possible: art, literature, athletics, music.
4. Develop skills you are good at, particularly athletic skills.
5. Have curiosity for life; don't be afraid to explore. Intellectual curiosity is essential. Don't stop learning.
6. On relationships: don't be afraid to commit yourself to another person.
7. Become cultured—you'll be at home with many different types of people.
8. Never jump to conclusions. Learn all the facts—particularly in relation to people.
9. Have a real zest for living. Get the most out of every opportunity.
10. Maintain a good, healthy life—it makes all the other things possible.

P.S. It is very important to be charitable when you are in a position to help others.

6

VITALITY

Diet affects our health, overall vitality and longevity.

There is wisdom in the body. Just think of these miracles that take place every day: the oat bran cereal you have while reading the newspaper this morning is the fiber that grabs bad cholesterol and ushers it out of the body. The yogurt at lunch is the calcium your body uses to build and maintain healthy bones and teeth. The carrots and broccoli you choose for dinner ultimately become the antioxidants that do battle with oxygen-charged molecules determined to damage cells. The juicy orange you devour as a snack is the vitamin C your body needs to produce collagen, a protein necessary for making connective tissue in skin, ligaments and bones.

Do you take time to think that a baked potato provides energy in the form of glucose for all your body functions? The coffee that kick-starts your day likewise has far-reaching effects: it quickens the breathing, strengthens the pulse, raises the blood pressure, stimulates the kidneys and excites the functions of the brain. Food can affect our moods, make us sleepy, clog our arteries. It creates substances that inflame joints, trigger headaches, stimulate insulin release and control blood sugar surges. Food stimulates the body to make cells that ward off infection, cause constipation or alter our entire immune system.

Just as we now know the devastating effects smoking has on our body, so we also realize the effect our diets have on our prospects for health, longevity and overall vitality. Scientific studies confirm that what we eat determines what happens at the basic cellular level, where all metabolic transformations move through endless cycles. That is where life begins and ends.

Why have I called this chapter on nutrition *vitality*? Vitality comes from the Latin *vita*, meaning life. The Oxford English Dictionary defines vitality as the ability of something to continue; the power of enduring; mental or physical vigor; liveliness. These are all traits that those of us concerned with passionate longevity want to possess. We can live without exercise, without work, family, friends; maybe this would only be existing, but it is life. However, we can't live without the six nutrients needed to sustain life— carbohydrates, protein, fats, vitamins, minerals and water.

Food provides the body with raw material for the production of energy, repairs damaged tissues and is essential for the growth of new tissues and the regulation of all physiological processes.

Now that we know the importance of diet for health, longevity and vitality, let's learn to make the right choices.

Carbohydrates—Eating for Energy

My favorite aspect of marathon training has always been the eating part. In my last few days prior to the grueling event, carbohydrate loading was mandatory. You've heard of the runner's high? I got high demolishing a plate of spaghetti, mounds of brown rice with vegetables, and several hunks of bread to soak up the tomato sauce. This loading was done for purely physiological reasons: to supersaturate my muscles with fuel in the form of glycogen. Carbohydrates are readily broken down into glucose, the body's main energy source; glucose gets stored in the muscles as glycogen.

Not all of us run marathons, but we all face complex and stress-filled days. If your marathon of career and family responsibilities leaves you without enough energy to get through the day, you also need a super-octane charge from complex carbohydrates. Carbohydrates include simple sugars and complex starches. Refined simple sugars are found in candy and soft drinks. Natural simple sugars are in fruits, juices and vegetables. Complex starches are found in fruits, vegetables, legumes and grains.

Refined sugar snacks—a candy bar, for example—might seem to provide quick energy. Unfortunately, there are no real nutrients in simple sugars. They lack the vitamins and minerals that help your body's engine perform at its very best. In comparison, the sugars found in fruit—the complex starches—provide both energy and lots of essential nutrients. Furthermore, complex carbohydrates (high in starches and fiber) are digested slowly, and thus provide the body with a consistent stream of energy.

At least fifty-five percent of our daily caloric intake should come from complex carbohydrates. Some experts even suggest sixty percent. What does this mean in the real world? One practical suggestion is to eat five or more servings of a combination of vegetables and fruits, plus six or more servings of whole grains or legumes daily. Some examples of foods high in complex carbohydrates are whole-grain breads, pasta, rice, beans, potatoes, corn, peas, carrots, beets and broccoli. One day's menus could look like this.

Breakfast	whole-grain cereal
	fruit
	orange juice
Lunch	sandwich on whole-grain bread
	fruit
Dinner	anything you like but include
	two vegetables
	one fruit
	two slices of bread

Pigging out on complex carbohydrates is not the road to good health. Excess carbohydrates—carbohydrates beyond what the body can store—are converted to fat and then stored—as fat! But with the steady increase in fat consumption in our diets, indulging in excess carbohydrates is rarely the problem. Eating fat will make fat. Combine one high-fat diet with a lack of physical activity and you have the formula for obesity.

Pass me the potatoes, please. Hold the butter and sour cream.

The Big Four Vitamins—Don't Leave Home Without Them

There has been a fundamental shift in the way the medical world views vitamins. Until quite recently, we were taught that most people get enough vitamins through their diet, and taking supplements just created expensive urine. Now the scientific community is researching the role vitamins play in promoting optimal health and preventing chronic disease. They believe that even with a healthy diet—low in fat and rich in fruits and vegetables—it's unlikely the body will receive the high levels of vitamins it needs.

Doctors strongly advise their patients to take these vitamins: E, C and beta carotene (the antioxidant vitamins), plus the B-vitamin folacin or folic acid. Antioxidants protect our cells by rendering harmless that nasty group of particles called "free radicals." Free radicals can damage basic genetic material and cell walls, and if left unchecked can lead to disease. Folic acid has been shown to prevent birth defects and cervical cancer; therefore, it is recommended for all women in their childbearing years.

To maximize good health, here are the recommended amounts of the big four powerhouse vitamins.

1. **Vitamin E**: 200–800 IU (International Unit) daily, recommended for all adults (for example, one tablespoon of canola oil contains 12 to 15 IU).
2. **Vitamin C**: 250–500 mg (milligram) a day. Supplements are advised for anyone not consuming several fruits or vegetables rich in vitamin C (one orange contains 70 mg) per day.
3. **Beta Carotene**: 6–15 mg a day (equal to 10,000–25,000 IU of vitamin A). Again, supplements are advised for anyone not consuming several carotene-rich fruits or vegetables daily (one sweet potato contains 15 mg).
4. **Folic Acid**: 400 mcg from food or pills for all women who may become pregnant.

Calcium

"You are perimenopausal," my physician announced one day. "That means you are around or near menopause, and this is why your periods are irregular." My first reaction was, "Impossible!" After all, as an athlete I felt twenty-five, and my friends told me I looked thirty-five. So what if my birth certificate read forty-five? Perhaps my body was confused. Was I ready for this next new phase of my life? My bedtime reading started to include books on menopause and osteoporosis. "Are my bones healthy and strong enough to get me through old age?" I wondered. I reflected on my calcium intake and life-style during the past four decades:

Childhood rated an A + + for high calcium intake, thanks to gallons of milk and tons of outdoor activity. Teen years also deserved an A, as I was still under parental influence, but I drank less milk.

Nineteen to twenty-eight years of age fell to C. My calcium intake was drastically reduced by three years of smoking, lack of exercise, alcohol on weekends, caffeine and chronic dieting. On the plus side, I had lots of sunshine, which forms vitamin D and helps absorb calcium.

Between the ages of twenty-nine and forty-five, I bounded back to A + +, thanks to an athletic life-style, balanced nutrition with dairy foods and lots of veggies and running outside in sun (but no suntanning).

Had I achieved top grades in peak adult bone mass? This bone density is the highest genetically predetermined value an individual attains during her lifetime. Bone growth slows at about age thirty-five, and then we begin to lose bone density. Prior to that, remodeling takes place; old bone is continuously being replaced by new bone, except during youth, when bone development exceeds bone removal. Other cells remove calcium and release it so it can be used for essential functions like muscle contraction, nerve transmission, regulating the heartbeat and blood clotting.

As menopause approaches, the ovaries produce less estrogen; this leads to a rapid and accelerated bone loss, most of which occurs in the first five to seven years following menopause. Bone loss can lead to osteoporosis, a condition that affects one in four postmenopausal women in Canada. Bones become fragile and brittle and they fracture easily. One out of every six men older than sixty is also affected by osteoporosis.[1]

For optimal levels of bone health, a panel of international experts on osteoporosis (Hong Kong 1993) recommended the following intakes for white women:

Premenopausal women age thirty to fifty: 1,000 mg daily
Postmenopausal women: 1,500 mg daily
Adolescents: 1,600 mg daily

---

1. Osteoporosis Society of Canada, Organization Profile 1990.

Requirements may differ in other ethnic groups (stats are unavailable) and may be less in people with lower protein intakes and small skeletal size.[2] These amounts are higher than levels recommended by Health and Welfare Canada.

The calcium in our diet can come from a wide variety of foods. Although milk and milk products are the best sources, calcium is also found in fruits and green vegetables (oranges, bananas, broccoli); breads and cereals (whole-wheat bread, bran muffins made with buttermilk); fish (sockeye salmon with bones, sardines); even beans and almonds. You may need calcium supplements in addition to your food intake to satisfy the recommended daily requirement. Check with your dietician or health-care practitioner to determine what you need. For those with lactose intolerance, a dietician can give you a balanced meal plan. Dr. Bonnick, head of the osteoporosis clinic at the Cooper Aerobics Center in Dallas, believes that calcium supplementation is mandatory for people who don't drink much milk or eat many dairy products. She explains that it's very difficult to get enough calcium from non-dairy foods alone.

How to Maximize Your Calcium Intake

"No one absorbs all the calcium he or she eats," says Dr. Harold Draper, professor in the department of nutritional sciences at the University of Guelph. "We absorb only about thirty-five percent of the total amount of calcium in our diet." Factors that decrease our intake:

1. Caffeine causes moderate calcium loss. The caffeine in one cup of coffee (150 mg) can increase calcium needs by 30 to 50 mg. Avoid consuming caffeine at the same meal with high calcium foods.[3]
2. Alcohol decreases calcium absorption and increases calcium losses.

---

2. Fourth International Consensus Development Conference on Osteoporosis, Hong Kong, 1993. R.P. Heaney. Bone Mass, Nutrition and Other Lifestyle Factors.

3. Bales C.W. Nutritional Aspects of Osteoporosis: in Lawton P (ed): Ann Rev. Gerontol Geriat 1989.

3. Dietary fibers, oxalic acid (found in spinach and rhubarb) and phytic acid (found in wheat bran) bind with calcium and keep it from being absorbed in the intestine. Try kale or Swiss chard, which are better greens for calcium absorption. If you take a calcium supplement, avoid taking it along with a high-fiber cereal at breakfast.
4. Smoking increases calcium losses from the body by lowering the estrogen content of the blood, thus weakening the bones.
5. Eating too much protein (having twice the amount you require) increases the loss of calcium in urine, leading to an increased risk of osteoporosis.

Quick Tips for a Calcium Boost
1. Make a yogurt shake or milk shake. In a blender put 3/4 cup low fat yogurt or skim milk, a banana and 1/2 cup strawberries. (more than 300 mg of calcium)
2. Stuff baked potatoes with a yogurt and herb mixture.
3. Make homemade broccoli soup and add skim milk; serve with a little grated Cheddar on top.
4. Use chick-peas (garbanzo beans) in soups, salads, casseroles, even tomato-based sauces. One cup has 300 mg of calcium. Or make hummus, a chick-pea spread of Middle Eastern origin.
5. For a snack, have low-fat crackers with low-fat cheese melted on top.
6. Low-fat yogurt with fresh fruit is a good dessert. Sprinkle some almonds on top; decorate with cinnamon and a touch of honey.
7. Add a tablespoon of blackstrap molasses to a cup of baked beans for a total of 300 mg of calcium.
8. Add low-fat grated Cheddar cheese or Parmesan cheese to salads, pasta, pizza. Just three tablespoons of parmesan cheese has approximately 210 mg of calcium.
9. A juicer is a convenient way to give your bones a blast. Blend five or six carrots, some kale leaves, a cup of parsley and an apple for about 460 mg of calcium.
10. Make a calcium-packed pizza with lots of shredded low-fat mozzarella cheese, broccoli florets, onions, parsley and mushrooms on a whole-wheat crust.
11. Bake muffins that include buttermilk, blackstrap molasses and fruit.

12. Use low-fat yogurt instead of mayonnaise for making tuna or egg salad sandwiches.
13. Forget peanut butter and jam. Have salmon sandwiches (with the crushed bones) for lunch.
14. For an appetizer, mix sardines with a bit of minced onion and spread on low-fat crackers.
15. Finally, don't skip breakfast. Kathryn Robins, former executive director of the Osteoporosis Society of Canada says, "By skipping the first meal, too many women miss an important opportunity to get the dietary calcium and many other nutrients they require for healthy bones."

Some Additional Facts
1. Current research shows high calcium intake has minimal or no protective effect against bone loss in the immediate postmenopausal period. But after this big drop, a high calcium intake substantially reduces bone loss thereafter.[4]
2. Thin women are at greater risk for developing osteoporosis. Fats act as carriers for the fat-soluble vitamins A, D, E, K. By aiding in the absorption of vitamin D, fats help make calcium available to body tissues, particularly to bones and teeth. Finally, a good reason to carry a little extra fat!

Iron

One day last summer, I arranged to meet my girlfriend Brenda for an easy ten-mile run. After running three miles we stopped at a fountain to get a drink. I bent over the faucet, felt dizzy and fainted on the grass. A blood test revealed that I had iron-deficiency anemia. Anemia is a condition in which our blood contains insufficient hemoglobin. Hemoglobin is the part of the blood that transports oxygen from the lungs to the tissues. In my case, the anemia was triggered by two factors: an increase in marathon training, which reduced my iron stores, and a temporary decision to eliminate red meat from my diet.

---

4. Fourth International Consensus Development Conference on Osteoporosis, Hong Kong, 1993. R.P. Heaney. Bone Mass, Nutrition and Other Lifestyle Factors.

Because of my experience, I decided to do a little research and discovered that iron-deficiency anemia is the country's most common nutritional deficiency. We need to eat substantially more iron-rich foods than our bodies require because only a small amount of the iron we eat is absorbed by the body. The iron from animal foods (heme iron) is more readily absorbed than that from vegetable foods (nonheme iron). About twenty-three percent of the iron in meats, fish and poultry is absorbed, compared to only three to eight percent from sources such as dark green vegetables, fruit, grains, legumes and eggs.

What are the requirements for iron? Women between the ages of thirteen and forty-nine need 15 mg of iron daily; women older than fifty require eight to 10 mg of iron daily. Men require 10 mg.

It is important to remember that vitamin C is an iron enhancer. It helps the body absorb more heme and nonheme sources of iron. So have orange juice with an iron-enriched cereal, and your body will absorb more iron from the cereal. Likewise, some foods are iron inhibitors. Having tea or coffee with an iron-rich meal reduces the absorption. Some iron-rich food sources are blackstrap molasses, green leafy vegetables (broccoli, bok choy), organ meats and eggs. Check with your health practitioner or dietician if you are thinking of taking iron supplements.

Liver

Forget the Pepsi generation! My parents came from the Geritol generation. My mother had "tired blood," so iron-rich calves' liver with onions was a regular item on our dinner menu. While other kids at school were eating bologna or ham sandwiches, I'd often eat chopped liver spread on rye bread. I've noticed that the world divides into two distinct groups: liver lovers and liver haters. Liver haters describe the awful smell and taste and expound on the high cholesterol content. They are also quick to point out that the liver is the detoxification center for the body.

They conveniently forget that liver is loaded with vitamins and minerals. Jane Brody, *New York Times* health columnist, says, "Liver is like a multivitamin-mineral tablet on your dinner plate." A two-to-three-ounce serving of liver supplies excellent protein, often hard-to-get trace minerals (iron, copper, zinc, manganese, selenium), magnesium, potassium, and all the B vitamins, including those especially needed during stress. Most importantly, the iron from liver (heme iron) is easily absorbed by the body.

If you need to disguise the taste, I recommend organic liver, nitrate and chemical free, which is available at health-food supermarkets. Remember: all you need is two to three ounces once every week or two for a healthy shot of iron, vitamins and minerals.

Fiber

I asked Maye Musk, the president of the Consulting Dieticians of Canada, how she advises her clients to get enough fiber. She replied, "The easiest way is to get it from breakfast. A high-fiber breakfast, like a third of a cup of Kellogg's Bran Buds with Psyllium, has eleven grams, and if you slice a medium banana on top, that's another three and a half grams, so that's fourteen and a half grams of fiber already. You're halfway to your goal of twenty-five to thirty-five grams for the day. For lunch, you could have two slices of whole-wheat bread or a whole-wheat bagel, half a can of tuna (no fiber), plus some kind of salad like a spinach salad or mixed greens. In the evening, have pasta, a baked potato with the skin, plus vegetables like half a cup of broccoli and half a cup of carrots." When you start increasing fiber in your diet, you are going to have good bowel movements, and you will require more fluids, especially plain water. Fiber absorbs water to produce a softer stool that can pass more easily through the intestines. You will also have more flatulence, especially until your body adjusts to the new diet.

There are two types of fiber: soluble and insoluble. Many foods contain both types, for example, legumes, fruits and vegetables. Insoluble fiber promotes more efficient elimination, and leads to a reduction of colon cancer and intestinal disease. Brown rice, wheat bran, vegetables, legumes and the skins of fruits and vegetables are excellent sources of insoluble fiber. Soluble fiber, on the other hand, lowers blood cholesterol by grabbing hold of it and ushering it out of the body. Oat bran, apples, prunes, grapefruit and legumes all contain soluble fiber.

Flax—The New Super Cholesterol Fighter?

The next dietary discovery seems to be flax, recently being studied by researchers. Flaxseed, grown in western Canada, is one of the richest dietary sources of linolenic acid, an essential fatty acid. It is also a good source of fiber. We already know the role of fiber in reducing cholesterol, so it may come as no surprise that flaxseed is winning rave reviews in its ability to lower cholesterol.

Baked bread and muffins containing fifty grams of ground raw flaxseed were given to a group of female volunteers at the University of Toronto. Researchers found, after just one month, that total blood cholesterol decreased by nine percent and LDL cholesterol (the bad stuff) decreased by eighteen percent. A similar study at the University of Medicine and Dentistry of New Jersey found comparable decreases in cholesterol. The participants in that study ate six slices of bread per day in which ground flaxseed replaced part of the flour.

Flaxseed is available in health-food stores and bulk markets that sell grains. Some bakeries sell flax bread.

Antioxidants—Protection Against the Enemy

We have one hundred trillion cells in our bodies. Just think about that for a moment and marvel! But one hundred trillion cells need ongoing maintenance, too. As a byproduct of normal cell function, waste products—oxygen molecules called oxidants—are created in our bodies and need to be eliminated in some way. So far, scientists have linked destructive oxygen reactions to at least sixty different chronic diseases, as well as to the aging process itself.

Enter the antioxidants, the body's police force. Antioxidants are produced from the food we eat; their main function is to fight off the oxidants. The most notorious bad-guy oxidants are the oxygen-free radicals. They can attack DNA, the genetic material of cells, causing them to mutate; this is the first step on the path to cancer. Free radicals can also affect LDL, low-density lipoproteins that carry cholesterol through the bloodstream, dropping it off where needed for cell building—and leaving any unused residue of cholesterol on the arterial walls. This sets off the process by which blood cells, full of LDL, block arteries.

Some oxidants, such as air pollutants and pesticides, come from the environment. Cigarette smoking is a major producer of oxidants, both for those who smoke and for those exposed to secondhand smoke.

How can we protect ourselves from all this internal wear and tear? The best ammunition in the battle comes from plant foods, the fruits and vegetables that are packed with antioxidants. Our bodies need foods high in vitamins C, E, beta carotene and the trace mineral selenium.

Some Major Antioxidants in Foods
1. **Beta Carotene**: found in carrots, sweet potatoes, pumpkin, broccoli, cantaloupe, mango.
2. **Vitamin C**: found in red and green bell peppers, broccoli, cauliflower, strawberries, spinach, tomatoes, citrus fruits.
3. **Vitamin E**: found in almonds, soybeans, roasted sunflower seeds.
4. **Selenium**: found in white tuna (choose the kind canned in water), roasted sunflower seeds, whole grains.

Remember: choose fruits and vegetables with color. The deeper the color, the more antioxidants.

Athletes need to insure that their diets include lots of antioxidants. Studies have shown that vigorous exercise increases the production of free radicals. This makes sense because athletes use more oxygen. In addition, exercise increases our rate of breathing, so during a vigorous workout, you may be taking in more ozone and other pollutants that boost free radical production.

So as part of your healthy, active life-style, increase your intake of fruits and vegetables. Some doctors are now recommending vitamin E supplements, as it's difficult to get sufficient amounts from food alone.

Protein

Do you know what three ounces of cooked meat looks like? Go to the meat counter of your favorite grocery store or supermarket. Ask the butcher to show you four ounces (fifty to a hundred grams) of raw meat. Remember: there's twenty-five percent shrinkage when meat is cooked. Memorize that size! Maye Musk, dietician, tells her clients that our meat, chicken and fish portions should be about the size and thickness of a deck of cards. Roberta Ferrence, PhD, associate professor with the department of preventive medicine at the University of Toronto, agrees. "Don't think of meat as the center of your meal. Think of it as a garnish, like a sprig of parsley."

That three-ounce deck of cards might look puny to someone used to sixteen-ounce steaks; nevertheless, it can provide a one-hundred-and-fifty pound adult with one-third to one-half of the day's protein requirements. Most of us eat at least twice as much protein as we really need. Only fifteen percent of our total daily calories should come from protein. Excess protein strains the liver and kidneys and promotes mineral loss (especially calcium). Surprisingly enough, excess protein also contributes to obesity. Yes, you can get fat from eating too much protein! Your body cannot store excess protein, so all that extra prime rib must be eliminated, converted to glucose or stored as fat.

Nearly all vegetables contain some protein, so with variety, even vegetarians can easily meet their daily protein needs. The richest sources of vegetable proteins are legumes—dried peas and beans, including lentils, chick-peas and kidney beans. How many grams of protein do we need daily? Dieticians and nutritionists determine our minimum needs through a formula, factoring in age, size and lean body tissue. Adults need 0.8 grams of protein per kilogram of body weight per day. There is no single answer for everyone.

A one-hundred-and-twenty-pound woman needs approximately forty-three grams of protein per day. The following menu provides forty-three grams of protein.

3 ounces white turkey meat	26.0 grams
(without skin, about the size of a deck of cards)	
1 baked potato (7 ounces)	4.0 grams
1/2 cup broccoli	2.4 grams
1 slice whole-wheat bread	2.6 grams
1 cup yogurt	8.3 grams
Total	43.3 grams

A 170-pound man would need approximately 61 grams of protein. For further information on protein, consult a nutrition book such as *Jane Brody's Nutrition Book*.

Water It Down

Water may well be our most essential nutrient; without it we would die in a few days. More than half the weight of the human body is water, the basis for all bodily fluids, including blood, urine, lymph, digestive juices and perspiration. The body depends on water for all cell processes and all organ functions. The exact amounts of water required daily will vary, depending upon the foods we eat, the temperature and humidity of the air, the amount of exercise we do and our individual rate of metabolism. Few of us think about the importance of replenishing our daily fluid loss. We get some water from the foods we eat (carrots, tomatoes, watermelon), and some water is produced as a by-product of metabolism. But we still need six to eight glasses of liquid—which can include juice, milk and soup—to make up the balance. Coffee, tea and cola are not ideal, as they have a diuretic effect, that is, they increase urine production. Plain old water is still the best source.

Vegetarianism

"Would you mind if I looked inside your refrigerator?" I asked Fay and Harvie Morris. Inside I was greeted by an artist's palette of colors: orange from carrots, cantaloupe and peppers; green from celery, lettuce, broccoli, beans; red strawberries and tomatoes; purple eggplants and plums; blueberries and apples. A nine-grain bread shared the top shelf with salt-free ricotta cheese and low-fat yogurt. Harvie (age ninety-three) and Fay (ninety) attribute their longevity to fifty years of vegetarianism. "We eat very simple, basic foods like brown rice, kasha [buckwheat groats], baked potatoes, lentils; we have a salad with every meal."

Dr. Dean Ornish, a research scientist at the University of California, would approve of the Morrises' life-style. His advice: "Just focus your diet on foods that are low in fat, high in complex carbohydrates and high in fiber. That is, fruits, vegetables, grains and legumes [beans, chick-peas, lentils]." Dr. Ornish puts patients with advanced heart disease on this diet and is able to make great improvements to their conditions. He recommends nonfat dairy products to keep total fat intake to ten percent of daily calories.

Sufficiency or Deficiency?

Are you thinking of becoming a vegetarian? Here's what you need to know to make sure your diet is healthy and balanced.

You don't have to be a total vegetarian to benefit from a vegetarian-style diet. Start by incorporating vegetarian dishes daily, and you'll soon become less dependent on animal proteins, which have higher fat and calories. I often make a vegetable stir-fry using onions, broccoli, red peppers, snow peas, celery, mushrooms and bean sprouts to serve with brown rice and lentils. Another favorite is couscous with chick-peas, steamed vegetables and herbs. Experiment with grains like kasha and millet, and legumes. Pasta with vegetables and daily salads are easy to prepare, low in calories and loaded with nutrients. Jane Brody, health columnist for *The New York Times*, says, "If you prepare a soup or vegetable casserole containing a substantial percentage of balanced vegetable protein, an ounce of animal protein will be more than enough to complete your meal." For some excellent vegetarian recipes, try Mollie Katzen's popular cookbooks, the *Moosewood* cookbook and *The Enchanted Broccoli Forest*.

If you decide to eliminate meat, chicken and fish, will you get enough protein? Yes, you'll have plenty from dairy products and eggs. Many of us eat more protein than we need. Remember, however, that the protein from vegetable sources is incomplete. This means it has insufficient amounts of one or more of the nine essential amino acids. Amino acids are protein building blocks.

One way to combine vegetable protein is to serve legumes with grains (buckwheat, corn, millet, oats and rice). For example, try rice with lentils; a peanut butter sandwich; bean soup with toast; falafels with pita bread; corn with beans. These are all complementary combinations.

Combine eggs or dairy products with any vegetable protein, for example in dishes such as rice pudding, macaroni and cheese, meatless lasagna, noodle pudding and pancakes. Combine legumes with nuts and seeds.

Recent research indicates that we don't have to combine complementary foods at the same meal to get a complete protein; we can eat them hours apart or even at different meals throughout the day.

For vegans only: vegans avoid all foods of animal origin, including eggs and dairy products, so they have to work harder to obtain an adequate supply of certain vitamins and minerals. For example, vitamin B_{12} is found only in animal products; it is necessary for normal metabolism of nerve tissue. A vegan may have to take vitamin B_{12} supplements or use fortified products such as soy milk. Likewise, vitamin D, commonly found in dairy products, can also be obtained from fortified margarine and by exposure to sunlight.

Vegans also need to ensure that there is enough iron, zinc and calcium in their diets. Vegans can get calcium from broccoli and kale, blackstrap molasses and most dried fruit and almonds. Iron comes from dark green leafy vegetables, beans and potatoes. Zinc comes from peas, lentils and wheat germ. If in doubt, have a registered dietician create a meal plan for you to ensure healthy eating.

Leaning Toward Vegetarianism
Is a vegetarian diet synonymous with low-fat eating? It should be, but too often it isn't. People who eat a lot of eggs, cheese, whole milk, nuts and seeds should be aware of the high levels of fat in their diet. Go easy on the eggs and use low-fat cheese and skim milk.

Fats—It's as Easy as Pie

Let's face it, even though we know we should reduce fat in our diets, many people still eat too much of it. Stand in any supermarket line on Saturday and see if there is a correlation between the size of the customer and the number of high-fat items in the buggy. Do you see rich desserts, ice cream, cream cheese, butter, cold cuts, bacon, steaks and roasts, cookies and potato chips? I am not calling these bad foods, but if you are getting more than thirty percent of your daily calories from fat, it's time to cut back. A low-fat diet shouldn't be a no-fat diet. We need fat in our diet, one tablespoon per day to maintain good nutrition; however, on average, we eat six to eight tablespoons of fat per day.

Leading cardiologists, cancer specialists and clinical nutritionists all agree that excess fat raises blood cholesterol, increases blood pressure and increases the risk of heart attack and adult-type diabetes. It is implicated in cancer of the breast, colon and prostate. Excess fat causes fatigue, back pain and stress on the weight-bearing joints of the body. In essence, excess fat affects the quality of life.

Dietary Fats
The following is a guide to the world of fats.

- Saturated Fats
  Substitute the word *implicated* for *saturated* because it's the worst kind of fat we eat. It's implicated in raising blood cholesterol and is a major factor in the development of heart disease. Saturated fats come mainly from animal sources—meats, dairy products (butter, homo milk). Two vegetable fats are also saturated: coconut oil and palm oil. The next time you pick up a bag of cookies, check the ingredients. If the label says, "may contain one or more of the following oils: coconut, palm oil or hydrogenated palm kernel oil," put the bag back on the shelf. The word *hydrogenated* describes a process whereby an unsaturated oil is changed into a solid—or saturated—fat. This is done for several reasons: to allow the oil to be more spreadable at room temperature and to give some products a longer shelf life. Unfortunately, certain types of unsaturated fats are adversely affected by hydrogenation, producing harmful trans-fatty acids, which raise blood cholesterol levels.

  In addition, if you see a label that reads "made with one hundred percent vegetable oil shortening," don't be fooled. "Shortening" is definitely hydrogenated fat, and therefore a poor choice for a healthy diet. Health leaders recommend that no more than ten percent of your daily calories should come from saturated fat.

- Monounsaturated Fats
  When you need fats for cooking, baking or salad dressings, choose the monounsaturated fats found in olive oil and canola oil. Monounsaturated fats lower bad LDL cholesterol. They also have an antioxidant property that fights off artery damage from LDL cholesterol. The Mediterranean diet includes olive oil on and in everything—poured on salads and cooked vegetables, used for sautéing and sauces and drizzled on bread in place of butter. Research has shown that people who follow the traditional

Mediterranean life-style generally enjoy longer life spans, lower incidence of heart disease and lower risk for some cancers.

- Polyunsaturated Fats
Polyunsaturated fats found in corn, safflower and sunflower oils contain essential fatty acids that help lower blood cholesterol; however, these fats are also implicated as a major dietary source of free radicals. Use sparingly.

Cholesterol

We need a certain amount of cholesterol to form hormones, nerve endings, vitamin D and bile, which is needed for the digestion of fats. But cholesterol can be either a friend or foe, depending on the way it travels through the body. Much of our cholesterol is carried through the bloodstream by potentially damaging carrier particles called LDLs, or low-density lipoproteins. LDLs are called bad cholesterol because an excess of cholesterol carried by them can lead to the building of harmful deposits, or plaque, in the arteries. This plaque causes a condition called atherosclerosis. In time, this hardened, sludge-filled growth narrows the artery and allows a clot to form, severely blocking the blood flow. The result: a heart attack. The other cholesterol carriers, known as HDLs (high-density lipoproteins), are considered good, as they play a role in preventing heart disease.

HDL, the cleanup crew, gathers up excess cholesterol and carries it back to the liver to be excreted by the body. It may also remove some of the cholesterol already deposited on the artery walls. So it's important to boost good HDL cholesterol and reduce bad LDL cholesterol.

Cholesterol comes from two sources. Some is produced naturally by the body's cells; some results from our intake of foods containing saturated fats or pure cholesterol, foods such as butter, cheese, eggs and animal fat. A problem arises when we eat too much saturated fat, which interferes with the liver's ability to remove cholesterol from the bloodstream.

According to Health and Welfare Canada's 1990 Guidelines for Healthy Eating, the link between saturated fat intake, elevated blood cholesterol and the risk of heart disease is one of the most serious diet–disease relationships for Canadians. The good news is that most people have a large degree of control over their cardio-vascular health.

Eight Ways to Increase HDL and Decrease LDL

1. Add dried beans or legumes to your diet. Soluble fiber helps lower blood cholesterol. According to James Anderson, MD, of the University of Kentucky School of Medicine, eating a cup of cooked dried beans a day suppresses bad cholesterol by about twenty percent. He says, "You can expect results in about three weeks." All types of beans work—black, kidney, lentils, chick-peas, soybeans.

2. Discover oat bran. Eating two ounces of cooked oat bran per day reduces bad cholesterol by sixteen percent. It can also boost HDL cholesterol by about fifteen percent after two or three months. Oats contain a soluble gummy fiber called beta glucans that jells inside the intestinal tract. This interferes with the absorption and production of cholesterol, so more of it is removed from the bloodstream.

3. Choose salmon. Fatty fish contain Omega-3 fatty acids, which boost HDL. Greenland Eskimos who live on a very high-fat fishy diet have low rates of heart disease. Says Jane Brody, "Eat more tuna, salmon, sardines, mackerel."

4. Give yourself an oil change. Is olive oil a miracle in a bottle? It's getting rave reviews from researchers and arteries. Unlike poly-unsaturated fat, which lowers both HDL and LDL, olive oil is a monounsaturated fat, which lowers LDL cholesterol and leaves HDL cholesterol intact.

5. Eat more fruits and vegetables. These foods contain vitamin C, vitamin E and other antioxidants. Antioxidants work by zapping oxygen-free radicals that otherwise turn LDL cholesterol toxic and dangerous. So increase your intake of red bell peppers, broccoli, oranges, carrots and cantaloupes.

6. Eat more apples and carrots. Apples and carrots contain pectin, a soluble fiber that helps lower blood cholesterol. Scottish researchers showed that eating seven ounces of raw carrots at breakfast every day for three weeks could reduce cholesterol levels by eleven percent and increase the amount of fat excreted by fifty percent.

7. Most important: cut back on saturated fat. Of all the foods you eat, those most likely to send cholesterol soaring contain

saturated animal fat, the fat found in meat, poultry and dairy products. It's essential to limit your choices of butter, whole milk, cheese, pork fat and poultry skin to help keep your arteries from clogging. Can you eat meat and still keep cholesterol down? Yes, if you trim off all possible fat. It's not the meat that's the culprit, but the fat that typically comes with the meat. A study done in Australia showed that healthy men and women put on a high-beef diet with almost all the fat trimmed had no increase in blood cholesterol. Remember: all we need is three ounces of meat daily for our protein source. Now what about eating foods that are high in cholesterol, such as egg yolks, liver and some seafood? Don't they contribute to high cholesterol? It may surprise you to know that high-cholesterol foods are a minor cause of high blood cholesterol. There is wisdom in the liver: when you eat too much cholesterol, your liver automatically pumps less cholesterol into your bloodstream. So levels remain about the same or do not rise much. "Saturated fats are four times more likely to raise blood cholesterol levels than dietary cholesterol itself," says Dr. John LaRosa, cardiologist, George Washington University. Does that mean we can pig out on egg yolks and other cholesterol-rich foods? No, because high-cholesterol foods can promote heart disease by stimulating the blood to form clots. Generally, heart authorities suggest a limit of 300 mg of cholesterol a day, or about four egg yolks a week.

8. Exercise. When you work off calories from eating those HDL-boosting foods you'll receive an additional benefit: aerobic exercise reduces LDL production and raises protective HDL levels. So lace up those walking, jogging and cycling shoes!

Be very careful with labels that scream *No cholesterol*. Many base that claim on the fact that their products contain no animal fat, the only source of cholesterol. And it's true—animals alone produce cholesterol. Plants and plant oils contain none whatsoever. But some plant oils, like coconut and palm oil, are very high in saturated fat, and these fats *do* raise cholesterol levels. "The crackers you buy may have no cholesterol but they're made with coconut oil—all saturated fat," says William Castilli, MD, director of the famous Framingham Heart Study. So watch out for this booby trap and read labels.

Nine Is the Magic Number

Before you read another word, get yourself a pen, a piece of paper and your pocket calculator. It's time to find out how much fat you're really eating. We start by remembering that nine is the magic number—there are nine calories in every gram of fat.

Now go into the kitchen and find a box of cookies or crackers with nutritional labeling.

1. Check the label for grams of fat per serving size.
2. Multiply grams of fat by nine.
3. Divide that number by total calories per serving.
4. Then multiply by one hundred to come up with the percentage of calories from fat.

For example, let's say one serving of your favorite snack food has "only ninety calories," and the label says there are five grams of fat per serving.

1. Multiply 5 by 9. (= 45)
2. Divide 45 by 90 (= .5)
3. Multiply .5 by 100. (= 50%)

In spite of having "only ninety calories," that's a very high-fat product; as we calculated, fifty percent of the calories are from fat! My rule is: it must be less than thirty percent or I won't buy it.

And before you put away your calculator, there's more.

Look at the types of fat listed on the label. You'll see monounsaturated, polyunsaturated and saturated fats. However, the grams of these three fats don't always add up to the total fat declaration on the nutrition label. What's missing? Food manufacturers are not compelled to tell you about trans-fatty acids, which result from the process of hydrogenation. Trans-fatty acids are the worst of all, because they raise blood cholesterol levels.

Here's how to determine the trans-fatty acid content of a labeled food.

1. Add up the total grams of polyunsaturated, monounsaturated and saturated fats.
2. Subtract that sum from the total amount of fat declared on the label.

The difference between the two is the trans-fatty acid content.

For example, let's say the label says, Total Fat = 8.0 grams.
On the package you see the following:

Polyunsaturated Fat	2.2 grams
Monounsaturated Fat	3.2 grams
Saturated Fat	1.6 grams
Total	7.00 grams

The total fat is eight grams minus the seven grams, calculated above, equals one gram of trans-fatty acids. And remember: the trans-fatty acids are extremely harmful!

Saturated fats should be no more than ten percent of your daily intake of calories. Warning: make sure that if you are tallying the grams of fat from one serving, you eat only one serving!

The Lean Mean Human Machine

Here's a quiz.

Picture two women. They each eat two thousand calories per day. They participate in the same exercise class. They have similar basal metabolic rates, that is, their bodies use up calories at about the same rate when they're not exercising. However, Woman A eats a high fat diet—forty-three percent of her calories come from fat— while Woman B eats a low-fat diet—twenty-nine percent of her calories come from fat. Who will weigh more? Woman A will weigh more than Woman B by about nine pounds. And where will this weight be concentrated? Mostly around the hips, buttocks, upper thighs and stomach.

It seems that almost every patient who consults me says these familiar words, "I'd be happy if I lost five to ten pounds." I promise that if you follow a low-fat diet (no more than thirty percent of your calories from fat) and exercise thirty minutes three to five times per week, you'll never have to worry about your weight again. And you'll feel great inside and out.

Can you eat your cake and have it, too? Yes! You don't have to eliminate treats. If you tell me, "I can't live without putting butter on corn on the cob," go ahead. As long as your overall fat for the day is low, you don't have to deprive yourself completely. Remember to be aware of hidden fats in foods. Some fat is part of the food naturally or is blended into the food when it is prepared. For example, seventy-five percent of the calories in hard cheese are fat calories; sixty-two percent of the calories in roast chicken (with the skin) are fat calories.

Walking Down the Aisle—at the Supermarket

It's Saturday afternoon and I've just paid for ninety-six dollars worth of groceries. Before I got to the supermarket, I planned to fill my buggy with a special selection. I would choose a wide variety of foods to satisfy these criteria: low fat, low sodium, high fiber and loaded with vitamins and minerals. So what did I buy? Come along with me for Elaine's Guided Supermarket Tour.

First stop: the produce section, my favorite area of any super-market. Quickly, I piled my cart with bananas, oranges, canta-loupes, peaches, kiwi fruits, fresh pineapple, romaine and leafy lettuce, a red pepper, fresh peas in the pod, mushrooms, tomatoes, bean sprouts, cucumber, broccoli, sweet potatoes and carrots. There was a new product beside the parsley called Veggie Wieners, a non-meat item made with tofu and soy protein, with only one percent fat. (I'll let you know how they taste.)

I skipped past the deli counter, stopping instead at specialty cheeses. The showcase included several low-fat choices (fifteen percent milk fat or lower); I found a Canadian Cheddar with only four percent milk fat! One thirty-gram serving (about a one-inch-square cube) has sixty-four calories, ten grams of protein, 1.2 grams of fat and eight percent of the RDA (Recommended Dietary Allow-ances) for calcium. What a perfect idea for my lunches this week! I'll make tomato, cheese and cucumber sandwiches with nine-grain bread.

At the fish and seafood counter, I was delighted to choose a piece of salmon (have to get my fix of Omega-3 fatty acids, which help lower cholesterol), perfect for the barbecue. At the meat counter, I checked out the specials and selected two packages of boneless, skinless chicken breasts. These are just right to stir fry along with vegetables and brown rice. Then on to Aisle Three, pasta sauces. My refrigerator always has at least two packages of angelhair pasta on hand, just in case I get into my "Type A—I'm starving and too tired to cook" mood. After perusing twenty-five varieties of assorted tomato and pasta sauces, I chose a low-fat, low-sodium brand to use with the pasta.

My supply of salad dressings was low, and I noticed many low-fat varieties. Feeling creative, however, I chose Dijon mustard, balsamic vinegar and extra virgin olive oil, to concoct my own instead. For a few moments, I was tempted by something called "light" olive oil. Could this be some new product lighter in calories and fat? On reading the label closely, I regretfully discovered that this product was lighter—but only in taste and color. There's a lesson here: be careful and read labels!

Continuing through the store, I bought a can of water-packed, solid white tuna and a can of chick-peas. In another aisle, I spotted a package of dry lentils; sometime this week they will be turned into a lentil and rice casserole, seasoned with fresh herbs from my garden. Must not forget the couscous, one of my favorite grain meals. In five minutes, I can prepare couscous with pine nuts and vegetables.

In the cereal section, my choices were bite-size Shredded Wheat and Bran Buds with Psyllium for a high-fiber breakfast boost. Both go well with a sliced banana and skim milk. For a refreshing drink, I bought low-calorie cranberry juice, to be mixed with salt-free soda and ice and garnished with a twist of lime. Forget the cookie and cake section. If I have company, I may make an apple crisp or buy gelato to serve with raspberries. Once in a while, an outrageous chocolate dessert comes into my house for a very special treat. I took a few minutes to check the ingredients on canned soups. One popular brand listed sugar, monosodium glutamate, caramel and 688 mg of sodium, and that was in plain beef consommé!

The dairy section was the home stretch, where I bought skim milk, buttermilk (it's low-fat), zero-fat yogurt and eggs. Usually on weekends, I make time to bake a batch of low-fat muffins with buttermilk, carrots and blackstrap molasses. Recently I stopped buying both butter and margarine and find that I don't miss either on my fresh bagels or nine-grain bread.

So there you have it: an inside peak at my grocery list, with lots of healthy choices that taste good, too. What's that you say? You want to come over to my house for dinner?

I asked Maye Musk, dietician, how she would grade my selections. She replied, "I'd give you an A for healthy choices with lots of variety." Now, before you rush off to duplicate my shopping list, a warning from Maye: "A person who eats meals out frequently would have a lot of food spoilage from the large number of fruit and vegetable items you bought." She reminded me that I'm cooking for two people (I have a twenty-three-year-old nephew), and intend to eat all my meals at home or pack a lunch for the office. A lot of people don't eat that way. So adjust your list accordingly, adding or subtracting according to *your* needs.

By the way, the veggie wieners were great!

Dembe's Top Ten Super-Nutritious Disease-Fighting "Don't Leave the Supermarket Without Them" Foods

1. *Broccoli*

   Broccoli contains antioxidants with high anti-cancer properties, particularly lung, colon and breast cancer. Broccoli is rich in cholesterol-fighting fiber and contains chromium to help regulate insulin and blood sugar. One cup of chopped broccoli contains ninety percent of our daily requirements for Vitamin A, two hundred percent of the vitamin C we need, six percent of niacin, ten percent of calcium, ten percent of thiamine, ten percent of phosphorous, and eight percent of iron.

2. *Sweet Potatoes*

   This blockbuster source of the antioxidant beta carotene can reduce the risk of heart disease, cataracts, strokes and numerous cancers. Women who eat one-half cup of sweet potatoes daily slash their risk of heart attack by twenty-two percent and stroke by forty to seventy percent, according to recent Harvard studies. Sweet potatoes also contain phosphorus, potassium, iron and calcium. Dr. Roberta Ferrence recommends making a sweet-potato sundae. It's delicious! Here's how to make it. Microwave a sweet potato and then cool. Make a sundae topping from a mixture of orange juice, skim milk, yogurt and a dash of cinnamon. Sprinkle a few almonds on top, then add a few pieces of chopped dried apricot. If I want something savory, not sweet, I'll put salsa on my sweet potato instead.

3. *Legumes* (beans of all kinds)

   These are potent weapons in the battle to lower blood cholesterol. In one study it was shown that one-half cup of cooked beans daily reduces cholesterol an average of ten percent. Legumes are high in fiber, and high-fiber diets are linked to reduced incidence of certain cancers. Legumes are a rich source of incomplete protein, iron and the B vitamins (thiamine, riboflavin, niacin and folacin). Try lentil-rice soup and chili con carne.

4. *Yogurt*

   "Yogurt is just about a panacea for women. It boosts immunity, delivers lots of available calcium and helps prevent vaginitis," says Dr. George Halpern, MD, from the University of California at Davis. Eating yogurt stimulates at least two vital components of immunity—natural killer cells and gamma interferon. The natural killer cells attack viruses and tumor cells. A year-long study by Dr. Halpern found that eating only six ounces of yogurt daily prevented colds, hay fever and diarrhea in both young and elderly adults. One cup of yogurt delivers 452 mg of calcium, the mineral we need to help prevent osteoporosis. Yogurt with live cultures is safe for some individuals with lactose intolerance.

5. *Salmon*

   This fatty fish, full of Omega-3 fatty acids, has been shown to boost the good cholesterol, HDL, even for those with normal levels. Omega-3 fatty acids reduce triglycerides, one type of blood fat that can promote heart attacks. Eat fish at least three times per week. Try mackerel, herring and tuna, as well.

6. *Olive Oil*

   Olive oil lowers bad LDL cholesterol without lowering good HDL cholesterol. This monounsaturated fat also helps keep bad cholesterol from being oxidized, thus protecting arteries from plaque formation. Buy extra virgin cold-pressed olive oil.

7. *Carrots*

   Carrots are a super source of beta carotene, a powerful anticancer, artery-protecting, immune-boosting, infection-fighting antioxidant. In one study, a carrot a day slashed stroke rates in women by sixty-eight percent The high soluble fiber in carrots reduces blood cholesterol and promotes regularity. High doses of beta carotene also reduce the odds of degenerative eye diseases. One large carrot contains eleven thousand units of vitamin A, as well as calcium, potassium, magnesium and trace minerals.

8. *Rice*

   Rice is the staple food of more than half the world's population. This great source of vitamins, minerals and protein contains practically no fat and is highly digestible. Whole brown rice contains a generous supply of B vitamins, plus calcium, phosphorous and iron.

9. *Fruit*

My favorites are apples (reduce cholesterol, high in fiber); cantaloupe (contains the antioxidant beta carotene); oranges (rich in antioxidant vitamin C and beta carotene); pineapple (contains manganese, a catalyst in the synthesis of fatty acids and cholesterol; thought to be an anti-inflammatory); strawberries (another anticholesterol super food); watermelon (an antioxidant; also contains vitamin C, lots of potassium, calcium, iron, magnesium). Don't forget peaches, mango, bananas and kiwifruit.

10. *Blackstrap Molasses*

Try it in baked beans and muffins, or pour a tablespoon out of the bottle and slurp it down. It's great and unbelievably nutritious. One tablespoon supplies eighteen percent of a woman's RDA of iron (as much as half a cup of cooked spinach); seventeen percent of the RDA for calcium; and as much potassium as a banana. Molasses is also an excellent source of B vitamins and is rich in copper, magnesium, phosphorus and vitamin E. Max Sharp, ninety-two years old, mixes blackstrap molasses and brewer's yeast into a glass of milk. This concoction may contribute to his longevity!

Other amazing foods that did not make the A list are cabbage, cauliflower, garlic, red grapes, kale, onions, parsley, parsnips, pumpkin, soybeans, enriched pasta, turkey (breast meat), millet, buckwheat groats, squash and liver.

Scrumptious Survival Suppers

Here is Dembe's list of food to have on hand when you're tired, starving, fresh out of ideas, but don't want to eat junk.

Dinner Possibility 1

In my refrigerator, I always have fresh pasta, the kind that comes sealed in a tray so it keeps for about a month. This will cook in only one or two minutes. In the crisper, there's also a package of broccoli florets that can steam in a couple of minutes. The cupboard shelves are stocked with a few jars of low-calorie tomato and pasta sauces. So, in about five minutes, I can sit down to pasta with broccoli in a tomato sauce, with a sprinkle of Parmesan cheese on the top.

Dinner Possibility 2

When I'm tired, I find it a chore to wash and spin-dry lettuce, so in the crisper I keep a bag of lettuce that has been washed, dried and pulled into bite-size pieces. I can easily toss the lettuce with an always-on-hand can of salmon or solid white tuna, adding vegetables such as cucumber, red pepper, celery or carrots. My weekly shopping list has zero-fat yogurt, so I can mix some with pepper, dill, lemon juice or parsley to pour over the salad.

Dinner Possibility 3

Have you ever tried couscous, the sensational North African cracked wheat? It's a cinch to prepare. Just boil 1 1/4 cups water, add 1 cup of couscous, cover and remove from heat. In five minutes, it's ready. I add a small can of chick-peas and whatever vegetables are on hand, raw or cooked. Sprinkle pine nuts, some orange sections or slivered almonds on top for a quick, nutritious meal. It also makes a great side dish.

Dinner Possibility 4

I keep individual pizza crusts in the freezer. Defrost and decorate with tomato sauce, red pepper, zucchini, snow peas, broccoli or any other vegetable. Add grated low-fat mozzarella, skim-milk ricotta or Parmesan cheese. Bake at 425°F for 7 to 10 minutes.

Dinner Possibility 5

Start with two healthy slices of whole wheat bread, top with slivers of tomato and peppers, and finally shredded low-fat cheese. Melt in the toaster oven for a few minutes and enjoy!

Elaine Dembe's Ultimate,
Zero-Fat, Nutritious Ice-Cream Experience

In the freezer, put any fresh fruit—strawberries, blueberries, raspberries, bananas in the peel; for peaches or apricots, cut up fruit first and remove pits. Freeze overnight. Remove and cut into small chunks if needed. If using bananas, peel the skins with a knife.

In a food processor or blender, put 1 cup fruit and one tablespoon of honey. Process until soft. Delicious!

Tips for Reducing Fat and Calories in Your Diet

1. Order a low-fat meal in advance when flying. Most major airlines are glad to accommodate special diets.
2. In restaurants, ask for salad dressings served on the side.
3. Instead of dessert, try cappuccino with a little sugar on the rim.
4. At home, use a smaller dinner plate, to make portions look larger.
5. Read food labels. Don't buy anything with more than thirty percent fat in it. Some foods, such as deli meats, are not labeled and are very high in fat.
6. Instead of butter, use herbs and spices.
7. Instead of butter and jam on toast, skip the butter; just use the jam.
8. In a restaurant, ask the servers not to bring butter with the bread.
9. Choose entrées that are steamed, poached, broiled or roasted in their own juices. Flash frying in a wok is another good choice.
10. Avoid foods that are sautéed or fried. Crispy fried dishes are especially poor choices.
11. In restaurants, split dessert with a friend.
12. Replace salad dressings and mayonnaise with low-fat yogurt.
13. Order vegetable-based soups in restaurants. Watch out for anything called "cream of."
14. Use a nonstick skillet for cooking.
15. Use olive oil or canola oil for cooking and salad dressings.
17. Start buying low-fat varieties of the products you now use. Example: hard cheeses should be less than fifteen percent milk fat or butterfat; try low-fat (one percent) mayonnaise, sour cream and cottage cheese.
18. Reduce the amount of oil in muffins and quick bread recipes; use part apple sauce. If a recipe calls for 1 cup of oil, use 1/2 cup oil and 1/2 cup applesauce.
19. Keep a pitcher of cold water in the refrigerator for frequent, refreshing drinks.
20. In restaurants, have bread, not bread sticks. Bread sticks can be very high in fat, especially the ones with sesame seeds. Three bread sticks have 150 calories and seven grams of fat, and forty-two percent of these calories come from fat.

21. There are many fat-free products available—even brownies! Try them.
22. If you know in your heart that you can't adhere to the recommended serving size of two cookies, and you must demolish the row, don't buy cookies.
23. Choose leaner cuts of meat, such as inside round, eye of round, rump roast and sirloin steak.
24. Having a snack attack? Try air-popped popcorn, rice cakes, light hot chocolate or a diet Popsicle or Fudgsicle.
25. Team your favorite vegetables with onions, leeks and garlic for more flavor.
26. Buy cookbooks that feature heart-healthy low-fat cuisine. I like Anne Lindsay's *Lighthearted* cookbooks. Put your recipes on a diet. Try a lower-fat version of a favorite recipe.
27. Peel butter. If you must have butter or margarine on corn on the cob, peel a sliver off a stick or spread with a potato peeler. You'll get about twelve calories worth of fat, compared to thirty-six in a pat of butter.
28. Eat your dressing with a fork. Dip your fork into the dressing, then stab the food. You'll get flavor with fewer calories.

If you need sound nutritional advice or you would like your daily meal plan personalized, consult your provincial dietetic association. They can give you the name of a dietician in your area. Unfortunately, "nutritionist" is not a protected title, so anyone can use it, whether the person has earned professional qualifications from a reputable university or not.

How to Live to Be 101

Ruth Atkinson Hindmarsh lived a remarkable one hundred and one years. Not long before she died, this wonderful centenarian said, "I have a date at my hospital next Wednesday. The doctors want to see how I've lived this long. I think the secret is my diet." She didn't recommend it for everyone who wants to live to be a hundred and one, but here is what Ruth ate:

"Three square meals a day—all kinds of plain food, not much fat. No milk except puddings. No salads. No bran or roughage of any kind. No raw vegetables. Easy on the red meat. Chicken and fish are okay. No fried stuff. Lots of potatoes, broccoli, carrots, turnips, parsnips and bread. One cup of coffee a day. I eat a banana at lunch every day. And I'm very keen on cookies and chocolate."

Was Ruth concerned that some nutritionists might not give her diet an A+? Her reply: "I'm living, so why worry? I take vitamins, calcium and potassium, too." She received full marks for life-style and attitude when she said, "I never drank or smoked. I played all kinds of sports as a girl and I've always been very active. Most of all I have some project going every day so I get up every morning at six-thirty. I really love life!"

Take a close look at Ruth's diet. She liked plain food; that means no sauces, which are usually fatty. Since it is very common for older people to have trouble with their teeth and dentures, many of them don't eat raw vegetables. Instead, Ruth ate cooked vegetables, which contain fiber. As for avoiding milk, she probably had strong bones from being fit and active all her life, and she took calcium supplements. Furthermore, you can eat the world's healthiest diet and still lose the benefit of good nutrition if you smoke. Throw in some excellent genes and you have Ruth's formula. You can't argue with longevity! I believe Ruth's passion for life kept her immune system strong and healthy, balancing out any negatives in her diet.

The 10 Secrets of
Ruth Atkinson Hindmarsh, age 101

1. Never have just one chocolate a day.
2. Keep physically active. People who sit, never get up.
3. Keep one or two passionate interests.
4. Live day by day.
5. Have a sense of humor.
6. Keep other people guessing—don't show your hand.
7. Plan something to do every day.
8. Don't drink or smoke.
9. Keep an optimistic attitude.
10. You're old when you feel sorry for yourself.

Epilogue: Dembe's Top Ten Food Truths
I think I've finally got it all figured out, this business of food and my body. Here is what I know at forty-six. You have my permission to copy this page and put it on your fridge. It's a summary of everything I have learned about taking responsibility for what I eat.

1. If I don't buy it, I can't eat it.
2. A little meal planning saves calories.
3. Eating fatty foods makes me fat.
4. Diets don't work—exercise does. Exercising four to five times per week allows me to indulge, but not excessively.
5. Food patterns that remind me of my childhood are hard to forget.
6. Restaurants are accommodating—order low-fat.
7. Small, painless changes in the foods I eat can make a big difference.
8. I really underestimate how much food I eat. I always eat more than the recommended serving size.
9. It's impossible to have cookies in the house because I have to finish the row. Desserts often look better than they taste, anyway.
10. I am human, therefore I am not perfect. When I eat out, I try to be careful, but I forgive myself for my indulgences.

7

RESPONSIBILITY

You must take control of your health.

*T*he doctor of the future will give no medicine but will interest his patients in the care of the human frame, in diet, and in the cause and prevention of disease.
—*Thomas A. Edison*

"It's scary these days if you get sick," remarked a physician recently. She was referring to the latest news of hospital waiting lists for patients who need immediate radiation treatment for breast cancer. Health care in this country is not well. Medical costs, like all government spending, have skyrocketed. Cutbacks have affected all areas of medical care—number of hospital beds available, delisting of unnecessary services, tightening up of rules on billable services, limited access to and availability of technology. One example: a patient can get an MRI scan in Buffalo in one week; in Ontario the waiting list stretches from one month to one year. Other areas experiencing cutbacks include reduced coverage for out-of-country health care, long waiting lists for surgery and reduced drug benefits. In addition, the government is looking at the cost-benefit ratio for complete comprehensive physicals for everyone; instead, it is now recommending age- and risk-specific tests. A woman who is at low risk for cervical cancer, for example, will have a PAP smear every three years instead of yearly.

What does all this mean for you and me? Now more than ever, the responsibility for health maintenance resides with the individual. We are seeing a change in emphasis. Fewer people are saying, "Health is not my responsibility," trusting doctors, medicine and hospitals. More people are willingly accepting responsibility for their health and well-being. After all, what is health care, anyway? To a great degree, health care is the sum of the choices made by an individual every day over a lifetime. It is a misconception that good health means access to a medical system. Those who stay healthy don't need hospitals or drugs. In the old medical model, we emphasize doctors and illness; under a holistic system, we talk about health care and well-being.

Let's look at one surprising statistic: fifty-four percent of all American deaths are the direct result of life-style choices—tobacco use, alcohol overuse, high cholesterol, imprudent dietary choices. (Canadian figures are not available but are probably similar.) Have you any idea what the consequences of tobacco use cost Canadians in extra health care, premature mortality and employment loss due to disability? In 1989, a staggering $9.3 billion! That obscene sum of money doesn't include the cost of smoking-related forest and property fires. Tobacco use alone is responsible for more than forty thousand deaths in Canada annually.

For those of you interested in taking responsibility for your own health and well-being, here are some basic activities included under the self-care umbrella:

- breast self-examination
- regulation of blood pressure
- weight control
- regular, nutritionally balanced meals
- proper dental care
- therapeutic and corrective self-care, such as increased fluids and extra rest for colds and influenza
- greater responsibility in taking over-the-counter drugs
- participation in a regular exercise program
- abstention from tobacco
- regular use of seat belts
- renewed interest in spiritual and mental well-being through social, religious and leisure activities
- support groups

In their book *Before You Call the Doctor*, authors Anne Simons and Michael Castleman emphasize that North Americans must get rid of one potent myth: the illusion that only doctors can cure us. The authors proclaim that doctors should be the health-care choice of last resort. The real health practitioners, they say, are the millions of people who practice self-care—the chicken-soup brigade.

Preventive self-care sounds like a great solution to our health-care woes; however, thousands of people are still not getting the message. Imagine the public outcry if 110 people died in airplane crashes each and every day because of negligent air traffic controllers. Yet 110 people die from the ravages of cigarette smoking every day in Canada. Here are some reasons we still have a long way to go.

- Many people forget that health begins at home, depending instead on their doctor to cure their health problems.
- Medicine is still oriented toward curing. Heart disease? No problem, we'll just do a bypass or transplant.
- Millions of people rely on a quick fix from pills, to keep them healthy. Between the pharmaceutical companies and television commercials, one could easily believe that relief is spelled T-y-l-e-n-o-l or V-a-l-i-u-m.
- Many of us operate under the illusion that disease will never happen to us, or we succumb to the defeatist attitude that says, "I've been living like this for so long; it's too late to change now."

Health care must change, and I believe it will, as we enter the era of the patient, a patient who is an active participant taking responsibility for health decisions. Dr. Tom Ferguson says, "Holistic health proposes that our health care system needs a new map. Self-care suggests that the wrong person has been holding the map."

How Can Self-Care Skills Be Learned?

Begin with your family doctor. According to Dr. Pam Letts, family practice is about relationships between the doctor and patient. "We should be educating our patients in wellness care, guiding them through the information they need, empowering them so that they know when to use self-care and when to call the doctor's office. It is not necessary for a doctor to treat every cold and flu." She joked, "Sometimes I think I should buy a stove for my office—to make chicken soup! " Dr. David Rapoport agrees. "Family practitioners are more important than they've ever been. Patients need guidance on

what amounts to a mine field of dangerous medication and dangerous investigations. The family doctor is your ombudsman."

If self-care is to become the cornerstone of health, then early
education is necessary. Health education must be made available in
schools through films, lectures, school projects and books. Similarly, parents have access to a wealth of material in libraries: books,
publications and health education monographs.

Many people visit a pharmacist first for minor problems rather
than seeing their family doctor. But remember, self-medication has
its risks as well as benefits and is *not* a substitute for appropriate
medical treatment.

Get involved! Anytime you have laboratory tests for blood or
urine testing, obtain a copy of the results from your doctor. You
should know your cholesterol level, for example, and understand
what the numbers mean. When I ask them about X-rays ordered by
their doctor, I often hear patients say, "No one contacted me, so I
guess they're normal." Call your doctor and find out the results;
don't assume anything.

Educate yourself. Buy a current book on home remedies or
natural and homeopathic healing. Public health departments have
up-to-date information on health issues. Read the newspaper and
health magazines; watch for television specials dealing with wellness issues. Above all, use common sense.

Important as doctors are, some people feel that there are limitations to the medical approach. The care is often fragmented. A
patient with arthritis sees a rheumatologist; a patient with skin
problems sees a dermatologist. No one doctor treats *all* symptoms
and conditions. Specialization is valuable, but we as patients are
whole beings, not merely a collection of symptoms. And what
about the healthy patient without symptoms who nevertheless
wants guidance on nutrition or exercise or stress reduction?

The holistic approach to health care refers to the treatment of
the whole person, as well as to the practice of healing and the
promotion of health. It is concerned with the physical, emotional
and spiritual aspects of those who need treatment. A holistic health
care practitioner views health as overall well-being, not merely the
absence of disease or symptoms. Such a practitioner also recognizes the importance of the patient's innate capacity for self-
healing. Patients are regarded as active partners, not passive
recipients of health care. Participation includes free-flowing

dialogue between doctor and patient, without an air of superiority from a doctor who claims esoteric and exclusive knowledge. Holistic medicine reminds me of the wisdom of a spiritual guide who said, "I come not to teach, but to awaken."

It is *health* care, not sickness care, that is the focus of all holistic practitioners. Dr. Robert Buckman, associate professor of medicine at the University of Toronto and author of *Magic or Medicine*, states, "If you look at the way most conventional doctors spend their time, they are almost entirely preoccupied with disease." That approach is fine for the patient with a serious illness requiring specific medical intervention. But at my clinic there is a place for organically healthy individuals who are nevertheless troubled by mechanical back pain, neuromusculoskeletal injuries, chronic headaches, sports injuries and stress-related conditions.

Many patients describe the circuitous route that has led them to choose chiropractic care and other alternative therapies over "regular" medical treatment. The deciding factors were often overall dissatisfaction with the medical care available for their particular complaint, as well as reluctance to treat their symptoms with medication. My patients express many reasons for exploring holistic health care: "There is continuity of care—the doctor who listened to and examined me also treats me." "I am sick of taking pills—the Band-Aid approach. At last the doctor is treating the cause." "I feel we have a relationship. The doctor cares about me, spends time helping me with all aspects of my health—nutrition, fitness, posture, stress, sleep."

In response to the growing interest in alternative health and the frustration with the limits of conventional medicine, more medical doctors are referring patients for alternative care. They are even coming for treatments themselves. Ultimately, the concern of all members of the health-care system should be for the patients— how will they benefit the most?

Holistic healers cannot lead others without first awakening themselves. When I first became a chiropractor seventeen years ago, my eagerness to fill in the "chief complaint" and "diagnosis" sections on the case history reports was perhaps typical of a new graduate. I viewed the human body mainly as a biomechanical model, and concentrated on pain reduction and the physical aspects of health. Misalignment of the spine was my focus; I was not really tuned in to the consequences of misalignment on the whole person. I could motivate patients to begin a fitness program, improve their diet and quit smoking; after all, I wanted to help them feel better. But during my own healing process eight years ago, I began to understand the emotional and spiritual complexities that must also be addressed for true health.

As I have evolved personally, my chiropractic practice has evolved holistically. Through my own growth, I learned that the body communicates important messages in the form of pain and disease with the goal of bringing us back into harmony. Unfortunately, many of us never learn to listen to ourselves and our signals.

Sometimes I tell my patients to pretend that their pain has a voice; I then ask them what the pain is saying to them. Their answers have been incredibly insightful. While I gently knead and manipulate those tight, tense muscles and stiff joints, many of my patients begin to understand their problems. Touch, or the laying on of hands, is a powerful part of much holistic health. Touch is potent; a hand massaging a sore shoulder conveys caring, compassion and comfort. One patient who had been seen by several medical specialists for recurrent whiplash pain joyfully announced, "You're the first person who has actually touched my neck!" I was saddened to think that technology has replaced humanness. Is this health care?

Ultimately, no matter what the doctor, chiropractor or massage therapist does or doesn't do, it is the patient who has to suffer with the sore neck. And it is the patient who must take responsibility for his or her health. Responsibility means listening to your body when it talks to you, emotionally, physically, spiritually. Responsibility means respecting your body through nutrition, exercise and life-style. Responsibility involves making choices, taking control, communicating your needs.

We can exercise responsibility for our health through use of alternative medicine and self-care.

Alternative Health Care

Think of the times in your life when you felt absolutely wonderful, your body flexible, pain-free and sparkling with energy. Emotionally you were at peace, no anger, fear or depression inhabiting the recesses of your mind. You were connected spiritually to nature, the universe and your true self. There was softness in your heart, allowing you to feel compassion, trust and love for yourself and others. You accepted that you were not perfect, yet you were enough. Perhaps this is the way you feel right now—whole and in harmony. Perhaps not.

Maybe you experience only fleeting moments of health as you frequently battle physical symptoms or emotional unrest. How do you cope with illness? Do you seek medical care or help from alternative therapy? Do you practice self-care? There are many different ways to look at the issues of health and sickness.

Most of us, when we get sick, see a doctor who has trained for years at a university. He or she (usually a he in days past) is associated with a hospital, refers patients to specialists, diagnoses diseases, repairs injury, treats specific symptoms and prescribes drugs. Doctors are enormously important in health care. For example, would you want anyone but a trained cardiologist to perform open-heart surgery on you or anyone in your family?

Critics of Alternative Care

Critics of alternative care are rightly skeptical about "healers" who foster false hope or claim they can cure anything. Unfortunately, traditional medicine is still too quick to dismiss therapies that are not scientifically proven, labeling positive results as merely "the placebo effect" whenever a patient is helped. In every profession there are charlatans. To protect yourself, get a referral from family or friends to an accredited doctor or therapist, or call the association that licenses that profession. Not all medical doctors practice "conventional medicine." There are a number of holistic physicians in Canada who do not prescribe drugs. To locate a medical doctor in your area who is holistic call the Consumer Health Organization of Canada.

Holistic Alternatives

Millions of people in the past twenty years have turned to alternative medicine. They are part of an enormous shift to holistic health care. According to a study published in the *New England Journal of Medicine*, one in three people in the United States used some form of alternative therapy in 1990. Chiropractic, massage and relaxation techniques were the treatments chosen most often. In fact, the number of visits to alternative practitioners (425 million) exceeded the number of visits to primary-care physicians (388 million). Thirty-three percent of individuals who used "unconventional therapy" did not report a specific ailment. Instead, as Dr. David Eisenberg, who led the research, said, "Many people use these techniques [massage, chiropractic, relaxation] to maximize their well-being." Of the people who did have a specific ailment, most sought alternative therapy for chronic back problems, headaches, sprains or strains, insomnia and arthritis, conditions that traditional medicine has often treated with drugs. Interestingly, seventy-two percent of these patients did not inform their medical doctor that they were going elsewhere.

The study also found that the use of alternative therapy was more common among college-educated people aged twenty-five to forty-nine with annual incomes of more than $35,000. Eisenberg summarizes, "It is likely that virtually all medical doctors see patients who routinely use unconventional therapies. Indeed, for medical doctors currently caring for patients with back problems, anxiety, depression or chronic pain, the odds are greater than one in three that a patient is simultaneously using unconventional therapy for these medical problems without disclosing this fact." I was amused to read the comments of Edward Campion, MD, in his article, "Why Unconventional Medicine?", an editorial accompanying the study: "Some of these treatments are probably quackery; some are just a version of the health spa." Dr. Campion did allow that "people resent the way visits to physicians quickly lead to pills, tests, and technology. Most now know of iatrogenic [doctor or drug-induced] disasters from medicine gone wrong. Consumers may seek out unconventional healers because they think their problems will be taken more seriously. They receive the benefit of time and attention." He concludes with this warning to traditional doctors: "We need to demonstrate more effectively our dedication to caring for the whole patient."

Dr. Pam Letts has a similar warning for family practice doctors: "People are defecting to alternative medicine because these practitioners are filling a gap. It behooves every GP to know about wellness, vitamins, nutrition and exercise. We as doctors should know what is appropriate in terms of referral to alternative medicine. Traditional doctors must be aware of their limitations in order to network patients to alternative health, which may be helpful. We need to be part of a health team."

Touch—The Laying On of Hands

Although many years have passed since I was a chiropractic student, something happened in my first-year human anatomy lab that I will never forget. One day we dissected a hand. During the course of the year, I had nonchalantly worked my way through the various neuromusculoskeletal systems of the body, easily able to disassociate myself from the reality of dissection. That particular day, I casually strolled over to my assigned cadaver and carefully unwrapped the plastic covering that protected the skin. A hand, lifeless, ice-cold, fingers slightly curled with yellowed nails, lay there in full view. A hand that once belonged to life, to a real someone; a hand that had once comforted, stroked, caressed, healed, held another's hand; a hand that could greet others, a hand that could wave goodbye. At that instant, I realized that nothing was more powerful or symbolic than touch; the human hand had a voice that could communicate every possible emotion and experience.

Touch is one of the most basic, natural and meaningful of human activities. For babies, being touched is as important as being fed, and can have a crucial effect on the growth of both body and mind. New research points to the possibility that certain brain chemicals needed for development are released strictly by touch. In a study conducted by the University of Miami School of Medicine, premature infants who were massaged for fifteen minutes three times a day gained weight forty-seven percent faster than those left alone in their incubators. The massaged babies also showed signs of a faster-developing nervous system through their level of activity and responsiveness to external stimuli.

Considering the importance of touch to human growth, it is not surprising that many traditional healing therapies have developed from this basic human need. Techniques that rely on touch and the laying on of hands are called bodywork. Most of the touch-oriented bodywork available today is part of the holistic approach to health. Some bodywork is designed to promote relaxation; some disciplines improve body alignment; others involve psychotherapeutic techniques. Improving the physical aspects of the body often affects the mental aspects; at the same time, working out our emotional problems often heals our physical pain. Here are some of the more common methods.

- *Massage* involves kneading of the muscles to stimulate circulation, relieve muscle tension, enhance joint flexibility and promote overall relaxation. Massage techniques vary. Sometimes deep pressure is used to treat sore or tense muscles; at other times smooth, gentle, rhythmical strokes assist relaxation. Massage therapy is an integral part of my chiropractic office; for conditions involving injury or strain, massage complements the work of the chiropractor to accelerate the healing process within the muscles.
- *Shiatsu treatments* rely on the manual stimulation of pressure points to bring the body's energy into equilibrium. In Japanese clinical practice, shiatsu has been used for centuries to relieve tension and a variety of physical illnesses.
- *Rolfing* is based on the idea that physical and emotional traumas and chronic tension have permanent effects on physical posture. Rolfing uses deep-tissue massage to restore skeleton and joints to normal alignment.
- *Alexander technique* and the *Feldenkrais method* are movement reeducation techniques. Both teach students to replace poor movement habits with healthier, more efficient ones. In Feldenkrais, increased awareness, a natural readjustment of posture, muscle tension and body image are facilitated through the touch of a therapist. The Alexander technique has been shown to expand the skeletal frame, lengthen the neck muscles and give the body a greater range of movement.
- *Reichian therapy* works to break down the "body armor"— chronic physical tension—that individuals accumulate when they hold their emotions in check rather than expressing them. Developed in the 1930s by Dr. Wilhelm Reich, the therapy uses physical manipulation combined with psychotherapy to dissolve energy blocks in the body.
- *Bioenergetics* includes many of Reich's techniques for physical and emotional release. A central feature of bioenergetics is the use of various physical postures to energize different parts of the body.
- *Trager* psychophysical integration uses massage techniques plus guided imagery to relax the body.
- *Therapeutic touch* doesn't actually involve touching another person; instead it means sensing and regulating the energies around the body to promote healing. Therapeutic touch is

used in delivery rooms, palliative care units and AIDS hospices. The College of Nurses of Ontario has recognized it as a healing strategy, and many nurses are being trained in its use. Research shows that it promotes relaxation, reduces pain and accelerates healing of wounds and fractures.

All these hands-on therapies stand outside the boundaries of conventional medicine. Like other forms of alternative health care, they emphasize prevention rather than diagnosis and cure. How do you select a treatment that is right for you? Do some research; ask friends and family for recommendations. There may be workshops in your area giving short demonstrations on a particular therapy. Check your local Yellow Pages for an index to specific bodywork. Going to the doctor for a pill is not the best way to maintain health, improve posture, reduce stress and tension and enhance well-being. The laying on of hands speaks volumes to body, mind and spirit.

Chiropractic—Making a Difference

I once heard a story about a tourist who was sitting on a beach. He was watching an older man who would walk a few steps, then stop and bend down repeatedly to pick something from the sand, then throw it into the water. Overcome by curiosity, the tourist finally strolled over to ask what was going on. The old man explained: "I'm throwing these starfish that have been washed up during low tide back into the ocean. If I don't save them, they'll die here from lack of oxygen." The tourist shook his head in disbelief and said, "There are thousands of starfish on this beach. You can't possibly help them all. And what about all the starfish on the hundreds of other beaches up and down this coast? You can't possibly make a difference." The old man smiled, bent down to pick up yet another starfish, and as he threw it into the ocean, he replied, "Made a difference to that one!"

For nearly a hundred years, chiropractic has been making a difference, patient by patient. Today it is the third-largest primary health-care profession in the western world (after medicine and dentistry.) My profession offers a natural and conservative approach to health care without medication and surgery. The Canadian Chiropractic Association defines chiropractic as "the science which concerns itself with the relationship between structure; primarily the spine, and function, primarily the nervous system, as that relationship may affect the restoration and preservation of health." Chiropractic (from the Greek, meaning "treatment by hand") is achieved through joint adjustment or manipulation, supplemented by physical therapy (massage, electrotherapy, corrective exercise) along with a focus on life-style counseling, prevention and patient responsibility for health. Studies in North America, Europe and Australia report that about eighty percent of chiropractic practice is for musculoskeletal pain, with low back pain the predominant presenting complaint. Another ten percent is for headache and migraine. The remaining ten percent includes a wide variety of disorders caused fully or in part by spinal lesions.

No responsible chiropractor today claims to cure organic disease through adjustment of the spine. Instead, "Chiropractors have built a reputation by treating patients who have had back pain for months or years and who haven't responded to the conventional bed rest, physical therapy and medication prescribed by most conventional doctors," says Scott Haldeman, MD, an Irvine, California, neurologist and chiropractor. "When these patients end up in the chiropractor's office, manipulation along with advice on building strength through exercise and proper diet can lead to substantial changes."

Many athletes have learned the value of chiropractic care for structural balance and mobility in order to achieve peak performance. Chiropractors are recognized as an integral part of many sports teams. The 1980 Winter Games in Lake Placid, New York, saw the first chiropractor accepted as a team doctor with the United States Olympic Team.

In North America, a candidate for entrance to a chiropractic college must have three years of university study in qualifying science courses. Chiropractic courses involve a structured four-year college program including basic sciences (anatomy, neurology, biochemistry, physiology, pathology, embryology) orthopedics, diagnosis, radiology, kinesiology, nutrition and chiropractic technique and principles. Government inquiries and independent investigations by medical practitioners have affirmed that today's chiropractic undergraduate training is equivalent to medical training in all preclinical subjects.

During the initial consultation with a chiropractor, there will be spinal evaluation, postural analysis and muscle testing, as well as specific neurological and orthopedic tests to determine overall function and range of motion of the spine and pelvis. X-rays may be required. In Ontario, Canada, where government benefits are available for up to twenty-two treatments annually, only eight percent of patients have used that maximum in recent years. As in medicine and physical therapy, some conditions require ongoing treatment, especially for cases of chronic long-term pain.

Many patients have already discovered the benefits of chiropractic care. As health care is poised to shift toward the promotion of health and wellness, chiropractic is firmly in place in the holistic model. Those of us who practice chiropractic are already making a "healthy" difference for millions of people.

Chiropractic has evolved from controversial beginnings to widespread acceptance. D.D. Palmer, the founder of chiropractic, believed that there was a universal intelligence in all living matter. Palmer thought disease could result from excess or deficient neurological function, and that interference with the normal transmission of nerve impulses was due to a "subluxation," or misalignment of the vertebrae. Palmer performed his first adjustment in September 1895. The patient, Harvey Lillard, had been deaf for seventeen years; he had his hearing completely restored. Many North American chiropractors today use the term "spinal dysfunction" instead of "subluxation."

Worldwide, there have been six formal government inquiries into chiropractic during the past twenty-five years. Chiropractic was found to be a safe, effective and cost-effective method of treatment; the studies recommended licensure and government funding. All six inquiries have criticized the level of antipathy and misinformation that exists between the chiropractic and medical professions, calling instead for cooperation in the best interest of patients.

Postural Vitality

If your new suit requires the services of an expert tailor to make it fit, perhaps your posture is the underlying problem. Poor posture can make a jacket gape, a stomach bulge and buttocks protrude.

Good posture, however, has advantages that go beyond looking good. It is a requirement for good health. Good posture allows the body to move more efficiently in a balanced and coordinated way. Good posture means you move effortlessly with vitality and energy.

Posture is the position in which all bodily structures relate to one another, whether you are standing, sitting, walking or lying down. At the center of the relationship are the spine and pelvis. If a person is viewed from the side, there are three normal curves, to give the appearance of a slight *s* shape. Any deviation from these normal curves, as in faulty posture, places abnormal stresses and strains on the spine and its supporting structures: ligaments, tendons and muscles. This can result in back pain and headaches.

In correct alignment of the body, an imaginary line dropped from the ear will go through the tip of the shoulder, the middle of the hip, the back of the kneecap and the front of the ankle bone. With correct carriage, the chin is tucked in, head up, back flattened and pelvis straight.

There are many reasons for poor posture, including structural abnormality in the skeleton. However, poor habits developed in our growing years are the cause of poor posture in the vast majority of people. Sitting hunched in a chair at school, lying slumped on a couch watching TV or stuck in front of a computer can lay the groundwork for poor adult posture.

Posture also mirrors our inner emotions, and we stand and move as we feel. It reflects our personalities, self-image and the confidence we feel in ourselves. Furthermore, increased weight puts stress on the skeletal system because the muscles have to work harder. And don't forget fatigue. It's hard to stand up straight when you're exhausted.

Clinically poor posture distorts the alignment of the vertebrae, decreases the range of motion in our joints and causes stiffness, fatigue and back pain.

Stretching and strengthening exercises for the abdominal, pelvic and spinal muscles can improve your posture. Combine these exercises with the correct stance, memorize and practice them daily, and you'll be well on the way to a noticeable improvement.

To find the correct standing posture, stand one foot away from a wall. Sit against it, knees bent slightly. Tighten abdominal and buttock muscles. This will tuck the pelvis back and flatten the lower spine. Holding this position, inch up the wall to a standing position by straightening the legs, but don't lock your knees. Now walk around the room maintaining the same posture.

Here are some tips to help you achieve and maintain good posture.

1. For proper sleeping posture, a firm mattress is essential. Never sleep on your stomach, as this increases the curve in your lower back. The ideal sleeping posture is lying on your side, knees bent.
2. Put soft chairs and deep couches on your *don't* list.
3. Never bend from the waist—only from the hips and knees when lifting objects.
4. If you stand for prolonged periods, rest each foot alternately on a low stool to reduce strain on your lower back.
5. When you are sitting, the small of your back should rest snugly against the chair.
6. High-heeled shoes strain the lower back. A moderate heel with a wider base of support is more sensible.
7. Avoid carrying heavy shoulder bags.
8. Maintain good muscle flexibility by stretching daily. This reduces fatigue, increases blood circulation and allows you to move in a relaxed manner.
9. Your computer may be giving you a pain in the neck! Make sure your computer and keyboard are properly adjusted to fit you. Be certain you have good lighting.
10. Your chair must fit the size, length and contours of your body. Check to see your lower back is properly supported, feet are flat on the floor, knees slightly higher than your hips. Above all don't sit for prolonged periods without taking a regular stretch and movement break.

Naturopathy

The naturopathic doctor views the individual as an integral whole, so symptoms of disease are seen as warning signs of improper functioning of the body or an unfavorable life-style. The naturopathic approach combines clinical nutrition, herbal medicine, homeopathy, manipulation, physiotherapy and Chinese medicine. Treatment is designed to support the body's recuperative powers using natural remedies along with changes in diet and lifestyle. I find naturopathy very helpful for myself and for my patients. A dry, scratchy throat is an early warning symptom that I may be getting a cold. With naturopathic remedies, my cold will be thwarted before it begins. Patients who are frustrated with drugs prescribed for insomnia, migraines or depression often respond very favorably to naturopathic treatment. To become a naturopath, students must have three years of premedical studies at a university, followed by four years of study at a recognized college of naturopathic medicine.

Homeopathy

All naturopaths practice homeopathy—a system of medicine based on the principle of "like cures like," meaning that substances that cause a disease or symptom in large amounts will also cure the same condition in minute amounts. For example, a substance like bee venom (apis) causes heat, stinging pain, redness and swelling if given to a healthy person; it can also be used homeopathically to treat conjunctivitis of the eye, which is manifested in redness, swollen eyelids and stinging pain. The German founder of homeopathy, Samuel Hahnemann, believed that symptoms are signs of the body's effort to throw off disease; once again, one must treat the whole person, not merely the symptoms.

Two people with the same disease are treated as distinct individuals; the homeopathic remedy matches each person's symptoms. Remedies administered as tiny pellets placed under the tongue or as droplets in a liquid are made from a wide variety of natural substances, using vegetable, mineral and animal sources. Because of the complexity of homeopathic prescribing, it is best to see a licensed naturopathic physician or practitioner with specific postgraduate training in homeopathy.

P-ILLS

Many drugs are necessary and lifesaving. What concerns me, however, is the overprescribing of drugs and "polypharmacy," the prescription, administration or use of more medications than are clinically indicated for a given patient.

In a 1988 health survey, the Canadian government found that forty-eight percent of Canadians take some type of medication in any given forty-eight-hour period, but only sixty percent of them do so on the advice of a physician. The National Alcohol and Other Drug Survey indicated the proportion of Canadians using prescription drugs thirty days prior to the survey. Five percent used narcotics such as codeine, morphine or Demerol; 3.6% used sleeping pills; 3.1% used tranquilizers and 2% used antidepressant drugs. Generally, usage rates were higher among women than men. Maybe these numbers don't mean very much to you, but to me they represent an alarming amount of sickness, suffering and lost productivity. And as we get older, drug use seems to skyrocket.

In the November 1993 issue of *The Drug Report*, a publication of the Ontario Medical Association's Committee on Drugs and Pharmacotherapy, the policy summary states, "Elderly people in Canada represent the fastest growing segment of our population and are the largest consumers of drugs. Their risk of adverse drug reactions, however, is four to seven times that of younger people and may be the cause of at least twenty percent of hospital admissions for acute care. Several studies have found that the physician's prescribing knowledge for elderly people is often inadequate, and inappropriate prescribing is common." Think of the significance of that one statement: at least twenty percent of hospital admissions for acute care may be due to adverse drug reactions in the elderly. Stated another way, out of every hundred beds occupied in any hospital, at least twenty people shouldn't be there. Those twenty people are someone's mother or father or grandparent— maybe yours. Now imagine the number of people at home who are unknowingly suffering adverse drug reactions that are not life-threatening. They're not even part of these statistics!

The report continues by suggesting that "cognitive and affective disorders [impaired thought and emotions] in the elderly may be due to adverse reactions to sedatives and hypnotic drugs [that is,

Valium, tranquilizers, sleeping pills]. There is also a strong correlation between the use of benzodiazepines [sedatives and hypnotic drugs] and hip fractures." During an eight-month period, from January 1993 through August 1993, the Ontario Medical Association received 905 reports of suspected drug reactions; reporting of adverse drug reactions by a physician is not compulsory, so there may be hundreds more. This is something that never should have happened.

A study published in March 1994 in the *Canadian Medical Association Journal* found that physicians who see the highest number of elderly patients also write the highest number of prescriptions. The lead researcher, Dr. Warren Davidson, chief of geriatric medicine at Moncton Hospital, says, "Physicians seeing a lot of patients in their office in one day are spending less time with each patient and prescribing more drugs. They are providing, perhaps, a poorer quality of care. Prescribing more drugs to elderly people may only make them sicker; people in their seventies are six to seven times more prone to suffer serious side effects to medication than people in their twenties." Dr. William Molloy, associate professor of medicine at McMaster University and coinvestigator of the study, says, "There is a major problem in our society with overprescribing to the elderly. I don't think you have to be a PhD or a doctor to know that. It's estimated that somewhere between ten and thirty percent of all admissions of the elderly to hospital are due to problems from overprescribing."

While there are still many people who think, "I mustn't question the doctor who is *the* health authority," there is evidence that people want more information about the drugs they are taking. Many are trying to second-guess their doctor's advice. Since January 1994, more than twenty thousand people across Canada, eight thousand in Ontario alone, have called the toll-free number of the Pharmaceutical Manufacturers Association of Canada to get information on how to use prescriptions wisely. Callers are sent information packages about specific diseases; about twenty percent have asked for details about hypertension or high blood pressure.

So where does that leave the patient who walks out of the doctor's office clutching another illegible prescription form? Here is some practical advice on pills for Patients In Love with Life.

- If you take several medications prescribed by more than one doctor, take everything to a pharmacist or doctor to check that you aren't taking some that are incompatible.
- Don't share prescriptions.
- Bring in all expired medications to a pharmacist for disposal. Once a year, there is a cleanup campaign for disposal of expired medication.
- When having any prescription filled, ask the pharmacist five questions. What is the name of the drug? What is the drug used for? When is the best time to take it? Are there possible side effects? Are there any possible interactions with other drugs? Some drugstores have a computer data base that keeps track of the drugs you're taking and can warn you of potential drug interactions.
- Every drug has side effects; if you have any unusual symptoms, call the doctor right away. Better still, ask the doctor about potential side effects while you're in the office. Some physicians hand out drug monographs to patients. These are pamphlets that describe everything known about the drug, in particular, adverse drug reactions and drug–drug interactions. Some three thousand physicians in Canada use a computerized drug data base system to record the drugs patients are using, to see which ones could potentially interact with each other. One expert on adverse drug reactions said, "If all doctors had this system in their offices, it would cut down tremendously on the number of problems with mismatched medicines."
- If your doctor prescribes drugs for a condition and you are uneasy about taking the drugs, speak up. Ask about alternatives, for example, ice instead of an anti-inflammatory, massage therapy instead of a muscle relaxant, chiropractic care for back pain instead of pills and bed rest.
- If the doctor suggests tranquilizers, ask about counseling instead. If you have insomnia, treat the cause, not merely the symptom. Sleeping pills are not the answer for long-term sleep problems.
- Says Dr. David Rapoport, "It's well known that doctors like to overmedicate women in comparison to the number of prescriptions they write for men. It seems as if there are doctors out there who would like a female to be on sex hormones

from age twelve until death." And speaking of hormones, within the next decade, about fifty million North American women will be reaching menopause—time to decide on hormone replacement therapy. Drug companies could potentially reap hundreds of billions of dollars—there aren't enough zeroes in my computer to show you just how much money they could make. They will be wooing you and your doctor with advertisements and promotional material. Some women *must* take these drugs; they should ignore the controversy and trust their doctors. However, for the rest of us, it is our responsibility to find out as much as we can to make an informed choice. Don't rely solely on your doctor. Read current books and literature on hormone replacement therapy. Many women are considering natural alternatives such as herbal medicines and naturopathy for hot flashes, exercise for weight gain and meditation for sleep disturbances.

The overuse of drugs concerns many of us. There is a word—*iatrogenic*—to describe doctor- or drug-induced disease. This could include the elderly taking too many drugs; women on hormone therapy for endometriosis who experience serious depression; arthritis sufferers on high doses of anti-inflammatories who develop stomach problems. Imagine being an elderly person hoping for some guidance from a doctor, perhaps really needing someone to listen to a concern, and leaving after a few brief moments with these words: "Here, take this pill." It will be very interesting to see the direction in which health care evolves in the next thirty years, when all of us baby boomers, mostly healthy and already dabbling in alternative health, become the next wave of seniors. Medicine may need a holistic transfusion to survive.

The Ostrich Syndrome

On Friday, March 4, 1994, John Candy died of a heart attack in Durango, Mexico. In his short life of only forty-three years, this comic genius touched many of us with his humor, his lovable demeanor and his teddy-bear girth.

On Saturday, March 5, 1994, I sat at my breakfast table reading the newspaper account of Candy's untimely death. A sad story was unraveled through the facts on the page. A heavy smoker, Candy had recently added another seventy-five pounds to his already overweight frame; he had a family history of heart disease. All I could think was, "What a terrible waste of an incredible human being!"

One of the comedian's friends, surprised at his sudden death, said he had spoken to Candy the day before: "He was fine." Other friends said they were unaware of any serious health problems. Fine? No health problems? A man who smoked excessively, weighed more than three hundred pounds and had a family history of heart problems?

It's not my intention to preach, to be judgmental or insensitive. Yet, how do we start taking responsibility, doing the things we know we should, all the while loving ourselves for who we are right now? How often do we hear someone say, "So what if I'm fat? I like myself the way I am." Or, "My grandfather smoked till he was ninety-five; it didn't kill *him*." And what about those of us who live with someone who has chosen an unhealthy life-style—smoking, drinking, poor diet? The battle between responsibility and acceptance troubles me. What is our responsibility? It's pure torture for us to watch our loved ones gradually killing themselves, yet we are often caught in a dilemma.

There's a fine line between nagging about bad habits and motivating someone to change. Motivating means setting a good example. It means never teasing or embarrassing someone about weight, tobacco or alcohol use. It means listening, not offering advice. It means respecting the other's right to grow at his or her own pace. It means providing healthy low-fat choices for an overweight child or spouse. And ultimately it also means saying, "I've done the best I could, now he or she has to do the rest alone." Several of John Candy's friends sensed his annoyance and aloofness, so they simply stopped talking to him about his overeating and smoking. Now he's gone. Through this chapter, we have talked about responsibility. Remember—that means taking responsibility for your own health, not everyone else's.

Some people don't really believe that a healthy life-style matters. And since we know lots of thin, fit nonsmokers who do *not* live to a ripe old age, it's easy enough to hide our heads in the sand—the ostrich syndrome. It's a lifelong struggle to reconcile who we are with who we could be. You wouldn't be reading this book on longevity if you didn't care about yourself.

The Ten Secrets to Preventive Health

1. Don't smoke. If you do, quit now! No more excuses—try patches, hypnosis, counseling, gum. Or try this approach: focus on becoming an athlete rather than becoming a non-smoker. You'll soon see that you won't want to ruin your body with toxins.

2. Exercise vigorously for at least thirty minutes three to four times per week. If you don't feel like running or going to fitness classes, take a brisk walk instead.

3. Change your eating habits for life. Choose lots of fruits, vegetables, whole grains. Decrease your total fat intake to twenty-five percent or less of total daily calories. Maintain a reasonable weight. Too thin is as dangerous as too fat.

4. Get as much sleep and rest as you need. The average is seven to eight hours per night, but you may function best with more or less sleep. Don't be afraid or ashamed to take naps.

5. Drink alcohol in moderation: no more than one drink per day on a regular basis, and no more than four drinks on social occasions (one per hour) if you're not driving. Never drink and drive; never drink if you're on prescribed medication. And speaking of driving, always wear your seat belt. As for so-called recreational drugs—thou shalt not!

6. Maintain a happy, optimistic outlook on life. Hardy people view change as a challenge and setbacks as opportunities to learn and grow. Keep stress to a manageable level. Get help when you need it. Talk with family, friends, clergy or therapist to sort out your problems and priorities.

7. Seek out a family physician who listens and cares. Have thorough, regular checkups, with appropriate age- and risk-specific tests.

8. Avoid medications wherever possible. Consider taking vitamins and minerals—calcium and vitamin D to prevent osteoporosis, antioxidants to prevent cancer and heart disease.

9. Don't forget your teeth: schedule regular checkups, brush twice a day, learn to love dental floss. Nothing sours life more than huge dental bills, gum disease, bone infections and painful abscesses—all preventable.

10. Above all, listen to your body, for it may be sending subtle messages you are ignoring. Remember, ultimately only you are

responsible for your body and your health care. Treat yourself with love and respect. After all, if you wear out your body, where are you going to live?

You can work on only one area of your life at a time. Perhaps you'll start by joining a health club or finally deciding to lose weight sensibly. The goal of healthy living is not a static one, because you can't ever say you are finished. Good health is a continuous process. It's never too late! People can make major health changes in their fifties and sixties—the human body is enormously forgiving, allowing us the opportunity to repack our suitcase for the journey of life.

The 10 Secrets of Bernie Herman, age eighty-three

1. To thine own self be true.
2. Never retire.
3. Get a profession.
4. You won't get anywhere without honesty.
5. In life as in card games, you play the hand that you draw.
6. What makes people old is how they think.
7. Use it or lose it—body and mind.
8. To be successful in business and in life, you have to be an optimist.
9. Work at having a happy, and lasting, marriage.
10. Learn to be patient.

8
CREATIVITY

*A person's mind must be constantly
stimulated.*

A few years ago, I experienced an explosion of creativity. My creative play took the form of writing poetry. What a surprise it was when I discovered I could compose rhymes in my head! My first few poems were safe, fun topics, mostly related to health and wellness: about Type A personalities, burnout, fitness, doing what you love. As I became more courageous, I wrote poems on relationships: men who can't make commitments; transitional men; special girlfriends; the single life.

My creativity became even more unblocked when I finally dealt with childhood issues. I had to go back to go forward. The healing process deepened when I began to deal with issues about parents, childhood and my ex-husband. I wrote poems about caring for my sick mother, my cherished memories of our fridge door, my ex-husband's betrayal. I cried and wrote and wrote and cried. The cerebral fireworks never stopped; ideas exploded in my head day and night. I kept a notebook and pen on my night table to record errant thoughts. Since then I've written more than forty poems. This has been the most playful, creative, cathartic period of my life.

Experiencing this burst of energy, combined with my research on wellness and longevity, opened a door to passionate and inspired living. The key was the rediscovery of creativity and play, the true fountain of youth.

We will explore the necessity for lifelong learning, the value of play and power lounging, creative thinking and activity, and the joy of living in the present. Keep reading and prepare to leave your grown-up inhibitions behind.

Lifelong Learning

"Use your God-given faculties and expand your mind," urged Rabbi Gunther Plaut, eighty-two, when I asked him what advice he would give to a child about life. He continued, "Go to school to *learn*, but don't assume that when you get a diploma, you know anything. A lot of professional people have forgotten to learn anything beyond their profession. Learning must never stop." When it comes to lifelong learning, Rabbi Plaut had a special role model— his mother. At the age of ninety, Selma Plaut enrolled as a mature student at the University of Toronto, studying French and history. Asked during an interview why she began studies at that point in her life, she replied, "All my life I've liked to learn. But I've gone through stages in my life—as my husband's helpmate, as the rabbi's mother—so learning had to stay in the background. But then, when my son retired from his pulpit, I thought I could begin anew. I wanted a chance to prove to myself that I was still able to learn." She did. At one hundred years of age, Selma became the oldest person to receive an honorary bachelor's degree from the University of Toronto. She lived for a remarkable one hundred and three years.

Beyond the creative reasons for learning, if you ever wanted a solid physiological reason for hitting the books at eighty or ninety, here it is: neuroscientists have discovered that the brain has an incredible capacity to change and grow, even in old age. Individuals have some control over how healthy and alert their brains remain as the years fly by. "Yes, it's the old 'use it or lose it' principle again," says Dr. Gordon Winocur, of the Rotman Research Institute at Baycrest Hospital in Toronto. "When a person keeps his or her mind active and stimulated, brain cells branch wildly, like the roots of a growing tree, creating continual networks of new communications. Normally with the aging process, some brain cells die, and dendrites tend to shrink. We have found, however, that when an older person, who may be unhappy and withdrawn, becomes engaged in life again, the intellectual stimulation spurs on renewal of brain tissue. Connections that were lost are reformed, and recovery occurs."

Dr. Winocur has some hopeful information to convey, especially for those concerned with warding off Alzheimer's disease: "Studies now show that the more educated a person is, the less likely he or she is to show symptoms of the disease. Life-style and education protect cognitive function," that is, thinking, learning and memory. Dr. Winocur has this advice for all of us interested in keeping our brain circuits buzzing: "Keep active with things you enjoy doing. A person's mind must be constantly stimulated. Take a course in something that's unfamiliar to you and intellectually challenging." So here's added motivation to learn a new language or study handwriting analysis.

Dr. Winocur has some final thoughts for baby boomers: "If you can lock into the things that you enjoy *now*, interests that you are passionate and excited about *now*, you'll be happier now, happier next year and happier in your senior years."

Creative Play: Sparks in the Dark

My dad was an inventor. During the war he designed the ratchet wrench, a tool used by all handy men and women, and the universal towing gear, a device for towing airplanes. I was able to observe his creative genius firsthand in the early 1960s during the Bay of Pigs crisis. Under threat of war, he invented Canada's first government-approved bomb shelter for homes; in fact, the prototype was installed under our house. Our family made the national news.

When I was growing up, one of the first lectures I received (Dad was big on lectures) involved creativity. "The world is just waiting for your ideas," he would say, "and all you need is one good one." Quite regularly, I would rush up to my father and excitedly announce, "Daddy, I have an invention!" He would hear me out, then patiently explain that either my idea had already been invented or it wasn't feasible. But he always encouraged me to keep thinking. Little did I realize that my mind was becoming imaginative, inquisitive and intuitive.

The creative process takes its root in childhood play. For the young, life is an adventure, full of make-believe. Children invent stories, games and imaginary playmates. Their creative drawings hang on that universal art-gallery wall—the fridge door. For children, play has no time boundaries. Children live in the flow, lost in whatever they are doing.

Adults possess the potential to be creative. We've all experienced times when we are playful, passionate, open, imaginative, curious, energetic and full of wonder—all childlike qualities involved in the creative process. Yet most of us have lost our childlike spontaneity. What happens when we become adults?

In trying to understand the way we lose our natural creativity, Teresa Amabile, a psychologist at Brandeis University, has identified six experiences that kill childhood creativity: surveillance—making kids feel they're constantly being watched; evaluation—making kids worry about how others judge them; competition—putting kids in win-or-lose situations where only one can come out on top; overcontrol—telling kids exactly how to do things; pressure—establishing high expectations for a child's performance; and time—stopping children in the middle of things they like to do. Does this sound like your experience of school?

What often emerges from this creative censorship is an adult afraid to play, invent, explore, daydream and risk. The creative process does take courage and trust: courage to face the possibility of failure, the inner strength to reveal our dreams and visions to the world outside; the tenacity to pursue goals without the guarantee of success; and trust in the personal wisdom that is guiding us.

If you think your creativity has been blocked by negative childhood experiences, here are some practical ways to open yourself up to this wonderful gift.

1. So you quit piano lessons thirty years ago; you hated practicing and now you wish you could sit down and play. Do it! Sign up for lessons. You'll be amazed how wonderful music school for grown-ups can be. Or change instruments; maybe you've always wanted to play the saxophone in a group. Why not?

2. Combine creativity with fun and fitness. Always wanted to tap-dance? Instructors claim this is the latest rage, thanks to the boom in large-scale Broadway musicals.

3. Explore the courses offered at your local community center or college; there are programs in calligraphy, sculpture, painting and drawing. By learning the proper techniques, you can silence your inner critic, who thwarts potential creativity.

Studying in a group of novices provides true support and encouragement.

4. Share yourself by teaching a skill to a child. Teach someone a song; show a youngster how to make Christmas decorations; build a treehouse with your grandchildren; design family stationery with the kids; write stories with your children.

5. Overcome your fear of failure by going on one of the Outward Bound wilderness experiences. Learn how to risk, explore, invent.

6. Have you ever considered taking acting classes? You may be surprised at the ways in which you will open up. One of my friends, who had unresolved conflicts with her mother, was able to confront these issues in a positive way after playing a role as a mother in an amateur production.

These are just some of the ways to get your creative sparks flying again!

Creative Thinking

For ideas to emerge, the mind needs to be free to wander without boundaries. Albert Einstein once asked a friend, "Why is it I get my best ideas in the morning while shaving?" These creative leaps often occur when we are not consciously thinking of a problem. Have you experienced flashes of insight? Solved a problem while pulling weeds out of the flower beds? Did you feel excited, bursting inside to share your ideas with someone? To produce something by your own thought and imagination is joyful and invigorating, whether you are splashing color on a canvas, writing a novel or creating a new computer software program.

These flashes of inspiration occur for all of us when we daydream. Daydreaming is a way to explore creative possibilities. When we are tense and focused on a specific problem, our minds seem to be full of repressive gnomes who guard a buried treasure of ideas; when we relax, we can discover jewels of insight.

How can we as adults deepen our creative capabilities? We can begin by exploring new ways of thinking and by looking at things in a fresh way. Edward De Bono, author of many books on creativity, invented the term "lateral thinking," a process that counteracts old patterns of logic and creates new ones. One of his methods is called "random input." Choose a noun from the dictionary at random and link it to your particular problem. For example, suppose you are looking for a catchy name for a new health-food store. Using De Bono's system you randomly pick the word "length" in the dictionary. Now start creating related thoughts: length of life, longevity, living long, lifelong. "Lifeline Health Foods" could be the name you want.

I asked eighty-year-old John Weinzweig, composer and professor of music at the University of Toronto, where the ideas for his musical compositions originate. He answered that an idea can come from any place at any time. He recalled one amusing incident. "I was at the cottage sitting at the piano working on a particular piece of music. A bird perched on a branch near the open window began to sing. He was interrupting my train of thought. Every few seconds this white-breasted sparrow would repeat a rhythmic motif." John listened to the bird's song and ingeniously incorporated it into his composition.

Creativity can be stimulated through games and puzzles. The game of Scrabble asks us to create words using random letters, then fit them into existing words on the board. Roger Von Oech, author of the creativity book, *A Whack on the Side of the Head*, has invented the "Creative Whack Pack." This deck of cards is divided into the four roles, or types of thinking, that make up the creative process. Instead of kings and queens, his deck contains the Explorer, who finds out new information; the Artist, the idea-generating self; the Judge, who makes decisions; and the Warrior, the kick you need to get your ideas into action. When you are solving a problem or looking for more insight into an issue, you pick a card to stimulate your imagination. Like De Bono, Von Oech believes we sometimes need a whack on the side of the head to jolt us out of the habitual thought patterns that prevent us from looking at things in a fresh way.

Creative Activity

Artistic play is the hands-on activity, the culmination of creative ideas, imagination, fantasy and play that becomes the canvas of any artist, whether it be a writer, dancer, painter, sculptor or musician.

"Creativity often comes from an emptiness, a part of you that is not being expressed," says Linda Montgomery, an artist and professional illustrator. "You may feel a longing to create, a pressure inside that builds as you grow older." The pressure may be expressed through the written word. Writing can be a cathartic process, allowing us to express feelings that are often partly submerged, like an iceberg. Once we put pen to paper, images and recollections of our life float to the surface. My poetry was the vehicle I needed to express feelings of emptiness about my life without parents.

Natalie Goldberg, author of *Writing Down the Bones,* wrote, "We have a great need to connect with our own mind, our true self. In writing practice, you enter your own mind and follow it where it takes you. All of us have a story to tell." Author Helen Weinzweig, now seventy-nine, remembers being typically caught up in the daily necessities of living and looking after her family, "doing all the right things," as she put it. She felt the one area that was hers alone was a love of literature. "At forty-five I began to examine different aspects of my life that had eluded me." Her creative energy took the shape of writing fiction. "Creativity puts me in touch with a part of me that was not known to me before. Some call it the unconscious, the imagination; others know it as contemplation. There is no limit to human ingenuity. In order to become a fully integrated human being we must discover that creative part of ourselves." Helen has been nominated twice for the Governor General's Award for fiction and is working on her fourth novel.

Other seniors are passionately involved in making music. One eighty-five-year-old woman is still playing her viola da gamba in baroque chamber music groups; her instrument, which looks a little like a cello, dates from the seventeenth century and always causes a sensation when newcomers see it. A retired biology teacher came back from a vacation and called his local community orchestra to see if they needed a volunteer usher for an upcoming concert. He chuckles as he remembers, "They told me to get over there immediately for rehearsal; they were desperate for more singers. That night I sang bass in the choir of Handel's *Messiah!*" He is now a regular member of the choir and sings at all their concerts.

For most of us, it is the *process* of creating, not the *product,* that really matters. The sheer enjoyment we feel from contacting and expressing our true self can be enough. Fay Morris, at seventy-eight years of age, decided she wanted to learn to play the piano. Now ninety, she has a teacher come every week. Harvie, her husband for seventy-one years, jokingly points out, "She'll never make Carnegie Hall." Max Sharp, ninety-two, is equally adept at needlepoint and golf; he shot a hole in one last year! "I've been doing needle-point for twenty-five years. All my nineteen grandchildren and thirty-four great-grandchildren have pieces of my work." When I visited Max's home I was astonished to see the numerous large, intricate, colorful canvases decorating the walls. He explains his passion: "Needlepoint keeps me alive; I never miss a day."

My feelings on creativity were expressed well by the late Rollo May, therapist and author of *The Courage to Create*. "Creativity is the answer to aging—listening to one's own inner voice, to one's own ideas, to one's own aspirations. It must be something fresh, something new. Some idea that takes fire."

Artist Henri Matisse had a fresh idea that allowed his creativity to flourish in the final stages of his life. Unable to get out of bed due to failing health, he used scissors to fashion paper cutouts. Then he painted them, using a long pole, from his bedside. Matisse consid-ered his activity a departure, not an end.

For ceramic artist Beatrice Wood, in her nineties, creative people are the people who are open to life and who listen to life as it comes to them. "Whatever I am, the song of life goes on. You can be creative inside even as you're washing dishes. To me creativity is more a state of the inner being than the outer."

Author Norman Cousins believed "that the tragedy of life is not death, but what dies inside us while we live."

Be Outrageous

Outrageous! How else to describe S.L. Potter, who at one hun-dred years old bungee-jumped two hundred and ten feet! Once this Californian "youngster" was on the ground, he asked for his dentures back. Was he scared? "Hell, no . . . I don't get scared," he retorted. His son Jim, seventy-two, said of his dad, "He's so inde-pendent. You can't change his mind."

Outrageous personalities possess a devil-may-care, madcap atti-tude full of joie de vivre. What about outrageous Joe Hillman, rollerblader extraordinaire? At eighty-two he "blades" five miles five times per week. For his eightieth birthday celebration, he rollerbladed five miles with his forty-year-old son; then, still wear-ing his sports gear (helmet and knee, elbow and wrist pads), showed up for the party given by his family and friends. Then there is outrageous Foofie Harlan. She's a cheerleader in Sun City,

Arizona. At seventy-eight, she does splits, handstands, front flips and cartwheels.

At eighty, Walter Stacks has a favorite motto: "Rest makes rust." There's no rust on Walter as he rides his bike fifteen miles to San Francisco Bay. Then he runs across the Golden Gate Bridge to Sausalito and back, a total of fifteen to sixteen miles. Then he plunges into the fifty-five-degree bay for a one-mile swim, only to get out and bike home! He has run more than a hundred marathons and was the oldest man to complete the Hawaiian Iron Man Competition at age seventy-four. He is beyond outrageous!

Donna Pasquale, ninety-one, has had a lifetime of living outrageously. Always ready for adventure, she was the first to sign up for the camel rides on a church tour of the Holy Land—when she was eighty-two. No one in her family ever remembers seeing her sick in bed; slowed down slightly by a bout of pneumonia a few years ago, she convalesced in the living room, refusing to go to the hospital. She learned to drive at age fifty-three and kept up her license until her mid-eighties. After all, it was much easier to get to her weekly bowling league outings in her own car.

Then there's Corina Leslie, age ninety-one, from Arizona. She celebrated her ninetieth birthday with a sky dive. Corina walks about five miles three times a week; stretches three times a week; golfs twice a week; and occasionally jumps on a trampoline.

All these characters and others like them possess two outstanding qualities: playfulness and an incredible sense of humor. Some examples—

From Allan Lamport at ninety-two: "People ask about my doctors. What do the doctors say? I tell them that I've tried to give most of them good advice but they didn't take it and they're not here now."

From Harvie Morris, ninety-three: "Enjoy life as it comes every day. Just to get out of bed in the morning is something. I mean to wake up breathing is even better!"

From Arctic Joe Womersley, only sixty-nine (or as he would say, *Sexty-nine*), when asked if growing old concerned him: "I don't know; I haven't gotten there yet."

You can be outrageous no matter what your age. I feel outrageous when I become Dr. E.D.C. and perform my rap songs on television or in front of a large audience during a motivational speech. Being a contestant on *You Bet Your Life* with Bill Cosby was, for me, the pinnacle of outrageousness. I wrote a special rap song for the show and performed it for Bill. I had a ball. Winning $620 was fun, too!

Think of times you have been off-the-wall outrageous. How did you feel? Did every cell in your body ooze with excitement, enthusiasm and energy? If we could capture those passionate feelings and bottle them, we would absolutely *live* every day of our lives.

Power Lounging

My office is full of stressed-out patients, the "hedonistically challenged." The faces are different but the bodies all feel the same, like concrete with muscles hard, stiff, inflexible and sore. The stories that go with the bodies are also the same. Here are a few.

From Susan, forty-two, with low back pain: "I'm a single parent with two children and a full-time job. Unfortunately leisure for me means chauffeuring the kids to after-school lessons and doing laundry. If I'm lucky, I go to a movie with a girlfriend once a month. I can only make it through a couple of pages of a novel before I start nodding off. I'd love to just get away somewhere but money is always a problem."

From Richard, thirty-nine, with neck and shoulder pain: "We've had widespread layoffs at work, so I've taken over someone else's responsibilities in addition to my own. I work ten-hour days, not including my forty-minute commute. Relaxation? What's that? The only time I stop moving is when I'm horizontal in bed. My wife and I are planning a vacation this summer—the first real one in two years."

From Donna, forty, with low back pain: "I am so stressed out! My mother has cancer and my husband's sixteen-year-old son moved in with us, so there's a lot more tension in the house. I'm not sure if I'll have a job next month and my husband's consulting business is really slow. On top of that I haven't had time to exercise and I'm putting on weight. I used to love gardening—this year I planted only a few annuals and I've hardly had time to notice them."

Add these three examples to my thousands of other patients with similar stories; then multiply by the number of chiropractic clinics in Canada, and you'll soon realize that there are millions of us suffering from stress-related complaints. Statistics Canada did a study on nine thousand adults and how they spent their time in 1992. Canadians were asked to assess their experience of the time crunch through questions on perceptions of time. Thirty-five percent of women and thirty-one percent of men agreed with the statement, "I feel that I'm constantly under stress trying to accomplish more than I can handle." Women with both full-time jobs and very small children scored the highest in the time-crunch scale. And time crunch eventually leads to body scrunch!

When you do start to relax, after a long, steady dose of stress or after one short, intense burst, an interesting phenomenon often occurs: the body falls apart. Has this ever happened to you: the day before you leave for a much-needed vacation, you are stricken with the flu? Or the day after a gruesome work project ends, your back goes into spasm? One of my patients with chronic lower back pain managed to hold herself together during her mother's month-long final illness; she coped with the subsequent funeral, followed by a week of mourning when relatives from all over the country descended on her home. Then she fell apart. I had to make a house call because she couldn't move.

It seems that we have the ability to glue ourselves together during stressful times. As soon as we let down our guard and say, "Now I have time to unwind," the body says, "Now it's time for me to have a nervous breakdown!"

Like letting a little air out of a balloon about to burst, we need to take regular, consistent breaks in our day before we, too, explode. When you do make the time, are you able to power lounge? Or is your leisure filled with work disguised as self-improvement programs instead of enjoyable and stimulating diversions?

Power lounging—a phrase to describe relaxation, leisure, time out—requires you to be engaged in life. And living, as opposed to existing, is the zone where we feel challenged and absorbed. Ironically, some of the most expensive forms of leisure are the least likely to provide this experience. Sitting on a yacht and watching big-screen television are purely passive activities, which do not engage your skills. Compare these expensive diversions to gardening, one of the best leisure pursuits: it's outdoors and involves physical activities such as digging, raking and planting flowers. Photography, woodworking, crafts, reading, fishing, golf, socializing with family and friends, dancing and exercising are other recommended leisure activities. What passions would you pursue if your work were to be taken away? Those passions should be your leisure pursuits.

Another aspect of power lounging is self-nourishment—taking time for the things we love without feeling guilty. One Sunday morning at a half-marathon road race, I struck up a conversation with a policeman on duty. "You should be running, too," I suggested, noticing his belly. He was about my age. He replied wistfully, "I used to exercise before marriage, three kids, ten-hour shifts and a thousand things to do around the house. I don't have any time for me."

Even the smallest of gifts can revitalize our bodies and minds. The gifts you give to yourself can be a fifteen-minute walk alone; the time to read a few chapters of a new novel; an uninterrupted bubble bath; playing the piano; listening to classical music.

What about you? Where are your needs on your list of priorities? At the bottom—after everyone else gets taken care of? Here's one positive suggestion for self-nourishment: make a list of everything big and small that makes *you* feel good. These nourishing and nurturing activities are ways for you to be good to yourself. Debbie, another patient, loves to make a cup of chamomile tea, sit in her favorite chair and sip it slowly, not moving for ten minutes. With a rambunctious three-year-old, that's a real holiday for her.

Beatrice Wood, at ninety, believes in self-nourishment. "I love getting in bed at night under the warmth of the electric blanket. I take a graham cracker with milk and I love it. I love looking at the mountains. And on a cold day I love getting into the hot tub. I think these are my greatest pleasures."

Ask yourself this question: Are there things I love to do but never have time to enjoy anymore? These are the very activities you need to include for self-nourishment, health and well-being.

Silence

Silence can be magical. After a record-breaking snowfall one December, I ventured out very early in the morning. It was dark except for some street lamps. I stood there awestruck in an enchanted winter wonderland. God, the artist, had painted the branches of the trees with a thick stencil-like brush of snow. The quiet beauty enveloped me. All the noise of the world seemed to be absorbed by the soft whiteness all around me.

Quiet time does not have to mean absence of sound; rather, it refers to a feeling of peacefulness and serenity. Remember your experiences of placid moments sitting by a lake with the haunting cries of a loon in the background; cross-country skiing through a dense forest; the gentle rocking of the train taking you home from work each day; reading a book in front of a crackling fire on a rainy Sunday afternoon; going for a run before the world has awakened, listening to the music of your footsteps; planting flowers in the garden.

Dr. Herbert Benson, in his book *The Relaxation Response*, explains that we must find a quiet environment, that is, unoccupied, uninterrupted time, to reduce the stresses and demands of twentieth-century life. He believes the key is breaking the train of everyday thought. If you are sitting by that lake but your mind is full of endless chatter or you're reliving an argument with your spouse, you're hardly quiet.

One of the most effective ways to reduce that inner chatter is through meditation. Sit quietly, eyes closed, and allow your mind to empty of all thoughts. Some methods of meditation involve focusing on breathing in and out and repeating a word (called a mantra) aloud or silently. The health benefits of meditation are well-documented: it reduces stress and lowers blood pressure and heart rate. Meditation is taught through yoga and meditation centers and special workshops. There are many books available on this health-enhancing technique, as well.

Meditation for patient Ruth Allen is self-love therapy. She begins her day with twenty minutes of meditation. "I feel an inner stillness, a clarity afterward. If I get busy with my work and miss a day I feel unbalanced or unsettled," she says. "At the start of my meditation my thoughts are scattered. My mind is like a puppy, scampering away, and then I bring it back; when it runs away again, then I have to guide it back. Finally it sits beside me and stays. My mind is then still and I am totally present."

Author Helen Weinzweig meditates by visualizing a tree. "When I want to still myself, I see the strong roots of a tree in the earth; the tree remains still and alive despite the pollution, acid rain, noise, attacks by developers. The tree changes with the seasons, renews itself with fresh leaves, gets rid of old branches and withered leaves in a storm, uses the sunlight and fresh air for new growth and expansion, and it all comes from within." What a powerful image!

My running is a form of meditation. Many times while running I will enter a trancelike state, unaware of moving my arms or legs. I call this my automatic-pilot stage. My mind will be empty, focusing only on the present: the trees, grass, sky, clouds, birds. I see and hear acutely everything around me. Jon Kabat-Zinn, PhD, founder and director of the Stress-Education Program at the University of Massachusetts Medical Center, says, "This form of meditation is called 'mindfulness'; it emphasizes paying attention from moment to moment."

Busy baby boomers who don't have time to sit and meditate for twenty minutes can still practice mindfulness anywhere, anytime. "It still requires a significant degree of concentration, but you can use whatever predominates in your awareness at the moment," says Kabat-Zinn. "You could be mindful of what someone is saying or you could bring mindfulness to eating or making love or driving. In effect your whole life becomes the object of your meditation." According to him, practicing mindfulness can have the same health benefits as meditation.

We can appreciate the health benefits of going away to a spa or retreat to unwind, destress and rejuvenate the mind and body. Silence and quiet in our home environment can be a "mental spa," a way to diminish that fast-forward, rushed feeling that leads to a chronic sense of time urgency and anxiety. Even ten minutes of quiet time each day can be restorative.

Here are some suggestions.

- Turn off the radio and television at home for a designated quiet time. Encourage reading and creative activities in your family.
- Put the telephone on automatic answer for part of each day.
- Find times during the day to be alone with your thoughts.
- Restore your sense of hearing through a visit to the woods; a whole new world will open up. Listen to the chirping of insects; the sound of wings as birds fly by; the subtle layers of sound from streamlets funneling into a brook.

Finally, meditation, like an empty seashell, will allow you to hear the roar of your own life.

The Precious Present

I've just returned from a dream run through the woods on a magnificent fall day; you know those magical, sunny, blue-sky kind of days with just enough breeze to coax the remaining leaves to join the piles of yellow, orange and gold crushed beneath the feet. I am mindful of everything about me—the warmth of the sun on my face; the familiar smell of autumn lingering in the branches above my head; the rhythmic crunching of leaves in tempo with my footsteps; squirrels, like athletes, long-jumping over mounds of leaves in search of food. I am not alone in my euphoric state. Others have come to celebrate these treasures in the forest: lovers holding hands, children collecting leaves for school, dogs sniffing each other to determine if friend or foe, a photographer with tripod hoping to capture on film what I feel in my heart—this joyful moment, this second of this minute of this hour of this day that will never come again.

At this instant, I am not thinking of the groceries I must buy that afternoon, or of the laundry in the hamper, or even who will win the World Series that night. I am totally present in the moment, aware of every smell, sight and sound around me. There is no yesterday or tomorrow, there is only now.

For me, a rather future-oriented person, savoring the moment is not a natural inclination. I spend much of my time looking forward to instead of just looking. The rediscovery of creativity and play taught me lessons; the more playful I was, the more present I became. Writing a poem, searching through my rhyming dictionary for just the right word, laughing or crying over a heartfelt line I wrote, that became my joy. The magic is in the process, not in the finished product patients take home and put on their fridge doors.

Running the New York City Marathon became 26.2 miles of present moments. I remember the overwhelming feeling of wonder being squished in with 27,500 runners, the helicopters whirling overhead, as we ran across the Verrazano-Narrows Bridge. I remember the cheering crowds, the little black kids in Harlem wanting to do high fives with their heroes, the Hasidic Jews in long black overcoats and top hats, the balloons, the marching bands, the volunteers at the water stations, the tall buildings in Manhattan. All those moments were more important to me than the finish line. It was the experience of getting there that I relished.

As I write this book, I keep returning to the image of the journey, an open-ended voyage of self-discovery. We discovered long ago, when we were children, many of the lessons we need to know today, lessons about playfulness, creativity and fun. Then life got in the way and we grew up. Remember, it's never too late to have a happy childhood. On our journey to passionate longevity, make sure to bring crayons, a toy, a song, a magic wand and some books—nourishment you need to become a creative adult.

The 10 Secrets of Allan Lamport, age ninety-two

1. Like yourself for who you are and keep that well-polished.
2. Live by elevated standards, without selfishly stepping on others to do so.
3. When you have time and knowledge, help others. The world's problems hurt us all.
4. Make yourself a part of the life of your children; they are a gift left in your care.
5. Learn to be on time! And since there is only one way to be assured of that, be ahead of time.
6. It is uplifting and satisfying to attend church when you can. *You have the time.*
7. Make your feelings happy ones with all the things you do.
8. Don't ever let increasing years bother you or interfere with your thinking.
9. Arise happy as you look in the mirror for the first time each day.
10. If you follow all this advice, you won't care about your age. The gift for a happy life is there if you will seek it.

P.S. Love your country.

9
FLEXIBILITY

Change is a vital part of life.

A girlfriend recently asked me if writing this book has put a damper on my social life. Well, let me tell you . . . How many people you know spend Friday night studying the sex life and molting behavior of crustaceans? Yes, you may be curious what these arthropods have to do with a book on passionate longevity. Read on to find out what I discovered about these fascinating creatures.

Lobsters and crayfish have a tough protective layer, or cuticle, that serves as an external skeleton, called an exoskeleton. This rigid outer shell allows the crustacean to increase in size by only so much, at which time the lobster or crayfish must molt, or deshell, to grow more. Pretend you are Larry or Lucy the Lobster. Things are getting pretty tight and uncomfortable inside your shell. You realize you have to change in order to grow; however, as soon as your protective layer comes off, you are vulnerable and defenseless. You know you can't go on living the way you are, but what if you get eaten by a predator? You innately understand that all change involves fear and resistance. In your little lobster heart, you know that soon after you venture out into the world naked, your soft, pink, flexible membrane will harden into a real shell, and you'll be bigger, stronger and happier than you are now.

Now while Lucy and Larry are molting in private, let's look at how we humans can make choices *now* that will lead to fulfillment in our later years. The time to assess our lives is now, at mid-life, when change is still possible, not when we're ninety, wishing, hoping, dreaming and, for many, regretting. Mid-life, in fact, may be the last chance we have to make some important life changes. Everything in life involves decisions. Perhaps the only thing standing in our way is the first step: the decision to change careers, to improve health, to start a family, to change a relationship, to heal our past. Ultimately, we learn the most when we decide to extricate ourselves from our shells and become open, flexible and courageous as we move forward through the undulating waters into new territory.

The Future in Retrospect

Grab a pen and a piece of paper. Let your imagination soar as you consider this: it's your eightieth birthday. You're fit, optimistic and healthy, happier than you ever thought possible. Looking back over your life, you see the many changes you've made in the past forty years to bring you to this state. What were they?

This question is designed first to propel your imagination into the future, and then to allow you to reflect, to see how you achieved that happy, healthy state. The thoughts and feelings that emerge from this exercise are *your* dreams for the future. Have you ever climbed in the mountains and looked out over the horizon? From that vantage point you can see peak after peak, some larger and some smaller, valleys, paths, streams, forests. From the bottom of the mountain looking up, you see very little of the panorama. Today, in mid-life, you are standing in the very middle of the mountain range, faced with many choices. Which route to take? You can climb on farther, stop for a rest, explore side roads and detours, stay where you are, follow a different path completely, even go back down to the foot.

I asked my baby-boomer patients to respond to my thought-provoking question. Their answers about the future were fascinating. Let me share some of them with you.

Seventy-six percent of the respondents made health changes. Some typical replies:

- practiced yoga and aerobics
- ate more fruits and vegetables, less fat
- quit smoking
- became a vegetarian

- took a vigorous four-mile walk daily
- finally made health and nutrition a priority
- lost weight on a regular fitness program

Sixty-four percent of the respondents were married. Thirty percent of that group made marital changes. Some replies:

- finally got out of unhealthy marriage
- got a divorce, met someone wonderful, happily married for thirty-five years
- had a one-month break from marriage every year
- married to same man since high school and still having sex
- sharing my life with someone I have deeply loved for fifty years

Twenty-four percent of the respondents mentioned money. Some replies:

- became financially independent
- stopped measuring success by dollars
- won three million dollars in the lottery
- became less money-conscious

Thirty-two percent of the respondents mentioned retirement or new careers. Some replies:

- retired at fifty-five, began second career in creative area
- retired at sixty, went into public service
- became a master gardener, then went into horticulture business
- retired at sixty, studied chef training, opened a small bakeshop

Fifty percent of the respondents made stress-related changes. Some replies:

- learned to relax, take naps regularly
- gave up things that caused me pain and aggravation
- got rich and fired stress-causing employees
- listened to me first, instead of doing what others wanted
- became more assertive
- practiced meditation
- finally learned to say no
- went to a therapist to learn to deal with my stuff

Thirty percent of respondents wanted to travel and pursue hobbies. Some replies:

- finally learned to play the piano and joined a small ensemble
- took up golfing, fishing, bike riding
- traveled around the world, my dream trip
- got rid of the television
- learned to play the saxophone
- spent most of my time reading, gardening, listening to music

Forty-two percent of respondents spent more time with their families. Some replies:

- strengthened family ties
- spent more time with children and grandchildren
- healed family rift, spent time with my family
- put work second, family first

Forty-eight percent of respondents moved from the city to the country. Some replies:

- moved to quieter community
- moved to a warm climate
- moved to country—slower pace, fresh air, less pollution
- dropped out of big city, enjoying small-town life
- living in home we built originally as a cottage on a lake

What did I learn from all this? When people are allowed to dream, they are willing to make changes to enhance their happiness quotient. I watched several people fill out the form without hesitation; they knew exactly what they wanted or could be like. Will they be able to make the jump from dream to reality?

Are you on the path of your dreams? If not, what changes do you need to make now?

Health Alert

Forty-three-year-old Bill Lindo studied the waistline of his rotund golf buddy and inquired, "What size pants do you wear?"

"Forty," came his friend's reply.

"I was stunned," admitted Bill. "That was my size, too! I couldn't believe I looked like him. At that moment I decided to change my life and get serious about my health."

This conversation on the golf course took place thirty years ago. Today, Bill, seventy-three years "young," is the oldest triathlete in Canada, competing regularly in swim, bike and run events. He has a resting heart rate of forty-two beats per minute (compared to the average of seventy-two). "I feel fantastic," he says. "I have more than enough energy to work every day and then do a strenuous fitness routine." For many years, it had been Bill's habit to work days, then go to night school to improve his education and ultimately provide a better life for his wife and seven children. His timetable created a sedentary life-style and a resulting weight gain. "I weighed a hundred and ninety-five pounds at five foot seven. I was having beer with the guys and eating a high-fat diet." A membership at the YMCA was the beginning of Bill's turnaround; however, the motivation from his business partner, Joe Womersley, gave him the fitness push he needed. Joe, you may recall, is the sixty-nine-year-old ultra-marathon Iron-Man triathlete who runs his age in kilometers every birthday. "I started to run with him and gradually increased my distance. I've run eight marathons, and my weight today is a hundred and forty-two pounds," Bill announced proudly.

"Has your fitness set a good example for your children?" I asked.

Bill was philosophical as he replied, "Fortunately, five of my kids are fit; the other two unfortunately smoke. I've learned from my own life that sometimes it takes a while to get the message."

Joseph Sorbara finally got the message after hearing his own diagnosis of diabetes combined with his father's prognosis from the same disease. At forty-nine years of age, Joseph was diagnosed with diabetes and high blood pressure, the very same health problems as his father. "The day before I was to begin the diabetes educational clinic at the hospital, my father had a stroke. By coincidence, he was in the same hospital. Each day I would go from the clinic up to my father's room and see my dad in a coma. That's not déjà vu, it's *pré-ja* vu! I realized that could be me in twenty years. I decided then and there it was not going to happen. I wanted to live to see my young children grow up." In Joseph's case, it was not a lack of fitness that triggered his condition. In fact, when I first met this busy lawyer fifteen years ago, he was running regularly and had completed marathons. Nevertheless, from poor health habits, he was carrying two hundred and thirteen pounds on a five-foot-six frame. Joseph explained his problem: "My weight was a joke with everyone. It was part of my image: the overeating, cigar-smoking bon vivant." A medical checkup for life insurance uncovered the diabetes. With a vow to get healthy, Joseph went on a fifteen-hundred calorie diet, lowered his fat consumption, continued to exercise and lost fifty pounds. Now, two years later, he has managed to maintain his weight and his resolve. Joseph looks lean, fit and healthy. "I feel great," he said. "Once I made up my mind it was easy. I'm a convert."

Arthur Scott's conversion came after a heart attack at age fifty-two. Even though he played badminton and tennis, it wasn't enough to dissipate the stress that was building. "I sometimes worked fifty-five hours a week," he recalled, "and when I wasn't working I was still thinking about work. I didn't relax a lot." Arthur had made one major health change seventeen years earlier—he had quit smoking—but it wasn't enough. A family history of heart disease, coupled with work stress, meant that he was walking a tightrope. The heart attack was no surprise.

"How has your life changed in the past eight years?" I asked. Arthur described a new life-style: "Now my health is a priority. I changed my diet, lost some weight and started a walking program through a rehabilitation center. Now I run, in addition to playing badminton and tennis. Most importantly, I took a serious look at my work. At first I thought of quitting; instead I reorganized my job functions. I also bought a condo in Florida for my eventual retirement, and for relaxation and respite from the winter. Many of us are too busy living to prepare for the future. In my thirties and forties I was only concerned with my financial future instead of preparing for a health future."

How would you rate your health future? Rosy red like the robust cheeks of a healthy, active youngster, or pale like the sallow cheeks of a geriatric smoker? Do you need a shock like Joseph or Arthur to make a change in your health status? For many of us, seeing our parents age or deteriorate can be a great motivator, especially when we now know that many ailments are within our power to ameliorate, mitigate or reverse. By the time I knew the importance of nutrition, exercise and vitamins in maintaining a healthy heart, it was too late to help my mother. She was overweight and inactive, depending on pills to function. Have you ever been to a nursing home? On the way to my mother's room, I would pass dozens of patients who wouldn't even be there if they knew what we know today about preventable diseases. That's the sad part; it's too late for them. But it's not yet too late for us. Some of us could have fifty or sixty more years of passionate longevity, if . . .

Small changes can make a difference. You can start with this one: stop using butter and margarine altogether; instead use olive oil sparingly. Here's another: walk briskly for thirty minutes three to five times per week. If you smoke, quit now!

The way I see it, you can make small, consistent health changes now or you can wait until your body gives you the early warning signals—chest or back pain, fatigue, chronic headaches. The choice for a quality life is yours. Remember: a healthy body will allow you to put the "passion" in passionate longevity.

Career Changes

"Remember the movie *Shirley Valentine*?" seventy-seven-year-old Ginger Eisen asked me. "That was me thirty years ago. I didn't know who I was. There was no point in seeing a psychiatrist—I knew what the problem was. I was missing self-fulfillment." Ginger worked before her marriage at twenty-four. For the next twenty years she did what most women did in those days—stayed home and raised children. "I always had big dreams," she reminisced, "and lots of energy." So when the kids were grown she decided to put that energy into a retail store. In 1961, she opened Ginger's Bathrooms. In no time, the business soared, and so did Ginger's spirits. She was ecstatic. This is how she described her success: "There is an opportunity for everyone in this world; the key is to follow your heart and work at something you love."

For thirty years Ginger devoted herself to the business she loved; then the recession hit. When Ginger turned seventy-four, her business went bankrupt. "I was devastated. It was like losing a child. I was emotionally as well as financially drained." Others in her position and at her age would probably have retired, but not tenacious, optimistic Ginger. And retirement didn't fit with her philosophy of longevity: "The secret is to keep working. I believe in the use-it-or-lose-it principle. If you are not using your mind, it atrophies." So two years ago she put her creative mind to work once again and came up with a timely new business. Her retail store specializes in bathroom designs for seniors and the physically challenged.

For those of you who need motivation as you contemplate

changes at mid-life, here's additional proof that it's never too late
for anything—even changes in your marital status. Ginger is a new-
lywed. Several years after her husband died, this widow fell in love
at seventy-five and married a charming man of eighty-five. That's
what I call amazing grays!

Ginger's story is inspiring for all of us who need to make a
change. Then there are those of us who are in the throes of a
change brought about by circumstances forced upon us. Robert
Reilly, forty-seven, is a case in point. For many years the manager of
a large rehabilitation company, he was frustrated with the organization yet not prepared to make a change. "It was the fear of the
unknown, my unwillingness to risk and the need for security that
kept me there. However, I always felt a war going on inside me, a
war between putting up with the bureaucracy and launching out
on my own. I wanted to do something creative and fulfilling," he
explained. The outcome of Robert's battle between safety and
uncertainty was decided for him. He was informed by his company
that downsizing measures would be taken in one month. Management couldn't be specific. "They just said people at my level would
be dropped, but they didn't say who they would be." I asked
Robert how he felt at this devastating news. Robert's reply? "I
realized I had two choices. I could either sell myself short, taking
the safe way out, and look for a regular job. Or I could believe in
myself and see this as a valuable opportunity for self-employment."
Robert began to prepare his departure plan: he networked, col-
lected information, registered a business name. In his mind everything would be in place for a swift exit.

And what happened? Robert told me this happy story: "When
they finally announced who the victims were to be, I think I was
the only one who left with a smile. My wife and I went out to our
favorite restaurant to celebrate my new direction." Robert is now a
consultant to private industry.

How has he changed through all this mid-life upheaval?

"When I finally made my career decision, a lot of things shifted
inside me. I felt this change would be a testing ground for validating
my life. I am finally finding out who I am and where I fit in this
world. I've also developed a new cooperative relationship with my
teenagers. The boys were thrilled with my new career choice. They

gave me advice and came up with some valid suggestions. Their support was very encouraging at a time when I was both scared and excited with starting out on my own."

Lil Brown "made her life happen" at forty-two. She stumbled upon a newspaper ad from York University inviting applications from mature students. "I thought, 'That's what I'm going to do,'" she said, recalling her decision twenty-three years ago. Was this a big leap for her? Yes! Even though this determined woman had already left a difficult marriage and lost one hundred and thirty pounds (from her peak of two hundred and forty-two pounds), she had only a grade-eight education. Nevertheless, she had been a voracious reader since age four, so she applied and was accepted part-time so she could continue her full-time work as a lecturer at Weight Watchers. She began with two courses, but soon realized that she lacked basic writing and note-taking skills. She had to take extra workshops just to get through those introductory subjects. Her first taste of success came when she saw her grades: an A and B in the two courses. She was ready for more learning. A professor encouraged her to enter the honors psychology program. Lil described her university days: "I loved it. I never missed a class. There I was with the twenty-year-olds but we were all equals. We were all learning from the same professor and writing the same exams." She knew one twenty-year-old very well: her daughter, Pearl, was in the same program. "We sat together, studied together and wrote exams together."

Lil, always a part-time student, graduated eight years later at fifty with an honors psychology degree. Was she finished with school? No way! She took a year off and then decided to go into social work. At fifty-eight she graduated with an honors degree in social work. She worked as a social worker for one year at a poverty clinic and had to learn poverty law to understand the legalities facing her clients. Was she finally finished with university? At fifty-nine, she went back to the University of Toronto to get her masters degree in social work. When Lil Brown graduated at the age of sixty she had three university degrees. Nevertheless, her challenges weren't over yet. "I was the only one in my class who didn't get a job! I had the maturity, the street smarts, the academic smarts, I even received an award for outstanding student. However, I believe my age was a factor." Instead, Lil decided to expand her small private practice and is now counseling families in crisis, as well as seeing clients with eating disorders and substance-abuse problems.

Has she reached all her goals? "I thought of doing my doctorate with the ultimate goal of teaching, but that would take another five or six years. Unfortunately, society draws certain lines. Once you hit sixty-five, the party is over for teachers. There is compulsory retirement. I am taking courses now in family therapy and I would love to write some short stories one day."

By the way, did I tell you that Lil, at sixty-five years of age, runs five miles a day, six days a week? "I also want to do some mountain climbing and tackle Mount Everest," she added.

The poet Robert Browning wrote, "Ah, but a man's reach should exceed his grasp,/Or what's a heaven for?" What mountains do you want to climb? What changes must you make to begin your journey up the mountain? Ginger took time twice in her life to reevaluate her goals—at age forty-four, then again thirty years later. Robert conquered his fear of change, taking advantage of a negative situation—company downsizing—and turning it into a positive career change. Not once did Lil let her age stop her from achieving her goal, finding work in counseling. How often do we think or say out loud, "I'm too old," or, "I'll be sixty by the time I finish this!" Let me open your eyes to these possibilities:

- getting a degree from university at eighty
- starting your own business at sixty-five
- learning to play the piano at eighty-five
- beginning a running program at seventy
- learning to drive at sixty
- inventing something at seventy-five

Every one of these possibilities has been accomplished by people who didn't let age or fear stand in their way. Be open to new ideas. Remember: *you* can change anything at any time if you really want.

Till Divorce Do Us Part

Cosmopolitan magazine would have been proud! The line I used was typical of something from an article on meeting an interesting man on an airplane.

"Excuse me," I began, looking at the handsome man sitting in the aisle seat; I noticed he wasn't wearing a wedding band. "I'm doing research for a book on baby boomers and changes at midlife. Did you have some significant changes in your late thirties or forties?'' He smiled and volunteered that his life had indeed taken a three-hundred-sixty-degree turn in the past seven years. I continued my questioning: "Would you share your story with me under conditions of anonymity? I don't even want to know your name or line of work."

"Sure," agreed the passenger in seat 4C, and began: "I married my high-school sweetheart just after we both finished university. We were the same age—twenty-one. Unfortunately, it was a shot-gun wedding. I know now that I married for guilt, not for committed love." He described the first five years as "good times interspersed with turbulence," as his family soon included three small children. His wife stayed home while he worked. In his thirties, he decided to go back to school to get his MBA. That's when he met *her*. She was in his class—brunette, brilliant and available. "I realized that if I was even contemplating having an affair, my marriage was already in trouble." Then came confrontation with his wife, confessions and counseling. The therapist explained that an affair is a symptom of a marriage gone wrong. "My wife and I were roommates, never soulmates," Mr. 4C admitted. After seventeen years of marriage they agreed to divorce.

"So what happened to Miss MBA?" I inquired sweetly.

Mr. 4C was philosophical: "We continued to see each other until I was transferred to Ottawa four years ago. Long-distance romances are tough." I wondered about his children. His reply: "I have a very close relationship with them and I see them every other weekend."

When I asked him what he had learned from all these changes in his life, he thought for a few moments, and said, "My kids are the most important aspect of my life, even more important than my work. I realize I can live alone and be happy, although I prefer to be in a loving, committed relationship. I'd rather be on my own than stuck in a marriage that is just going through the motions. I can make a major, traumatic life change and survive. Finally, I've learned that family and friends can help me get through anything!" The airplane landed, we said goodbye and the passenger in seat 4C disappeared into the terminal. What did I learn from all this? Pick out a stranger in a crowd from a certain age group and the story he or she will share is almost predictable. For baby boomers, the story will be about significant change.

Change, although stressful, is necessary. A vital part of life, it is an opportunity for something new. For Dorothy, now seventy-three, her forties signaled a new beginning, a new life of independence, freedom from a difficult marriage. "Somewhere within me, I found a strong woman, courageous enough to leave my marriage at a time when it was shameful to be divorced. When I left, I had no money in the bank and no furniture; all I had was a secure job. I found a little apartment, made some new friends and never looked back. It was such a wonderful feeling to realize I could manage on my own. I was free at last!" Dorothy has lived on her own for thirty-three years. Does she ever feel lonely? She answered my question confidently. "No. I have family and friends. I date, I read, I travel regularly. People worry about being lonely. Instead they should do some volunteer work and help others."

Any advice for those baby boomers who are in unhappy marriages? "You only live once. Why live in a situation that makes you unhappy? Many people think they are trapped. Anybody can change anything if they want: health, career and marital status."

I know about changing one's marital status. In my twenties I was a WISW (wild immature single woman); then I changed to a CFMW (career-focused married woman). Eventually I became an MSW (mature single woman). I did have to take a special night course in Neediness 101 before graduating to MSW—I had to learn the difference between "alone" and "lonely." Initially, I did not know how to be alone with myself and instead looked to inappropriate men to fill in the empty spaces. With time I learned to fill the spaces with my own creativity and energy. I now understand the meaning of the phrase, "Be your own best friend." I remember distinctly the night I became an MSW. For the first time ever, I decided to go to a funny movie, alone, on a Saturday night, traditionally a night reserved for couples. I had a perfectly wonderful time with myself and a box of popcorn. With a strong sense of self and the ability to enjoy who you are, you will be in good company all the time. From this position of strength, you can make stable and mature choices. Learning to be happy when you are alone is a necessary part of maturity, no matter what your marital status.

Many of us are like frogs lined up at the starting line called divorce; we all have different paths and time frames awaiting us. Some frogs sit there for a while, contemplating where they have been. Some jump forward with a huge leap into remarriage. Still others go sideways on a convoluted path; they date for a while and realize they like living alone Monday to Friday but enjoy company on weekends. Some enjoy long-term, committed relationships but still maintain separate living quarters. Whatever fits you, live it— single, married, divorced. One final comment: daily I hear complaints from women who are on their own and would love to meet "a nice guy." They don't want a husband, just someone to share a dinner or a movie once in a while. Where can you meet this nice guy? He won't find you in your apartment or home. Get out there in the stream of life.

- Take some courses that interest you.
- Pursue a new hobby.
- Go to the library, church or synagogue.
- Find a part-time job working in an elegant men's wear store.
- Invite all your single friends together for a party and have each woman bring two of her platonic male friends.
- If you are daring, put an ad in the personals column of the newspaper and carefully screen all replies.
- Read the newspaper daily. The business section usually has a column listing weekly seminars and financial forums. You can be sure that many interesting men will attend. Go, meet new people and expand your business acumen at the same time.
- The activities of large cities are often covered by a monthly magazine that focuses on theater, art, film and concert events, for example *Toronto Life* or *New York*. Choose the events that interest you, then go alone or with a friend, and be open to adventures.
- Do some fund-raising, volunteer work, political canvassing.

Remember: there is a scent of desperation and neediness others can easily detect. When you are happy just being you—involved in life and the community—you'll radiate the energy that will attract that special someone.

Loss

"You should see my telephone index book," said ninety-two-year-old Mrs. F as we sipped tea in her lovely home. "There are so many names I've had to cross off over the years. I've lost some friends who were much younger than I." Loss is a natural part of life—loss that comes with age; loss of mates, family and friends; loss of health and mobility. "It's not what happens to you that matters," she told me firmly, "it's how you cope." Mrs. F speaks from experience. When she was fifty, her sixty-three-year-old husband had a stroke, which left him partially paralyzed and speechless. "I didn't believe the doctor's gloomy prognosis for one minute. I told my husband, 'You'll walk and you'll talk.' I believed it and I made him believe it." She read books on speech therapy and neurological disorders so she could understand his condition; she worked on his facial muscles and taught him to speak. With therapy he eventually regained most of his mobility. For almost twenty-five years Mrs. F cared for her husband until he died at the age of eighty-seven. About the loss of her husband she remarked, "The way one dies should reflect the way one has lived. He had spirit until the very end. He went with peace, quiet and dignity. We had a good life together."

Elsie Palter's attitude to loss is similar. At eighty-three she firmly believes, "Everything in life is finite. You have to accept that. Every living thing comes to an end. It makes you realize that you are part of the universe and you can't expect to be an exception. That's why every single day counts for me." Recently David, her husband, died. "I treasure the good times we enjoyed all these years. We were blessed with a happy marriage, totally fulfilled with children and grandchildren."

Dorothy, seventy-three, is also philosophical about loss. Sharing her feelings about her mother's death, she observed, "A little bit of you goes when your parents go. You are never quite the same afterward. But you have to get on with living. Time certainly helps heal the pain."

Does she believe in an afterlife? Dorothy explained her feelings: "I think heaven and hell are right here on earth. The good things that happen are the heavenly part and the unpleasant things are the hell you have to live through." She experienced the hell part three years ago when she was diagnosed with breast cancer. When the decision was made to perform a mastectomy, her positive attitude prevailed. "I said to myself, 'They are cutting away the cancer,' not, 'I am losing a breast.' I wake up every morning and say, 'Thank you, God, that I'm here.' I've been dealing with things on my own most of my life and felt I could certainly handle this, so initially I balked at the nurse's suggestion to go to a cancer support group. When the nurse said that maybe I could help others deal with their losses, I changed my mind and decided to go. In helping others, I have been helped myself."

"How have you been supportive to the others?" I asked.

Dorothy described her involvement: "I listen when they share their pain, anguish and fear. I tell them I know what they're going through. I understand. Take that fear, I tell them, put it in a box and place it on a shelf. There are times when you'll be tempted to bring the box down and live with it. That's okay. Over time and with courage comes acceptance. My philosophy is this: I get up every day and that's the day I want to face."

Loss is change that is imposed on us. Whether it is the loss of someone we love or loss of our own health, we are traumatized. Every loss we experience needs to be grieved. If death is expected due to a lingering disease, one grieves during the actual process of dying. There is time to prepare for the inevitable, to say goodbye. When one loses an elderly relative, it often doesn't seem as sad; at funerals and memorial services there is a tendency to focus on celebrating a life rather than mourning a death. Haven't we all heard people say, "He or she had a good long life" or "I should be so lucky to live that long." Nevertheless, the definition of what is "old" or what constitutes "a long life" is changing. Remember when living to "three score years and ten" was a goal? Now, we remark, "He was only seventy."

When I was twenty-two, my father died. He was seventy-six years old and had been ill for six months with cancer. What sustained me through this loss was knowing that I still had my mother. But when Mom died three years ago, I felt a huge loss. The feeling of being alone in the world without parents enveloped my heart. Some call it the "orphan syndrome," the feeling of being very mortal, very responsible and very empty. I have found, however, that whenever I reach out, there is always someone there. The seniors who were interviewed for this book have not only taken me into their homes; some have taken me into their hearts. There are now several white-haired, passionate individuals I can chat with on the telephone, new friends who love to get together for tea. I feel comforted and consoled by their presence.

I have been using my personal experience of loss to help my baby-boomer patients as they, too, begin to deal with aging parents, ill parents, loss of parents. These losses force us to face our own mortality. Wendy Cecil Cockwell's loss of her mother made her feel that she was bumped up one step on the ladder of life. She explains, "As long as one's parents are alive, many of us feel we have some sort of protection that says, 'I'm not next.' Once both parents are gone, that invisible shield is gone." I am also able to share with patients the wisdom of my senior friends and how they dealt with the many losses that can be expected by the time one reaches eighty or ninety. Their answers are all the same: family and friends sustained them; death is a part of life; grieve and then get on with living; be thankful for the time you had together; take one day at a time; don't feel sorry for yourself; time heals anything; prayer and spirituality give you strength. Keep the memory of your departed friends and relatives alive; share stories and anecdotes. Don't be afraid to talk about them.

A sense of humor helps, too. I smiled when I read an interview with the late Ruth Atkinson Hindmarsh in the Toronto *Star* just after her one-hundred-and-first birthday. Commenting on the loss of her contemporaries, she said, "Too many old friends have cashed in lately." "Cashing in," "kicking the bucket," "gone with the wind" are some of the humorous terms I heard seniors use to describe their own inevitable deaths. Harvie Morris, ninety-three, told me an amusing story. His son had arranged for a driver to pick up Harvie and his wife five times a week at 5:20 a.m. to take them to and from their fitness workouts. One day their regular driver had car trouble and ordered a replacement. Harvie described the result: "I was waiting to be picked up at the Inn on the Park when this black stretch limousine pulls up and a new driver asks if I'm Mr. Morris. I thought it was a hearse, so I told the driver I wasn't ready for him yet!"

Oil of Delay

Recently I dropped in to a bar to meet a friend for a drink. Looking around, I realized that I was the oldest person there. I was surrounded by twenty-year-olds. For some baby boomers, looking in the mirror is a daily reality check. Have you noticed that your cute little laugh lines have become wrinkles and the highlighting doesn't keep pace with the gray hair?

For many of us, the change in our appearance is experienced as a loss. For so many years we have taken our youth for granted. The

Pepsi Generation is now buying bifocals, antiaging creams and hair-loss miracle drugs. No matter how fit and healthy you are, aging is inevitable.

Like so many other changes mentioned in this book—changes in career, health and relationships—the way we cope with the change in our appearance reflects our overall sense of self. When we're happy, doing what we love, feeling creative and fulfilled, appearance is at the bottom of our list of worries. We need to find more elegant and attractive older men and women as role models, people whose love for life shows on their faces. Katherine Hepburn, Paul Newman, Sean Connery—these people are not afraid to show their wrinkles and bald spots.

As I wrote in the "The Body Image Rap":

> Here is the truth on perpetual youth
> Laughing each day chases wrinkles away.
> Fitness and nutrition instead of cosmetician,
> Forget all the creams, improve your self-esteem,
> Liking who you are, not found in a jar.

Confronting Demons

For years, I've had one persistent demon—a fear of drowning. When I was eight years old, I nearly drowned in the Severn River, a popular cottage area in Ontario. In terror, I struggled against the river's currents and managed to dog-paddle to a nearby wharf with Olympic-style effort. Since that one frightening experience, I've never been comfortable near or on lakes.

You can then imagine how I surprised myself a few years ago by eagerly agreeing to go on my very first camping and canoeing trip in Algonquin Park. In the weeks leading up to my departure, I tried to focus on the fun I would have with nine women friends, sleeping in tents, exploring the uniquely rugged and uninhabited island landscape of the park. I tried not to think of our main mode of transportation—a tippy canoe. Every participant would be equipped with a life jacket, but I felt I needed extra protection. Just in case, I bought an orange inflatable water-ski belt which I planned to fasten around my waist at all times.

Five days before our departure, I developed a sharp pain in my lower back. At first, I thought I had somehow strained a muscle; I soon realized that my subconscious was arranging the pain so I would cancel the trip. My fear of drowning was living inside my right sacroiliac joint. Well, I did go on the trip, sore back and all, and survived. I even ventured out alone in the canoe (armed with life jacket *and* water-ski belt) and paddled to the middle of the lake. I returned triumphant. With renewed confidence and courage, I was able to confront other fears in my life. I took up downhill skiing for the first time that winter. I conquered my fears of heights, falling, breaking bones, tearing ligaments and, most of all, my fear of speed.

Fear. A four-letter word powerful enough to keep us stuck in jobs and relationships that make us sick; it prevents us from exploring new friendships, new challenges, new activities. Fear imprisons; by our self-limiting beliefs and anxieties, we stand in our own way.

One of my patients, Mr. R, suffering with headaches, has been in a mind-numbing government job for more than ten years. The position is not challenging, and he regularly complains that he is miserable. In fact he is so unhappy I have rarely seen him smile. Even his wife remarked that he comes home depressed from the office. When I try to motivate him to explore new avenues, he resists. The excuses proliferate; his fear is speaking when he says, "There's a recession; at least I have a job; I'm not trained for anything else; I'm too old to change." Ten years from now, Mr. R will still be complaining unless serious health problems emanating from chronic unhappiness force him to change his life.

Take risks. Fear is normal and universal. Successful people experience fear, but they cope with it, working with their fear so it won't defeat them. One of my patients with the very common fear of public speaking took a course to deal with his anxiety. He now addresses corporations regularly without trauma.

Fear distorts our thinking. Once we meet the fear head-on, we soon realize that it is often blown out of proportion in our minds. Think of something you once hesitated to tackle because of fear; with hindsight that obstacle now seems easy to overcome.

Reesa Kassirer, social worker, offers some advice for dealing with a common fear—the fear of change. "Rather than fearing our transitions, we have to embrace them. Change is the best learning experience." She speaks with firsthand knowledge. When she was forty-eight, she was fired from her job in social work as a result of departmental changes. "I was totally devastated," she recalled. "I felt inadequate, without a future." She was motivated, however, to explore new areas she hadn't previously considered. A new employer generously paid for a special training course, which enhanced Reesa's therapeutic skills. As a result, an opportunity arose that changed her life. These skills led her into private practice. Now, twenty years later and happy with her career, she says with certainty, "Being fired was the best thing that ever happened to me because it opened doors I was not even aware of or looking for. I probably would have stayed where I was even though I wasn't happy because I had a secure job. You never know what is going to be around the next corner."

We *choose* to let fear stop us from taking that first step to new horizons—whether it be fear of rejection, fear of poverty, fear of aging or physical fears (heights, crowds and so on). Dr. Pam Letts, a family physician who does counseling with her patients, agrees. "The people who live their lives the most fully are those who take the most risks. There's an increased chance of failure, but also far greater chance of success. Sometimes you fail and still survive. Once you've gone through that, there's not as much fear the next time."

Lately, I have been having discussions with many patients in their forties who are eager to make a life change. They are sick and tired of being sick and tired—tired of working, tired of the daily routine. Many have worked steadily for fifteen to twenty years, but have never been able to take more than the standard two-week holiday. They have decided to take a leave of absence from work, destination unknown. One woman is planning to travel extensively during her time off. All of them want to reconnect with themselves while searching for the answer to the question, "What am I going to do with the rest of my life?" Are these people afraid that if they get off the treadmill they will never be able to jump back on again? No. They're not sure what they want right now, but they realize that an inner voice is urging them to take a sabbatical to reevaluate and rejuvenate. "Why wait until a serious illness forces me to take the break I desperately need?" one woman asked.

Start small. Do your fears sometimes seem as insurmountable as Everest? Sometimes the most simple tool or approach is also the most effective, such as this basic truth: things will stay the same unless *you* change them. So expand your comfort zone by taking a risk—one small or bold stroke that will empower you. Take swimming lessons or public speaking courses to conquer your fears. Afraid of meeting new people? Make a point of chatting with one new person in your office. Fearful of change? Start by making small shifts in your behavior—finding a new route to work, changing your style of dressing, learning a new hobby or skill. How about taking tap-dance lessons, flower arranging, piano lessons? This will help you get used to the idea of change. Fearful of starting your own business? Brainstorm with people who have already taken the step. Want to make a relationship change but afraid of being alone? Talk to friends who are living on their own. Plagued by phobias—fear of flying, fear of heights, enclosed space? Join a self-help group. It has been proven that self-help groups help relieve anxiety.

Healthy people learn to cope with old fears through new insights and behavior patterns. Don't be too hard on yourself: change doesn't happen overnight.

Inner Change—The Magic Zipper

Can you imagine if we could see
Deep inside our chest cavity?
A Magic Zipper to let us peek
Inside our hearts—what truths would speak?
All our memories stored inside
Those we remember and those we hide.
Permanent records of what we feel,
The heart knows wounds that need to heal.
Plastic surgery for the soul
Smooth life's wrinkles, make us whole.
Erase scar tissue and ease the pain,
Open our hearts to love again.

How did we ever live without therapy? I began my process of inner change—pulling down the "magic zipper"—at Esalen, a retreat in Big Sur, California. In my group sessions, many participants had giant invisible locks on their zippers. They had the key yet didn't realize it. Some had their zippers undone partway, but then got stuck. Others had tried to force their zippers by ripping them from the bottom. That never works. No one can rush or force the process. Inner change has no beginning or end. We never know precisely when that shift in attitude, belief or understanding will come. Through this process, we constantly evolve; like the ebb and flow of waves in the ocean, we never know where one wave ends and another begins. Some therapists describe this process by using the image of the layers peeled away from an onion until the core is reached. And, as with peeling an onion, there are always tears. At Esalen, our group facilitator, Janet Zuckerman, taught us to work from our heart and gut. She said we spend ninety-five percent of our time inside our heads trying to figure things out logically and analytically. Inside our hearts are unexpressed feelings, she explained, keeping us stuck in all our unfinished business from the past.

Often a crisis—marital, family, work—starts the therapy process. For Mr. WP, the loss of his business in the recession was his catalyst for seeking help. He needed to deal with his feelings of inadequacy; his financial failure caused changes in his family dynamics, as well. He spent much time at home, feeling like a failure, while his wife had to work to make ends meet. When they reluctantly decided to put the house up for sale, the children were upset that they would have to move away from their school and friends. Mr. WP's therapy process involved his entire family, giving everyone the opportunity to express fears and hopes for the future. As a result of their new insights, the family became closer to each other. "With my family behind me, I had the strength and the courage to approach one of my business competitors for a job," Mr. WP explained. "I am now climbing out of my financial hole, and things are a lot brighter. Therapy helped our family cope; today we are much more open to discussing our feelings as new issues arise."

Sometimes a change in attitude comes about without therapy. When his fifty-year-old wife was diagnosed with uterine cancer, Mr. MB was devastated. A self-proclaimed workaholic, he described the change that happened to him. "You soon realize what is important in life and what things you should worry about. I used to be very cautious about spending money, always too busy to take a holiday. After my wife's radiation treatments, we traveled to places we only talked about before. On vacation, I could see I hadn't relaxed in years. I decided my health needed an overhaul. I began exercising and lost weight. I felt great. Our relationship became much closer. Now, fifteen years later, I can look back and say that my wife's cancer was a turning point for me. We have a wonderful marriage, living life to the fullest."

Many of my patients in their thirties and forties are looking at some of the unresolved issues, the scar tissue that builds up over a lifetime. One woman in therapy finally decided to end a long-term extramarital affair and is choosing to commit herself whole-heartedly to her marriage. One man is now making peace with his absent father through therapy. Another woman is examining the pattern that pushes her to keep choosing inappropriate men. Another man is having a "mid-wife crisis," sorting out his feelings for his wife and his girlfriend. One couple started therapy to deal with their difficult child; after looking at their own childhood issues, their marriage improved. Some patients who share their unhappiness with me balk at my suggestion of therapy. They resist my advice and refuse to discuss it further. These individuals talk about wanting change, all the while actively or passively resisting it. Whether through lack of self-acceptance or low self-esteem, they are unable to confront their fear or face the risk that comes with change.

What are the alternatives to therapy? One can start with the many excellent self-help books available. Talking to someone you trust—a close friend, a minister, rabbi or family doctor—is another possibility. Or start keeping a journal; certain patterns will become clear over time.

It is not a coincidence that so many baby boomers start questioning their pasts in their thirties and forties. Twenty-year-olds aren't usually ready; they're too busy starting a job and getting a life. Sixty-year-olds have already resolved many of their inner conflicts. Mid-life is a traditional time for reevaluation. If life is a journey, picture mid-life as the crossroads. Which road are you going to take and why? Maybe you want to sit down for a while on that bench by the side of the road to contemplate. See that detour sign over to the left? Perhaps you're afraid to venture off the beaten path. The pavement doesn't look very smooth, and there are lots of bumps and potholes, but maybe that is the road you should be taking. Besides, the route may be more peaceful and interesting the farther along you go. Some of us are frightened of going forward and think we can always hitchhike back to where we came from. Just remember: very few are going that way, so it could be a lifetime before you get a ride.

The 10 Secrets of Sam Sigesman, age ninety-two

1. Say "thank you"— you can never say it enough.
2. Don't think of your age. As long as you're capable of doing things, giving advice and making people happy, that's the main thing.
3. Family support will get you through anything.
4. It's important to help people.
5. Respect your parents.
6. Get an education or you haven't got a chance to make it.
7. Work like hell and fight your way up the ladder to success.
8. Give and take is the secret to a successful marriage.
9. In life, you need honesty amd integrity.
10. Be kind to people.

10

SPIRITUALITY

*Those of us who believe in something, live
longer, happier lives.*

Beliefs are very personal. Sometimes I have to be careful about what I say and to whom I say it. With only my intuition to guide us and no scientific proof, I hope to show you that there is no such thing as coincidence! Many of us have had the experience of thinking of a friend we haven't seen in ages; the phone rings, and there she is on the line. Life is full of coincidences. But why do they happen? Do they have any meaning? Can we control them? Carl Jung, the renowned Swiss psychiatrist, was so intrigued by coincidences that he coined the term "synchronicity" to describe the occurrence of two events, in close proximity of time, which have no causal relationship yet appear related. In the glossary to *The Essential Jung* I found a description of this fascinating concept. Jung states, "Meaningful coincidences are thinkable as pure chance. But the more they multiply and the greater and more exact the correspondence is . . . the more they have to be thought of as meaningful arrangements." Jung found that coincidences happen far more often than would be expected by random chance, increasing in frequency if we are open to them. There are so many inexplicable happenings in the world, everything from ESP to psychic healing to miracles. No one really knows why or how they occur. In our western scientific tradition, dismissing what we can't see or measure is common; skeptics would explain coincidences as merely insignificant, randomly occurring events, but I'm not so sure. How do we know that they aren't part of a universal plan?

The German philosopher Arthur Schopenhauer would say, "Of course they're part of a plan!" In his essay "Transcendent Speculation on the Apparent Deliberateness in the Fate of the Individual," he explains that when we reach an advanced age and reflect back over our lives, there appears to be harmony, meaning and consistency. Schopenhauer uses the wonderful metaphor of the novel and compares our lives to an immensely long, complicated but well-planned epic with a cast of thousands. The people we meet, even those who come our way by accident, influence us; we in turn affect their lives. Furthermore, the plot of this "novel" does not unfold at random; we are on a journey guided by an inner compass that brings everyone correctly onto the path that is the only one suitable for us.

Coincidences happen every minute of every day. How do you explain the ones that happen to you? My heart tells me, "Elaine, there's a message here. Don't ignore it." Many of us believe there are reasons the journey of life often meanders; paying attention to coincidences may alter our course. Coincidences encourage us to ask questions without assuming that there is only one right answer. The rightness doesn't matter; what you believe and perceive reflects your understanding of reality.

In my studies on longevity, I have learned that those of us who believe in *something* live a longer and happier life than those who believe in nothing. That something might be a commitment to an organized religious denomination, or only a vague belief in the goodness of humanity. Nevertheless, all religions and philosophies of life seem to have two main themes in common: a belief in our interconnectedness, and a recognition that life has a purpose. Coincidences demonstrate that we are somehow related to each other, our lives fitting together in the overall scheme of things where nothing happens by accident.

My philosophy has always been simple: when I make my final exit, I want to be able to feel that somehow my life has made a difference to my family, friends and patients. This is my way of recognizing my connections to other people; I treasure that kinship. Healthy people are rarely loners, living in isolation; rather, they share their talents and energy, strengths and weaknesses, with others. In fact, all the long-lived seniors I interviewed emphasized the importance of both people and purpose in their lives: friends, family, causes, volunteer work, hobbies. Each one had, in ways large and small, made a difference to someone. I never asked them directly about coincidence, but they often talked about luck, about mysterious good and bad events that shaped their lives. Many said they were lucky to have good health. Or they thought they were lucky to have had the right parents. Maybe they were the right children, children who listened, learned and lived their parents' advice; maybe they made their own luck or serendipity, those happy accidents of life when wonderful and helpful coincidences occur.

Is good luck a matter of random chance or coincidence? Is it a case of "the harder I work, the luckier I get"? I believe that lucky people move through life with a different attitude, hearing, sensing, feeling differently from others. How do they do it? Here are some practical suggestions for improving *your* luck and making coincidence work for you:

C is for curiosity. Don't be a passive listener. Ask questions. You may find something you've been searching for.

O is for openness. Be open to the mysterious ways of the universe. There are many valid experiences that can't be explained scientifically.

I is for intuition. Listen to your instincts. What is your intuition telling you? Go with it.

N is for network. Meet new people. Share ideas, goals, beliefs. You never know how a new person will fit into your life. Why are certain people part of your journey? Is there something you need to learn from them?

C is for change. Be flexible about sudden changes in your life. Missed the bus, plane, train? Maybe there is something you were meant to do instead. Your delay may allow you to connect with someone new.

I is for impulsive. Do something adventurous, like hiking in the Rockies or learning to water-ski. Break up your routine, and your luck will often improve.

D is for determination. Successful people are tenacious and persistent. Many have "failed" their way to success by never giving up. Problems are opportunities waiting to happen.

E is for education. Never stop learning. Spend the afternoon at the library. Take a course. Read journals and newspapers. Be prepared for ideas that pop into your head from left field.

N is for notes. Write down the coincidences and lucky events that have happened to you, then analyze them. Trace back through the steps that allowed them to occur. For example, "because I arrived at work thirty minutes early today, I decided to do X which then led to Y."

C is for connections. Look backward at your life and sideways at other people's to see connections, kinship and similarities. Explore the ways in which we are joined to each other. Why is your best friend in your life? Have you been unconsciously forging new links to a certain someone?

E is for energy. Look after your body and mind through fitness and nutrition. Fatigue will keep you stuck in a rut. You need energy to go, move, change, do.

Nurturing Nature

Of all my childhood memories, one stands above all the others—the weekend hikes with my family along the magnificent Bruce Trail. Surrounded by the treasures in the woods, the beauty and stillness, I developed an intense passion for nature. We were always equipped with pails to gather any luscious raspberries and plump blackberries discovered along the roadside. Nature had fashioned its beauty in so many ways—mysterious ear-shaped fungi on the trees; pale green milkweed, jackets split open to reveal symmetrical brown seeds; dainty purple violets amid clusters of pure white trilliums; towering, mossy tree trunks stealing the sun. When my father placed his finger across his lips, all of us, including the dog, knew this was his signal that deer might be close by. We were often rewarded by his sixth sense; for a fleeting moment, we would spy those elusive animals playing in their natural habitat. Every hike was a gift, an opportunity to view an assortment of wildflowers from nature's bounty. I learned to value their simplicity, their silent beauty. These trips in the woods inspired hope, love and peace.

Nature is a remarkable teacher. Several years ago, when I traveled to Big Sur, California, to sort myself out, I sat for hours on a rock, mesmerized by the sound of the foamy white waves of the Pacific Ocean. Watching the ebb and flow, my spirit reawakened; I left the darkness of grief, loss and pain and ventured out. The sound of the waves, like the rhythmical breathing of a gentle giant asleep at my feet, was intensely soothing. As a chiropractor, I knew that touch healed people; at Big Sur, nature touched me, and I began to heal.

Nature teaches us that nothing ever stays the same; the only constancy is change. And the potential for change is the source of hope. Today might seem bleak and depressing; tomorrow, fresh ideas and renewed energy might present a solution for an unsolvable problem. Think about the devastation of a forest fire—the blackened earth, the scorched trees, the deathly silence. A few seasons later, there will be intense green growth, new plants that thrive on the acid soil, birds returning to nest, and the cycle of nature continues. Human life can experience the same renewal from the ashes, too.

The knowledge that we are part of this wondrous universe is a source of strength for us. The experience of coincidence teaches us that all human beings are connected in some way to one another. The study of nature teaches us that we are also connected to every living thing—plants, animals, birds, even the water and the earth itself. No human being is ever obliterated; all of us who walk this earth return to the earth, dust to dust, our molecules transforming over and over again through countless centuries. It is comforting to realize that we are joined to a force that is grand, stretching for centuries into the past and into the future. This is as close to infinity as we can imagine.

Is there anything more sensual than nature? Hearing a crash of thunder, smelling lilacs in the spring, tasting wild raspberries, touching soft, fuzzy pussywillows, seeing a rainbow—these experiences excite every one of our five senses, creating a childlike feeling of joy and wonder. Our cities, like concrete beehives, can be noisy, deadening and uninspiring. A walk in the park can reawaken our senses, inspiring us to feel at peace with ourselves and our world. "I feel very connected to nature," said Rose Wolfe, chancellor of the University of Toronto and one of the younger seniors I interviewed. "I especially love trees. Someone wanted to cut down a tree in my front lawn—a large willow. I almost went crazy. That tree was my friend. For me trees symbolize peace and tranquillity."

Look for ways to rediscover your first home, to nurture nature all year round, not just on summer holidays at the cottage. Gene Wilhelm, a former vice president of the National Audubon Society who now leads workshops on natural awareness called "Earth Strolls," recommends that you get to know one place well. Find a spot outdoors—a park, a mountain, a forest, a nature trail. Visit this place regularly, daily if you can. Once there, relax and open your senses. What do you see, hear, smell? Does it feel different in the morning and in the late afternoon light? You might want to record your experiences and observations in a diary. This process will establish a true physical and spiritual connection with your place.

For me, longevity is not just about living long. It is about loving life for as long as possible. Many lessons about living and loving life can be learned from nature. Just look and you will see examples of change, tenacity, continuity, growth, renewal and healing. In studying nature, we may find what we are searching for—ourselves.

Prayer—Window to the Soul

An ancient native American proverb says that each human being is like a house with four rooms: the physical, mental, emotional and spiritual. We must visit each of these rooms daily, even if it's just to air them out. Prayer is one way we open the windows to the heart and soul, the room of our spirit.

The spiritual side of human life is often neglected in our secular society, yet many other cultures are much more willing to address the needs of the soul. The soul, like the body, wants to be nourished, exercised and inspired regularly. We often turn to prayer in times of crisis—serious illness, bereavement, suffering. But prayer also belongs to every day, a response to all events, both happy and sad. The need to pray goes far beyond our formal involvement with organized religion; it transcends theology books and Sunday school. You might be surprised to learn that nine out of ten Americans pray frequently and earnestly, and almost all say that God has answered their prayers.

Many of my senior friends mentioned religious beliefs and traditions when talking to me about the values that sustained them in times of crisis. Phrases like, "I thank God for all my blessings," were frequently repeated to me by these wise and experienced men and women. Major-General Richard Rohmer believes, "It's important for all society to have a relationship with a supreme being—something that you can't touch, reach, see, that you believe is there. There has to be some explanation for all the things we see on this earth—life and the whole of creation." Prayer nurtures our relationship with that unseen but very vital reality.

As we reach mid-life, we seem to be more open to the spiritual side of ourselves, more willing to think about the big questions that have no easy answers. Prayer is one way to experience ourselves as both body and soul, regardless of our background or involvement in conventional religion. Prayer is a conversation between oneself —the creature—and the Creator; *Life* magazine calls it, "the flight of the alone to the Alone." We don't necessarily need churches or temples, Bibles or prayer books. We do need the willingness to share our whole self with our creator, God or whatever name we use to identify this supreme Being.

My friend Bertha Madott gives workshops on prayer and spirituality and has shared some of her experiences with me. "A wise saint once said, 'When it comes to prayer, we are all beginners.' I always tell people to start with what they know. Prayer belongs everywhere—at home, on the subways, in restaurants, not just in churches."

Life magazine sums up the universality of prayer. "It says what human beings in all lands and ages have tried to say to God. Help me. Heal me. Love me. Inspire me. Save me from my enemies and from myself. And promise me that when my body dies my soul will live forever."

Amen!

Choosing Happiness

One year in April, I enjoyed a holiday at a Florida spa—four stress-free days to indulge in reading, writing, running and relaxing. My appreciation level for tropical foliage and sunny eighty-five-degree temperatures was at an all-time high after an unusually hard winter of cold, icy weather. Thinking about this holiday, I was grateful for the airplanes that made it possible to trade in a wintry climate for a tropical one in just three short hours. Running joyfully along a paved path, framed on one side by a velvet-green golf course and on the other by a dense jungle of palm trees and flowering hibiscus, I was filled with thankfulness—thankfulness for my satisfying work, my good health and my five precious senses that were being stimulated on my run. I stopped to watch a mother duck with little ones in tow, quacking and paddling across one of the many ponds that dotted the golf course.

It was then that I experienced firsthand the relationship between happiness and thankfulness. How can any of us feel gratitude when we are miserable? Unhappy people filter out the wondrous beauty of the universe, focusing only on the black clouds that they allow to permeate their inner core.

Millions of words have been written on happiness. For some, happiness is like an elusive butterfly, always just out of reach. However, Nathaniel Hawthorne suggested that if you sit very still under an open sky, the butterfly will light on your hand. During the quiet moments of sitting, one simple truth emerges: the capacity for happiness exists in each one of us, rich and poor, healthy and sick alike. Unfortunately, many people think: "If only I were in a relationship, I'd be happy." When we become consumed in the "if only things were better" syndrome, we postpone happiness while life goes slip-sliding away. Happiness is not about the future and tomorrow, dreaming or fantasizing about happier times to come. It's about living with contentment today in the here and now. Why spend your life—the only life you'll ever have—waiting? Waiting for Christmas, for a new relationship, for a better job and more money! Meanwhile, the real joys and pleasures of living today are ignored.

Happy people have found something in life to be passionate about, something that makes them eager to get out of bed in the morning. As the late scholar Joseph Campbell said, such people are "following their bliss."

True happiness requires unconditional love for yourself. You must accept yourself as you are, never perfect but uniquely *you*. To find this unconditional love of self, we must be willing to grow and change while accepting our limitations. And once happiness with self is realized, we are then ready to give to others.

Happiness is also about relationships. We all need to give and receive love. Psychologist Dr. Joyce Brothers says, "I don't think you can be happy without some love in your life. It doesn't have to be love of man for woman. It can be love for God; it can be love of mankind. Relationships with people—friends, partners—can be used to promote happiness, but not if you seek happiness through them. The more you pursue happiness, the less likely it is that you're going to find it." Happiness is not caught in a net through frantic pursuit; marriage and friendship can't guarantee happiness, no matter what romance novels and fairy tales suggest.

Happiness is associated with some of the other secrets to passionate longevity: physical activity, nutrition, rest. I am not alone in encouraging people to take responsibility for bodily health. Comedian Dick Gregory linked health with happiness: "A real secret of being happy is good health. It's diet, proper rest, proper maintenance of the body, proper exercise and the proper amount of water. Children get the exercise, they get the proper rest and they leap out of the bed ready to take on the day. When they wake up the next day, Wow! That's happiness, man." Good health is usually the first item on our thankfulness list, yet many of us do not take good care of our bodies. Obesity, chronic pain or fatigue can have a profound impact on anyone's happiness quotient. Feeling energetic and alive is a byproduct of good health and a component of happiness.

Happiness is not constant. Happy people still feel sadness, frustration, hurt, guilt; they experience conflict, failure and grief. The attitude we bring to these situations makes the difference. The courage to face challenges while stepping outside our comfort zone, the willingness to grow, change or listen to another's viewpoint—these are the hallmarks of a happy person. Looking at the vagaries of life, psychologist Abraham Maslow wrote, in *Motivation and Personality*, "Permanent happiness isn't possible. What people must strive to attain instead is the permanent ability to return to happiness after periods of stress or grief. This capacity is the distinguishing feature of self-realized, full-grown adults." For youth, happiness often depends on a date for the prom, a pimple-free face, the latest fashion gear. Compare this to the serenity and acceptance of an older person, standing at a grave site burying a dear friend or spouse, stricken by grief but aware that life goes on and happier days will return.

Married for sixty years, Pearl and Sol Zucker believe that contentment is the secret to happiness and staying young. "We never had too much," says Pearl, eighty. "We lived in England, went through the war years, deprivation, rationing, yet we sailed through it. We always had a positive outlook. I'd say, 'It's not going to last forever, things will get better.' " Adds Sol, eighty-six, "We never wanted or craved a lot. We were satisfied with what we had. After all, just how much does one person really need?" Sol's comment reminded me of something my father used to say about the endless pursuit for riches: "You can only wear one pair of pants at a time!"

Does this mean we can still be happy in the hospital, at a funeral, on unemployment insurance, after a relationship ends? Yes! And this feeling of contentment at the very core of each person doesn't need to change. We can lose sight of our right to happiness, burying our potential under tons of garbage—the problems of everyday life, unfulfilled dreams, unrealistic expectations. Remember, misery is optional and happiness is a choice waiting to be uncovered; somehow as we age, we have the insight and understanding to accept this.

So, for all you baby boomers wanting to find something you already have, here's June Callwood's advice from her book *Emotions*: "Happiness takes practice. Most people need to start small." Start with what's closest at hand, maybe with nature, and work on exploring all your senses. For example, when you leave the house in the morning, stand still for one minute and listen, *really listen*. Do you hear birds, children's laughter, the sound of traffic? Savor that minute; think about what you are hearing. Is the bird calling a mate? What games are the children playing? Are the people in the cars going to work? Then reflect on yourself—part of a world where birds sing, children play, people work. Now, choose to be grateful for your self—your place in the world, your very existence. Following this exercise for each of the five senses will open you up to new possibilities of happiness and feelings of gratitude. And while you're standing there, learning to appreciate the gifts of your own senses, the elusive butterfly of happiness may light on your shoulder.

Joy for the Ordinary

Think of a time in your life when you experienced a moment of transcendence, a moment when time ceased to exist and you were completely filled with ecstasy. You may have felt this euphoria after making love, hearing an incredible piece of music, seeing a beautiful sunset, witnessing the birth of a baby. Athletes talk about experiencing a runner's high, the feeling that they could run forever. Abraham Maslow called these awe-inspiring moments "peak experiences," brief snapshots of heaven on earth that connect us to the universe, giving us a sense of the profound and a glimpse of the oneness of all things.

An Attitude of Gratitude

Gratitude is not a topic most of us regularly discuss with each other unless we are directly asked, "What are you most thankful for?" When I asked this question of Rabbi Gunther Plaut, eighty-two, he answered without hesitation, "My daily prayers include gratitude to God for the wonderful opportunities I've had, for good health, a wonderful wife, great kids and grandchildren and the opportunity to wake up every morning and have many things to do that I *must* do—not just aimlessly puttering around the house." When I asked my senior friends the question, the answer was the same: good health, family, children, productivity. When life is reduced to its most simple truths, what else is there for all of us?

Abraham Maslow, the psychologist, also sees the link between happiness and gratitude. As he says, "People who are happy have all their faculties in play. They relish life, quirks and all. In a word, they are capable of gratitude." We have much to be thankful for, so many blessings to count, yet often our hearts are filled with envy, wanting to be somewhere else, trying to be someone else. This one-liner sums up these negative feelings: "No matter how many hot dogs we eat at home, they always taste better at the ballpark." My father would have retorted with a famous Yiddish saying, "If everyone hung their problems on a fence for everyone else to see, you'd end up taking your own problems back." To this day, I am grateful to my father for teaching me that truth.

We learn lessons from our peak experiences. Sometimes these come from the pleasure of reaching a goal; the day I ran my first marathon in less than three hours remains a high point in my life. Other lessons teach us the power of beauty and nature, the preciousness of life, the need for trust, the rapture of love. According to Maslow, "The emotional reaction in the peak experience has a special flavor of wonder, of awe, of reverence, of humility and surrender before the experience as before something great." What is the difference between such moments of transcendent joy and ordinary, garden-variety happiness? Jesuit priest Edward J. Lavin describes joy as "the exuberant external face of happiness. Whereas happiness is a condition of longer duration, caused by the proper fit of our lives into the puzzles of reality, joy is more like a single event, an expression of something that invades our lives in a single, quick, unexpected flash."

The peak experiences of life are wonderful, but a whole lifetime can be frittered away while we wait for these flashes, all the while missing the small joys or miracles that happen every day. Unfortunately, the adult mind, unlike the child's, views the events that happen with regularity as familiar, and what is familiar can become stale or boring. Don't we *expect* the rising and setting of the sun, the changing of the seasons, the continuous cycle of birth, maturation and death? In our rush to become grown-ups, we may have left behind some of our youthful spirit, innocent freshness, curiosity and spontaneity.

One consistent quality my senior friends possess is a joy for the ordinary. Simple things tickle their spirits—things many of us don't even notice as we go about our busy day. They get excited watching goldfish in a backyard pond; marvel at the miracle of a hosta plant that knows when to emerge in exactly the same formation and location as last year; rejoice while playing a game with a grandchild. It is precisely this joie de vivre that is life-affirming and life-enhancing. I am convinced that many seniors (which should be spelled *seen-years*) know the secret to stave off old age: become as childlike as possible. As Georgina Madott, sixty-eight, said, "I hope I die before I grow up!" There is a myth that prevails about aging. The term "second childhood" often denotes a progressive, inevitable breakdown, mental and physical, of body and spirit. Such a decline does happen to a small percentage of people. However, it is not years alone that cause deterioration; it is how we have learned to *live* them. Continued productivity, stimulation through new experiences and renewed creativity maintain those seen years as keen years. The expression "use it or lose it" applies to the mind and spirit as well as to the body. "Old age" should be a time for self-development and expansion instead of obsolescence.

From Type A to Wait a Day (or Two)

"What pearls of wisdom from seniors have you taken to heart and used in your daily life?" a friend asked me recently. I hesitated only briefly, then spoke the word that is generally not part of the vocabulary of a Type A personality: "Patience." I tend to be a reactive, I-can-fix-it, make-it-happen, change-it, why-wait-do-it-now person. "Not a good idea," cautions Major-General Richard Rohmer, seventy. He developed the ability to temporize from the late John Robarts, former premier of Ontario. "As his chief of staff, I would present him with a daily agenda. He would take a situation and, instead of acting upon it immediately, he would say, 'We'll deal with that next week or maybe the week after.' If you leave a decision for a while, instead of making it under pressure, often the situation sorts itself out or the circumstances change for you. And how you feel about something on day one can be quite different from how you feel on day ten." Thinking about Rohmer's words, I could instantly recall times when I had impulsively blown up on day one, instead of trusting circumstances to unfold as they should and letting things be. Eleanor Mills, eighty-one, has a similar philosophy. "If you are feeling really dug over and nothing seems to be right, don't brood on it. Things often resolve without intervention. Let things simmer in your mind; very often they sort themselves out. Impulsiveness doesn't work. Sit back and observe the situation, rather than leap into it."

When I asked Sigga Moore for her ten secrets for living, this energetic, passionate eighty-two-year-old replied, "An important one is to be patient and sit it out. You'll be amazed at how often things work out on their own."

So there you have it, good advice for all those who tend to tackle life's challenges by jumping in feet first and thinking afterward. Patience—the capacity to wait for the right opportunity—is definitely a virtue. That's not to say that we can't make a decision right away on some things, and often it's necessary to do so, especially in our frenetic fast-forward make-up-your-mind world. But as Father Edward Lavin writes, sometimes we should be like the lioness, "waiting in the high grass for her prey to pass by, making no movement for hours except for gentle twitches of her tail." I can just picture that magnificent beast—watchful, assessing, alert, contemplative and composed. She has just the right temperament to make the right decision with patience.

Memories: They're All in Your Mind

Arthur Soler gave me a precious gift: he told me his secret to enjoying life. Over lunch, this remarkable company president shared his philosophy: "The most important thoughts we have in our minds are all the wonderful experiences we've ever had. I keep a mental file of all these memories. Any time I have another pleasurable experience I file it. Right now I could tell you twenty incredible experiences I've had, just like that. If I am unhappy about something, I can draw on these memories and I am instantly filled with joy. When people focus on their problems, they ignore all the outstanding experiences and pleasures they have had in life."

I asked Arthur to share just one memory. "My mother, who is over eighty, is the most beautiful person I've ever known. If she died I would be very sad. What will sustain me is remembering all the extraordinary things she did for me. Three months ago she opened her heart and said, 'When I die, just remember, nobody could have ever loved you more than I did.' I will never forget this."

That day I had an opportunity to try Arthur's approach. My lawyer telephoned about some frustrating business; after I hung up, I could feel my stomach churn. I took a moment to reflect on some joyful memories: seeing my first double rainbow; graduation day, when I became a chiropractor; my first leading role, in Christopher Columbus, a grade five school play. I remembered treating Mel Gibson when he had a sore back; my mother's delicious cheese blintzes with sour cream; crying with joy as I watched the Christmas Day parade at Disneyland. My mind filled with happy images: seeing the Beatles on the *Ed Sullivan Show*; my brother Steven with his favorite childhood friend, his Howdy Doody puppet—I savored each thought with pleasure. In a few minutes my heart was so full of joy there was no room for any negative emotions.

Now it's your turn. Make a list of all your wonderful memories. Try writing them on three-by-five-inch file cards, then carry them with you in your purse, briefcase or car. Stuck in a traffic jam or feeling stressed at work? Read your list and you'll feel uplifted.

Having trouble sleeping? Fill your dreams with sweet memories instead of worries. Don't postpone joy. It's there inside of you—all you have to do is *remember*.

Arthur shared another important secret to enjoying life: "Most people are so busy planning their retirement that they forget how to live today. We are always postponing things for the future—one day I'm going to do this or that and then I'll be happy. I cherish every second of every minute of every hour of every day that I live. I truly know how to enjoy each day."

He's right. No one can promise you tomorrow—you may not be here. The key is to be conscious of the present moment. Suck the juices out of life each day, then spit out the bad parts and savor the rest. When I left the restaurant after lunch with Arthur, the sky somehow seemed bluer.

The Meaning of Life

Feeling bored on a rainy Sunday afternoon? Looking for something to do to kill a few hours? Try answering this simple question: What is the meaning of life? Finding the answer, if indeed there is an answer, is one of the most difficult and personal quests, one that has challenged philosophers throughout the ages. Some believe there is a universal meaning, a supreme goal inherent in every human experience, which is connected to one's faith—to fulfill God's will, to serve and then return to our creator. Some believe that life can be given meaning through our contributions to the whole of society: to make this world a better place than we found it through loving others, expressing compassion, achieving balance and harmony with every other living thing in creation. Others believe they are here to write their own story in the book of life. These are issues we can think about for a whole lifetime.

Perhaps a more appropriate question for the scope of this book is: What is the meaning of *my* life? For if my life has no meaning or purpose or spiritual dimension, what's the point of wanting to live to a ripe old age? Furthermore, as our life experiences change, our meanings change. Today one could be consumed with the relentless pursuit of the almighty dollar; tomorrow one might focus inward, on self. Soul-searching, or the process of looking inward, in turn forms the basis for other complex questions: Who am I and why am I here? These are questions, says Rabbi Gunther Plaut, that were asked in the beginning. He explains, "When Adam and Eve transgressed the Divine Word and had eaten the forbidden fruit, God asked the basic question, 'Where are you?' We too are always asking ourselves the question, 'Where am I in life?' We may answer, 'I thought I'd get there, but I know I can't, so where can I get? Did I succeed? Did I fail? Am I satisfied with who I am?' These are frequent questions when we reach transitional ages."

Some of the answers to these almost overwhelming questions may flow out of our relationships with others and the many roles we play—parent, spouse, child. Other insights may come from our work and our spiritual beliefs. Questions beget more questions. We must also ask ourselves, "What fulfills me? What allows me to feel love, joy and wonder?" If we examine the moments when we are most happy and joyful, our raison d'être may be revealed.

I believe that each of us here on this earth has a special purpose or mission; we find our truth through the lessons we learn from everyone who comes into our world, from the guidance of our intuitive inner voice and from our connections to the deepest rhythms and "synchronicity" of the universe, the earth or God. Our special purpose may be to learn to love ourselves and others unconditionally, to care for and help others in need, to heal others through a special talent or gift, to love and nurture a child. There is something inside each of us that feels naturally right, something that resonates in our heart; our life purpose may be about creating, inspiring, teaching, understanding, sharing or seeking. I believe every person in the world is as unique as his or her fingerprints; each person has one particular set of circumstances, thoughts, experiences and beliefs, making one individual canvas in the art gallery of life.

Are we all seeking a meaning for life? Throughout this book, I have used the word "passion" to describe the feeling of joy that comes from a life lived on purpose. I have stressed that it is never too late to discover one's passion. For baby boomers who know intuitively that something is calling to them, discover it, then grab it. Otherwise life is reduced to a hollow, meaningless existence, merely going through the motions. To those trapped in a rut of dissatisfaction, Joseph Campbell asked, in *The Power of Myth*, "What good was your life? You never did the thing you wanted to do in all your life!" It is truly a tragedy when a talented and gifted person does not live up to his or her potential.

Psychologist Abraham Maslow believed that each of us has a

need for "self-actualization," that is, the need to become whatever we are capable of being. Individuals who are self-actualized are those who can best use their own special talents, capacities, potentialities. A self-actualizer wishes to grow, to find out "who he is, what he is, what he likes, what he doesn't like, what is good for him and what bad, where he is going and what his mission is." Maslow held the view that each person is unique, and therefore no two people can follow exactly the same path to self-actualization. He believed there is an order or hierarchy of needs, ranging from basic biological needs, such as food and shelter, to more advanced psychological needs such as self-esteem and self-actualization.

Sometimes it is possible to find meaning for ourselves at the very bottom of Maslow's scale, that is, even when our basic survival is in question. Psychiatrist Victor Frankl, in *Man's Search for Meaning*, described the horrors of life for himself and his fellow prisoners in a Nazi concentration camp. Stripped of all dignity, treated like an animal, starving, cold, with no hope for tomorrow, how could anyone find life worth living? Frankl answers by quoting the philosopher Nietzsche, "He who has a *why* to live can bear with almost any *how*." The why for Frankl was love. In his despair, he began to think of his wife, who was in another camp. "Then I grasped the meaning of the greatest secret that human poetry and human thought and belief have to impart: The salvation of man is through love and in love. I understood how a man who has nothing left in the world still may know bliss, be it only for a brief moment, in the contemplation of his beloved." Frankl believed, "Everything can be taken from a man but one thing: the last of the human freedoms—to choose one's attitude in any given set of circumstances." Even when life hands us those painful, tragic situations— the death of a child, an incurable disease—Frankl still maintained, "What matters above all is the attitude we take toward suffering." He illustrates his belief that there is meaning in suffering by telling a story about a patient who was severely depressed for two years after his wife died. Frankl asked the man, "What would have happened if you had died first?" "This would have been terrible," replied the patient; "how she would have suffered!" Whereupon Frankl replied, "You see, she has been spared suffering, but now you have to pay for it by surviving and mourning her." The patient left Frankl's office full of gratitude and filled with a sense of inner peace for the first time in two years. As Frankl wrote, "Suffering ceases to be suffering at the moment it finds a meaning, such as the meaning of a sacrifice." Like Frankl, I, too, believe that attitude is everything. No one can get inside our heads and tell us what to think; we have the freedom to choose where we focus, what scenarios we replay in our minds. However, it takes a very special, spiritually evolved individual to understand and accept the meaning in suffering. Not everyone can do it. Think of the negative, bitter people you know. Some of them even advertise their cynical views on their T-shirts: "Life's a bitch, then you die!"

Then there is the attitude of Chris DeMatteo, a mailman. When asked about the meaning of life, he replied, "Life is what you make it. When we're born, we each start out with a blank canvas. God provides the paint and brushes. The rest is up to us. We can either make Rembrandts or rejects of ourselves. The lives we draw, the colors we choose—they're all our decision."

Before we know it, the canvas is finished and we must turn in our paintbrushes. Life is so short, we've had barely enough time on earth to allow the paint to dry. Jesse Jackson, Baptist minister and civil rights leader, describes the brevity of life as "the dash between our birth date and our death date." I asked my senior friends whether they had any regrets as they contemplated the last scenes being painted on their canvas. They all spoke about not wanting to look back on their lives with regret; they wanted their final years to be peaceful and harmonious with the people they loved. They all seemed to realize the importance of forgiveness, that special healing from the inside out. Perhaps the meaning of life can be summed up as a question we can ask about all our relationships, including the one we have with ourselves. How well have I loved?

Forgiveness and "New Eyes"

About seven years ago, I suffered one of the deepest hurts in human experience—the pain of betrayal. I felt like an explosion had ripped my heart apart, spilling out every emotion that had ever existed inside of me. I cried, I screamed, I plotted revenge. Night after night, for months on end, I relived conversations, scenarios and innuendoes, trying to make sense of the constant nagging questions that haunted me: How could he? How could she? With support from family, friends and professional therapy, after reading dozens of books and with the passage of time, the rawness of the wound is gone. Only some remnants of scar tissue remain. When I think about my life now, I feel as though I've successfully crossed a bridge and I'm standing on the other shore, grounded, safe and secure. There is, however, one more obstacle for me to face; not a small stone, but rather a boulder, which is still blocking my path to complete freedom. Forgiveness is, for me, the final hurdle. Only through "new eyes" is forgiveness possible.

In his book *Forgive and Forget*, Lewis Smedes tells a wonderful fable about a righteous but cold man who caught his wife in the act of adultery. Conscious of his reputation for goodness, the man took great pleasure in pretending in public to forgive her sins, but deep in his heart he hated her for betraying him. His fakery did not sit well in heaven. Each time he felt his secret hate, an angel would drop a small pebble into his heart, causing him immense pain. The pebbles multiplied with each mean and unforgiving thought. Finally, in complete agony, as the pain intensified and his heart grew heavier and heavier, the man prayed for help. The angel took pity on the unhappy man and appeared to him, explaining about the stones of unforgiveness. The man begged the angel to take the pebbles away, but the angel refused. Only by forgiving his wife could the man be free of his pain. The angel suggested that the man look at his wife with new eyes, seeing the reasons for her adultery, the loneliness and unhappiness that drove her to another man. And each time the man did look at his wife in this way, seeing her as a fallible human being who made mistakes, the angel removed one of the pebbles. As the weight lifted, the man discovered his own warmth and humanity for the first time; he treated his poor wife with greater affection, and she, in turn, began to love him as he wanted. And the angel looked down on them both and smiled.

With my new eyes, I am able to see what forgiveness really is: the decision in one's heart to let go of the pain, the burden, the connection with the past, the link that chains us still to the person who has hurt us. Only through forgiveness can those emotional bonds be broken, allowing us to experience liberation for the first time. Some people maintain the attitude, "Why should I give that *?!*! the satisfaction of forgiveness?" or, "They don't deserve to be forgiven!" Those with this attitude fail to realize that forgiveness is something we do for *ourselves*, for *our* peace of mind, for *our* health and well-being. In fact, holding on to grudges and animosities affects our health, both physically and emotionally. We have already seen in the chapter on unity and the mind-body connection how emotional stress changes the way the immune system functions. The link between anger and heart disease is also well-documented. Describing the cancer-prone personality in his book *Getting Well Again*, O. Carl Simonton, MD, cites "a tendency to hold resentments and a marked inability to forgive" as part of the process through which some people develop serious illnesses. Obviously, keeping our hurts buried inside can be extremely detrimental. But where does forgiveness originate?

Religions have long recognized the importance of forgiveness to both the individual and the community. "Jesus taught that unless you forgive others you will not experience forgiveness from God," says Reverend Peter Moore. "Think of the words of the Lord's Prayer: 'forgive us our trespasses as we forgive those who trespass against us': words familiar to hundreds of millions of Christians throughout the world." The Bible says, "You shall not take vengeance and you shall not bear a grudge," the standard for Jewish ethical behavior since the days of Moses. On Yom Kippur, the Day of Atonement, Jewish tradition states unequivocally that a sinner must ask and receive the forgiveness of anyone he or she has sinned against during the past year before he or she can hope to obtain divine pardon. Yom Kippur is not only a personal day of atonement; it is also the day on which the entire Jewish community, worldwide, stands before God and seeks forgiveness and divine guidance. I remember reciting the Lord's Prayer every morning in public school, a jumble of memorized words without much significance at age six or seven. Through my parents' teaching, however, I readily understood making up with my brother after a fight; saying "I'm sorry" if I hurt someone; feeling remorse when I had disobeyed. Forgiveness, like all essential moral teachings and virtues, is taught by our parents and reinforced in our religious schools, churches and synagogues.

While apologies are acceptable behavior for children's transgressions, how do we as adults come to terms with the horrible tragedies and crimes that are seemingly unforgivable? I posed that question to a very special patient of mine, Lesley Parrott. In 1986, her eleven-year-old daughter, Allison, was abducted and murdered; in spite of a massive police search, the perpetrator was never caught. "I knew my whole life could be overwhelmed and consumed by this," Lesley explained. "I quickly realized that if I didn't move forward, I would lose my life and my family. Forgiveness, which has always been a deeply held belief of mine, is the only way to move on in life." Lesley then said something which surprised me: "I hope the person who murdered Allison can become whole again." What a rare human being to feel this way! Says Reverend Moore, "Part of forgiveness is wishing the people who have wronged us well. But what we are wishing for them is a whole and healthy understanding of what they have done to us." The thought of wishing my ex-husband and ex-girlfriend well, prior to hearing this explanation, would have been very difficult for me. Now I understand that forgiveness does not mean letting anyone off the hook; nor does it in any way condone unacceptable or immoral actions. Forgiveness doesn't mean you have to forget, either.

Forgiveness, like grief, has no timetable. It takes as long as it takes. No one can tell anyone else when it's time to forgive. Smedes believes we forgive in four stages: hurt, hate, healing (you are given new eyes) and finally the coming together (you invite the person who has hurt you back into your life; if you don't wish to see them, or the person is deceased or unknown, then you have to be healed alone). Because forgiveness is an inner process, something we do for ourselves, it is not absolutely necessary to see or talk to the person at all.

The healing process that leads to forgiveness is like a slow dance —two steps forward, one step back, maybe even a few steps sideways before we go forward again. We can't hope to move forward unless we first deal with hurt and anger, two emotions that precede forgiveness. While I can't possibly do justice to these vital issues in this limited space, I would like to highlight some key points you may find helpful.

1. Writing is healing. Start to express your feelings of anger and sadness with pen and paper. Don't edit your thoughts; let them come out in any way they want—phrases, single words, drawings, dreams. Or write a letter (which you have no intention of mailing) to the person who hurt you. The important thing is to confront that hurt and rage in a positive way.
2. Do something physical—run, bike uphill, pound a pillow with your fists, scream at the top of your lungs in the car with the windows rolled up and the radio blasting. When you express anger, your perceptions will change.

3. Get some professional help. Talk to a therapist; Gestalt therapy is particularly useful. Take a workshop on forgiveness at a retreat like the Esalen Institute in Big Sur or the Omega Institute in New York. Do bodywork that specializes in opening up your feelings, such as bioenergetics or Feldenkrais.
4. Read. Go to your local bookstore or library. Try *Forgiveness: A Bold Choice for a Peaceful Heart* by Robin Casarjian; *A Path with Heart* by Jack Kornfield; or *Forgive and Forget* by Lewis Smedes.

When I began interviewing my senior friends about longevity, I did not initially broach the subject of forgiveness. They did! They spoke very definitely about the necessity of healing family rifts, letting bygones be bygones, making peace with the past. None of them wanted to die full of regret and sadness, often the result of our unhealed, wounded relationships. As I sat with them, listening to their wisdom, it became clear to me that forgiveness is something we must all face, now or later. My own time for forgiveness emerged while I was writing this chapter. Forgiving ourselves is part of the process, as well. I have begun to accept the humanity of those who were once close to me, as I accept myself. The boulder blocking my path is now gone; with my new eyes, I can see that the path to passionate longevity is directly in front of me.

Two Inches Equals One Lifetime

For the longest time, I skipped the obituary page entirely, and then a few years ago I began to glance occasionally at the names in the columns. Now I admit to being a regular reader of the obituaries in my daily newspaper. Thankfully, most of the time the names are unfamiliar to me, but each two-inch space tells a poignant story —a summary of someone's life, someone's mother, father, grandparent, son, daughter, friend.

It's funny about life. No matter how many zeroes are attached to our bank balance, the quantity of square feet we call home or the number of hours toiled at the office, most of us still end up with the same mathematical equation—roughly two inches equals one lifetime, unless you're really famous, and then you might rate a full page. It doesn't matter how many frequent flyer points you've accumulated, when we all depart for our final flight, no carry-on luggage is allowed. We enter the world naked; we exit with one set of clothes. But what legacy do we leave behind? Who do we leave behind?

On Wednesday, April 3, 1991, my mother died at age seventy-six. To the kind lady at *The Toronto Star* whose task it is to write the obituary notices, I send a special thank-you. You were sensitive and caring while I sadly attempted to fill that two-inch space. I am choking back tears even now as I write this. You used the words "devoted mother." I never told you what those words really meant for me. You never tasted my mom's famous tomato-soup cake or her homemade thimbleberry jam. Did you know she had a wonderful smile and a funny bump on her wrist that I sometimes touched? I didn't tell you about the wig she wore as her hair became thin and gray. I wish you could have watched her create a beautiful flower arrangement from our garden. Did I mention that she stood on her sore, bunioned feet every morning for thirteen years to make the thickest, healthiest sandwiches for Steven and I for school lunches? You never heard her voice yell the same words every morning for those thirteen years, "Elaine, hurry up! You'll miss the school bus!" No, all you wrote was "devoted mother," two words that spark millions of fond memories, enough to fill an entire newspaper.

The last question I asked seniors during my many interviews was the most difficult for me. It was so personal, so telling: "How would you like to be remembered?" Most paused to reflect before answering. Some answers:

- as a nice person
- as a kind person
- as a good friend
- as the best grandmother
- as a wonderful father
- as someone who helped people
- as someone who made a difference
- as a pleasant person who did things well
- it doesn't matter: it's what you do when you're alive that counts

That last comment came from Sigga Moore, eighty-two, now widowed, once happily married, a devoted mother, cherished grandmother, churchgoer, volunteer, friend. She also bakes a delicious date-nut bread, which we enjoyed with tea during the interview.

Now ask yourself the same question: "How would I like to be remembered?" When you think about the answer now, as Sigga says, you'll be clear on how you want to live today.

Becoming Real

Every once in a while a book comes along that we adopt into our hearts forever. *The Velveteen Rabbit*, read by millions of children, was given to me by my wonderful friend Samena Jeffery just three years ago, and has since etched a permanent impression in the corridors of my heart. The enchanting tale begins at Christmas, that magical time for all children; a little boy received a splendid, stuffed velveteen rabbit with pink sateen ears. The boy loved the rabbit for at least two hours, but with competition for his attention from so many other toys, he was distracted, and the rabbit was forgotten. For a long time, the rabbit lived in the toy cupboard or on the nursery floor, snubbed by some of the more expensive mechanical toys. A wise old skin horse who had lived in the nursery longer than any of the other toys befriended him. One day the rabbit asked the skin horse, "What is real?" The skin horse replied, "Real isn't how you are made. It's a thing that happens to you. When a child loves you for a long, long time, not just to play with, but really loves you, then you become real . . . It doesn't happen all at once. You become. It takes a long time. That's why it doesn't happen to people who break easily, or have sharp edges, or who have to be carefully kept. Generally, by the time you are Real, most of your hair has been loved off and your eyes drop out and you get loose in the joints and very shabby. But these things don't matter at all, because once you are Real you can't be ugly, except to people who don't understand."

As the story unfolds the boy reconnects with his forgotten bunny and they become inseparable companions. Nighttime would find them snuggled up together in bed, the boy's hands tightly clasped around his fluffy friend all night long. As the skin horse predicted, over time, from endless cuddles and hugs, the rabbit's fur became shabbier, the seams on his tail came apart and the pink nose wore thin where the boy had kissed him. His hair was being loved off. In essence, the rabbit was becoming real. I don't want to spoil the story, so you'll just have to read this charming fable yourself, to find out what happens.

Becoming *real* is the essence of passionate longevity. It takes a long time for *real* to happen; we need a lifetime to understand the process fully. Maybe by the time *real* happens to you, you'll be "old" like the seniors I met while writing this book. But remember, it doesn't matter what you look like on the outside. All the seniors were real inside; like the skin horse and the velveteen rabbit, their hair had been loved off, and some were loose in the joints, too. Real is what life is all about—giving love and being loved for who you are. But everything must begin with self, so real starts with accepting, respecting and loving yourself; it includes accepting the responsibility for your physical, emotional and spiritual health— everything from fitness to family to forgiveness. As we have explored throughout this book, real happens when we listen to our hearts and do the things we know we must: change jobs, begin a fitness program, choose lower-fat foods. We move one giant step closer to real when we begin to own our emotional stuff—resolve our issues; make peace with the past; learn to forgive. Real involves patience, resiliency and tenacity, hanging in the way the velveteen rabbit did, even when life seemed bleak and his true purpose for being was unfulfilled. In the skin horse, however, he had a wonderful, kind friend with whom he could share his feelings. Friendships can be the family we never had, or have lost through time. When we are real, we are not afraid to ask our inner child to come out to play silly games, draw, paint, sing or dance. Becoming real means growing wise, having learned many of life's valuable lessons. You can be mentor, teacher, guide for the younger ones. Here is the essence of love—giving to others, caring and sharing. The only way one learns to love is by being loved, the most basic of all human needs. Isn't that what we all want—to love others and be loved, to be transformed to real?

Throughout this book, I have used the term "passionate longevity" to describe the link between living long and loving life. Rabbi Gunther Plaut explains what the *passion* in passionate longevity really means: "You take your first breath through *your* lungs, not through somebody else. We start with our breath, our thinking, our needs. But if that is all your life is, you are very poor. There are people who have a lot, but they are very poor people. They don't know how to share or how to give. Some people love or care for the world, but can't quite care for their neighbor next door; they want justice in the world and racial equality, but 'please, no blacks on *my* street.' They are poor also. In all of life, you have to be passionate about human beings and about the world. Your passions have to go beyond yourself. If your priorities exclude others, you've got no passion at all."

Your suitcase for the journey to passionate longevity must be quite full by now. There is still enough room for whatever you need to take on your travels through life. Thank you for allowing me to accompany you this far. Have a *passionate* journey!

The 10 Secrets of Gert Kushin, age seventy-eight

1. Don't take your health for granted—it's a God-given gift.
2. Don't be selfish—be grateful for the things you have.
3. It's always nice to compliment people even if you don't know them—it's also nice getting compliments.
4. Tell those close to you that you love them—you might not have another chance.
5. Listening is very important.
6. We all need spiritual guidance.
7. When you're feeling down, pick yourself up and do something, such as have coffee with a friend.
8. Take your blinkers off and see people for what they are. We sometimes make hasty judgments about people.
9. If I "could have, should have and would have," things would have been different. We can't live in the past; it's already gone.
10. On staying healthy: use the power of positive thinking. "Please God, I have a lot of unfinished business; let me live another five to ten years!"

RECOMMENDED READING

Berman, Philip L. and Connie Goldman. *The Ageless Spirit*. New York: Ballantine Books, 1992.

Bonner, Joseph and William Harris. *Healthy Aging*. Claremont, California: Hunter House, 1988.

Bortz, Walter. *We Live Too Short and Die Too Long*. New York: Bantam, 1991.

Bridges, William. *Transitions*. Boston: Addison Wesley, 1980.

Brody, Jane. *Jane Brody's Nutrition Book*. New York: W.W. Norton & Co., 1981.

Chopra, Deepak. *Ageless Body, Timeless Mind*. New York: Harmony Books, 1993.

Friedan, Betty. *The Fountain of Age*. New York: Simon and Schuster, 1993.

Gawain, Shakti. *Creative Visualization*. San Rafael, California: New World Library, 1978.

Goldberg, Natalie. *Writing Down the Bones*. Boston: Shambhala Publications, 1986.

Johnson, Spencer. *The Precious Present*. New York: Doubleday, 1984.

Kinder, Melvyn. *Going Nowhere Fast*. New York: Prentice Hall, 1990.

Moyers, Bill. *Healing and the Mind*. New York: Doubleday, 1993.

Paulus, Trina. *Hope for the Flowers*. New York: Paulist Press, 1972.

Redfield, James. *The Celestine Prophecy*. New York: Warner Books, 1993.

Rountree, Cathleen, *On Women Turning 50*. New York: HarperCollins, 1993.

Seligman, Martin. *Learned Optimism*. New York: Simon and Schuster, 1990.

Sheehan, George. *Personal Best*. Philadelphia: Rodale Press, 1989.

Sher, Barbara. *I Could Do Anything If I Only Knew What It Was*. New York: Delacorte Press, 1994.

Siegel, Bernie. *How To Live Between Office Visits*. New York: HarperCollins, 1993.

Smedes, Lewis. *Forgive and Forget*. San Francisco: Harper SF, 1991.

INDEX

About the Author

Dr. Elaine Dembe, born and raised in Hamilton, Ontario, is one of Canada's authorities on stress management, wellness and motivation.

Chiropractor, marathon runner (she ranked 11th in Canada for her 1982 marathon performance of 2:53:53) and recipient of the International Award for Amateur Sports, Dr. Dembe has a thriving Toronto-based practice and is the only chiropractor on call at the Chief Protocol Office of the Government of Ontario for visiting royalty and dignitaries. Among the many celebrities she has treated are Mel Gibson, Kris Kristofferson, Paula Abdul, Phil Collins, Bryan Adams, Celine Dion and Lindsay Wagner. For two seasons, from 1985 to 1987, she was also chiropractor to a number of the Toronto Blue Jays.

A speaker with The National Speaker's Bureau, Dr. Dembe—who has appeared on numerous radio and TV shows—lectures extensively on wellness, longevity and back care to corporations, institutions, service clubs and conferences.